Play™ Tennis

High Performance Training Tips

Carl Petersen, BPE., BSc (PT), MCPA
Nina Nittinger, Dipl. KFFR/Sports Mgt.

Racquet Tech Publishing

An imprint of USRSA

Vista, California, USA

Racquet Tech Publishing
(An imprint of the USRSA)
330 Main St.
Vista, California 92084
760-536-1177
www.racquettech.com

Published by Racquet Tech Publishing under licensing agreement from:
Fit to Play Int. Inc.
1303-289 Drake St.
Vancouver, BC
Canada V6B-5Z5

First edition, 2003
Second edition, 2006

Library of Congress Control Number: 2005938184

Cover design and interior illustrations by Kristine Thom.

Front cover tennis photograph is courtesy of Bruno Herdt (1954-2005), Actionphoto GmbH, CH-8269, Switzerland.

Inside action tennis photographs courtesy of: Jon Pesochin, Green Tea Photography Ltd., www.greenteaphotography.com; Bo Mon Kwan; Kiwican Photography; Tennis BC, www.tennisbc.org; Carl Petersen, www.citysportsphysio.com.

Inside exercise and lifestyle photographs courtesy of: Carl Petersen, www.citysportsphysio.com; Nina Nittinger, www.MAPP-coaching.com; Greg Griffiths, www.mountainmoments.com.

The Athlete Self-Screening Exam™ (Tests 1-6), Chapter 24, pages 317-325, are the property of Randy Celebrini and the OnFieldClinic. All copyright laws apply.

Chapter 9, Stroke Fundamentals Training, pages 141-157, is the property of Tennis Canada. All copyright laws apply.

Printed in the United States of America

ISBN-13: 978-0-9722759-5-8
ISBN-10: 0-9722759-5-9

Dedication

Carl Petersen

This book is dedicated to my parents, Art & Eileen Petersen, and grandparents, Halford & Gretta Campbell. They taught me about sport and life and gave me the opportunity to pursue my dreams. Most importantly, they made me realize that being hardworking, organized and ambitious is not a character flaw.

Nina Nittinger

I would like to thank my parents, Prof. Dr. med. Hans Nittinger and Ute Nittinger, for their support throughout my career. I would also like to thank Carl Petersen for being the best physiotherapist, friend, and business partner. Great appreciation to the coaches, physiotherapists, scientists and all the people I have worked with who have taught me a lot about myself and the fascination of tennis.

Contents

Contents

Contents

Contents

Acknowledgements

The principle authors would like to thank the many athletes, coaches, mentors, and sport science and medicine personnel from a variety of nations with whom we have had the opportunity to work. They have been an important part of our education, experience, and life over the years. Their knowledge, enthusiasm, hard work, and dedication has been truly admirable and refreshing.

We would like to thank specifically all of the contributing writers for their work and lending their expertise helping in organize this project. The writing of a tennis book such as this, although a task primarily undertaken by myself and Nina, is in reality the bringing together of training and coaching ideas, concepts, and information developed and put forward by colleagues, friends, clinicians, coaches, and experts in the field of tennis and sports training. To these people and many others in the background thank you for your help, constructive criticism, and encouragement. Your support has played a large role in the successful completion of this second edition of the book.

We would also like to thank the physiotherapists and office staff at City Sports & Physiotherapy Clinics for their help and patience during this project.

The authors would also like to thank the following athletes and exercise models for photo use: Paul Baccanello, Ryan Clark, Natalia Cretu, Shannon Cuciz, David Chu, Daniel Chu, Rhav Datt, Eunice David Ashley Fisher, Melanie Gloria, Zenya Kasabuchi, Corrine Issel, Sylvia Kerfoot, Amanda Mankovits, Erica Mahon, Atonio Matic, Kate Pace-Lindsay, Stas Pakhomov, Tania Rice, Michelle Ruthven, Nicole Sewell, Tara Simpson, Michelle Summerside, Ryan Oughtred, Alizee Paradis, Vasek Pospisil, Christina Risler, Andrea Van der Hurk and Petra Vogel. Your patience and help is very much appreciated.

Preface

Success in tennis and other sports combines hard work, talent, the support of coaches and parents, and dedication to a goal to be your best. For many athletes, giving their best also means becoming the best in the world. Over the course of your tennis career, you will face many different challenges. One aspect of our sport that is completely controllable is physical conditioning. It is the focus of every top athlete. Conditioning is about getting as much as possible out of every training session, having the physical preparation to withstand slips and mishaps, and building the confidence to know you have prepared to the best of your ability. This is how to become a champion.

Fit to Play™ Tennis: High Performance Training Tips is the latest resource to help you become a better player and athlete. The authors and contributing writers have decades of combined experience working with athletes from a variety of nations; sports; and Grand Slam, World Cup, World Championship and Olympic competitions. We hope *Fit to Play™ Tennis* will be an important tool assisting you in your preparation to be your best. Success takes an uncompromising commitment to training hard, playing well, and a belief that you can win.

We have applied our collective knowledge and experience along with the research and resources of our peers to provide tennis athletes with the latest information on smart training concepts. It is our belief that improved knowledge and education regarding training, injury prevention, and recovery techniques, both physical and mental, offer athletes of all ages a long healthy playing career.

Introduction

Making Yourself a Better Player and Athlete

Carl Petersen

To be competitive on a consistent basis you must be in great shape. The training and competition schedule along with associated travel can be grueling, and the physical, mental, and emotional demands of the sport can all take their toll, leaving you vulnerable to injuries. Developing proper training, injury prevention, and recovery habits early and sticking to them will help optimize performance. As an athlete, you must strive to develop a training and competition attitude that helps you improve both as an athlete and a person.

Successful athletes require physical ability, technical skill, and mental toughness. Designing programs to ensure optimal tennis training and high performance is both an art and a science, with some trial and error added in. The science to justify training technique is rapidly catching up to the art of past, current, and future training. The high performance training tips in this book are designed by physiotherapists, coaches, physicians, and other sport medicine and science personnel based on current research and numerous years of practical experience working with high performance and recreational athletes from a variety of sports.

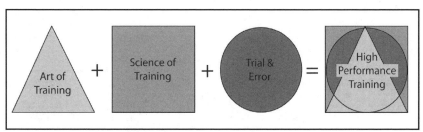

The art and science of training

1

DON'T JUST PLAY TO GET INTO SHAPE; GET INTO PROPER SHAPE TO PLAY.

To ensure proper training and practice progressions, to optimize training and performance, and to outsmart your injuries, it is important to look at all of the factors that affect your physical training and performance.

Factors affecting training and performance

- Your chronological age.
- Your training age (how many years you have been seriously training).
- Your body type.
- Your pre-existing general and specific fitness level.
- Your strengths and weakness as identified by your coach, physical therapist, or strength and conditioning coach.
- Your strengths and weaknesses as identified by sport-specific field testing and lab testing where appropriate.
- Your general health status.
- The rehabilitation status of any of your past or current injuries.

The Fit to Play™ training model uses the concept of "interconnecting gears" to illustrate the importance of different factors in producing optimal performance and outsmarting injuries. This is a concept first described by sport scientist Dr. Howie Wenger from the University of Victoria, British Columbia.

Training gears. *Implementation of a training program requires management of many interrelated factors (adapted from Dr. Howie Wenger).*

For the performance gear to turn smoothly and efficiently, you must have control of the primary training gears including skill, strategies, physiology, environment, recovery, and psychology.

Performance is your central gear, and all of the other gears have an effect on its movement and ultimately affect performance. Some athletes can have success with high abilities in certain areas but not others; however, to perform optimally and consistently, all of the gears must be working. The performance gear must turn smoothly and efficiently in order to perform at a high level. Your training programs should be designed in consultation with your coach, a sports physiotherapist, a strength and conditioning specialist (fitness coach), and sports science and medicine personnel, if available.

Multidimensional training. *Because performance is multidimensional, so must be training, and optimal performance depends on a well-designed, structured program.*

THE MAIN RESPONSIBILITY FOR YOUR TRAINING AND PLAYING PROGRAM DESIGN AND IMPLEMENTATION RESTS WITH YOU.

THE S'S OF SMART TRAINING

The responsibility for making yourself a better player and athlete falls directly on your shoulders. To optimize your training and performance, improve recovery, and outsmart your injuries, you need to develop and build a good six-point plan that includes:

1. Structured training and practice.

2. Structured yearly planning and periodization.

3. Structured environment.

4. Structured mental training.

5. Structured physical/medical assessments.

6. Structured recovery and injury prevention.

4

This book is organized into six parts, detailing this six-point plan for structured training both off and on court. A short overview of each step follows.

S-1. Structured Training and Practice

- Develop specific training and competition plans.
- Consult with a coach sports physiotherapist, strength and conditioning specialist, or fitness coach.
- Develop contingency plans for adverse weather conditions (indoor courts or daily physical training adjustment), training partners, facilities available, and fatigue level.
- If you're not working with a coach, choose your practice partners wisely.
- Find a like-minded training partner with whom you can decide on a practice plan and take turns running the practice sessions.
- Organize the training sessions into three parts:
    1. Warm-up.
    2. Specific drills or exercises.
    3. Cool-down.
- Specific drills should progress in stages from learning a new skill, technique, or tactic to practicing it with drills, playing points, and match play (speak to your coach for suggestions on structuring your practice sessions).
- Remember that properly structured competition can be the most desirable form of training.
- Ensure appropriate equipment and clothing (shoes, clothing, sunscreen, hats, etc.).
- Use video analysis to optimize biomechanics of strokes and help identify areas for improvement.
- Include appropriate recovery strategies after each training session.

(Turn to Part I for more high performance training tips.)

PRACTICE IS PART OF YOUR JOB AS A PLAYER. SURE IT CAN BE HARD WORK, BUT IF YOU LOVE THE GAME AND WANT TO IMPROVE, IT IS WHAT YOU HAVE TO DO.

S-2. Structured Yearly Planning and Periodization

- The yearly planning and periodization of your training season must include pre-competition training, in-competition maintenance, and post-season recovery breaks.

- The main objective is to balance the intensity, volume, and density of training, competition, and recovery.

- Your competition season should be planned for playing your best at tournaments by dividing time into three phases:

Off-court training. *Tennis training involves both off-court and on-court training, skills development, and competitive practice.*

  1. Pre-competition (preparing for a tournament).

  2. In-competition maintenance (playing tournaments).

  3. Post-competition rest and active rest (recovery after a tournament).

		v	w	x	y	z	aa	bb	cc	dd	ee	ff	gg	hh	ii	jj	kk	ll	mm	nn	oo	pp
Dates	Month	Sep		Oct					Nov				Dec					Jan	97			Feb
of	Weekend	15	22	29	6	13	20	27	3	10	17	24	1	8	15	22	29	5	12	19	26	2
Camps &	Domestic																					
Comps	International																					
	Location																					
	Training Phase																					
Physical	Suppleness																					
Component	Stamina Aerobic																					
	Stamina Anaerobic																					
	Endurance Strength																					
	Base Strength																					
	Maximum Strength																					
	Speed Strength																					
	Event Spec. Str.																					
	Agil/Bal/Co-ord																					
	Active Rest																					
Period-	Macro-Cycle																					
ization	Micro-Cycle																					
	Peaking Index																					
Sport	Monitoring																					
Science	Medical Control																					
	Sport Psych																					
	Sport Vision																					
	Therapy																					
Forms	Team Dryland																					
of	Home Dryland																					
Preperation	Ski Camp																					
	Recovery/Regen																					

Periodization chart

- Within each training and playing cycle, you need to include on-court training, tournaments, off-court fitness and conditioning, and rest and recovery strategies. The amount of each will depend on the purpose of the cycle.
- Yearly planning and periodization will reduce the risk of boredom, staleness, burnout, overtraining, and injury.
- Planning gives the player and coach a better understanding of the overall training program, its goals, and its implementation.

Turn to Part 2 for more high performance training tips.

PERIODIZING YOUR IN-COMPETITION PLAN WILL OPTIMIZE PERFORMANCE AND DECREASE INJURY POTENTIAL.

S-3. Structured Environment

In order to play and train at your best, you must manage all the areas that affect your performance, not just what happens on court. The multifaceted needs of today's athletes cannot be met by the coach or parents alone. As training age increases and training demands become more comprehensive and sophisticated, you will need to draw upon the advice and knowledge of other professionals such as sport physicians, physiotherapists, mental trainers, nutritionists, strength and conditioning coaches, and other sport scientists to ensure a safe, effective off- and on-court conditioning program.

Optimizing training, performance, and recovery and outsmarting your injuries require proper management of several factors:

- Proper nutrition before, during, and after training or competition.
- Adequate hydration.
- Jet lag and travel concerns.
- Environmental concerns such as playing and training in the heat and at altitude.
- Doping and ergogenic aid concerns.
- Staying healthy on the road.

Turn to Part 3 for more high performance training tips.

S-4. Structured Mental Training

- Keep a journal or diary and use it.
- Ensure that resources for appropriate sport psychology or mental training are available to you.
- Set goals with your mental trainer or sport psychologist.
- Practice imagery, distraction control, and relaxation techniques.
- Examine your athletic requirements in the context of your daily life, considering such things as social climate, school, work, family, interpersonal relations, and daily stresses such as exams, deadlines, and personal conflicts.
- Plan well to achieve good balance between training and relaxation.
- Use video feedback and mental review of practice and tournament situations to practice mentally without the physical overload to the body's tissues.

Turn to Part 4 for more high performance training tips.

S-5. Structured Assessments (Medical and Physical)

Medical

- Comprehensive pre-participation medical screening including ligament laxity tests, blood work, and urinalysis.
- Get prompt help for any and all injuries and illnesses.
- Keep readily accessible the telephone, fax, and e-mail information of your health care professionals.
- Carry first aid supplies and have ice available for prompt attention to sore muscles or joints.

Physical
1. Sport Specific Assessment

- Prevention of injuries can be facilitated by preseason screening.
- Screening is best done at least 6-8 weeks prior to the start of your heavy tournament period.
- A sport-specific assessment by someone who knows what to look for may save you a lot of pain and frustration later in the season.
- Have your physiotherapist screen you for potential vulnerable or problem areas such as:

- Previously injured or chronic injury sites.

- Abnormally tight or loose joints and muscles.

- Weak or easily fatigued muscles.

- Postural problems.

- Malalignment issues.

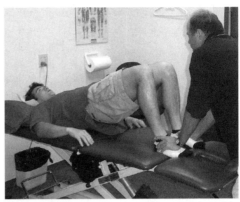

Sport specific assessments. *These can be critical to your long-term success.*

- Doing a comprehensive orthopedic assessment along with the Athlete Self Screening Exam™ and the Fit To Play™. Additional Functional Strength Tests will give you some ideas as to potential areas that need to be addressed.

OLD INJURIES ARE PERHAPS THE BIGGEST RISK FACTOR FOR A NEW INJURY.

2. Field Testing and Laboratory Assessments

- Physiological assessments including field tests and selected laboratory tests will provide objective insight on:

  - How your training is progressing and what you need to work on.

  - Your strengths and weaknesses .

  - How you compare to your peers.

- Test protocols should be set and reviewed based on current research and practice.

- Reassessment with the same tests, testing conditions, and preferably the same tester should be done several times per year.

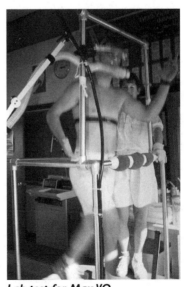

Lab test for Max VO$_2$

- Work with your sport federation or a local sport scientist and develop a protocol of tests based on the facilities and equipment available to you.

Turn to Part 5 for more high performance training tips.

S-6. Structured Recovery and Injury Prevention

Injury prevention and management must be an integral part of your off- and on-court training program. There are several key components to successfully out-smart your injuries.

Proper Training and Recovery Strategies

Training and competing are never 100-percent injury free. You are working hard, pushing yourself to the limits to achieve your best performance, and injuries are an ever present danger. Furthermore, due to the asymmetrical nature of many sports, tennis included, the most common injuries are of the overuse variety. The cumulative effect of pounding around the courts and repetitive actions such as hitting ground strokes or overheads can cause tissue breakdown and inflammation (micro-trauma). However, injuries can be minimized and controlled with proper recovery strategies and a sensible injury prevention and management strategy at the heart of your training plan.

The benefits of structured recovery sessions are well documented, both in terms of improved performance and decreased injury rates. Athletes, coaches, and parents need to be aware of techniques in order to outsmart injuries following heavy workloads. The best planned and periodized training program is of little use if you are always injured and unable to train or compete effectively.

Recovery. *Proper recovery strategies are essential to maximize workout results.*

Develop a Team of Sports Medicine and Science Specialists

As the athlete progresses up the competition ladder and the sophistication of performance increases, the coaches and parents must act as coordinators for the sport medicine and science needs of the athlete.

There are many types of specialists that an athlete might include on his team:

Specialists

- Physical therapists.
- Other therapists including certified athletic trainers, registered massage therapists, osteopaths, and chiropractors.
- Personal trainers, strength and conditioning specialists, and exercise physiologists.
- Medical doctors and surgeons (all specialties including wrist, knee, etc.).
- Sport psychologists, mental trainers, and psychiatrists.
- Podiatrists (foot doctor) and orthotic technicians.
- Dieticians.
- Optometrists/ophthalmologists (eye doctor).
- Dentists.

Choosing Your Team

As a high performance athlete, you are faced with many decisions about your health and well-being. Whether you are trying to improve your performance on court or treat and outsmart injuries, finding the right sports medicine and science specialist is important.

Tips to help you make the right decision

- Beware of people who make unrealistic claims.
- Check the credentials of the specialist to save yourself from ineffective training and/or treatment.
- Is the specialist licensed or unlicensed, board-approved or certified? Are the sports medicine and science personnel and other professional health care providers licensed and/or certified, have formal training, and regularly attend continuing education courses?
- Does the specialist have any advanced training such as a fellowship, doctorate, or clinical specialty?
- How many years of general and sport-specific experience does the specialist have?
- Can the specialist supply you with references with whom you can speak?

The members of your team should understand their role in the overall scheme of off- and on-court training, treatment and care, and have a good understanding of health issues related to tennis. As well, they should possess certain qualities.

Introduction

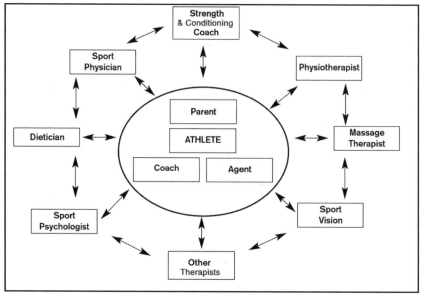

Your performance team *(adapted from Bruker & Khan, 2002)*

Team members should be

- Well respected and recognized in the field (ask other athletes and coaches).
- Good communicators.
- Good listeners.
- Confident in themselves, recognize their scope of practice, and recommend referrals where appropriate.
- Able to emphasize the importance of physical, mental, and emotional health and well being to ensure a long playing career.
- Realistic about setting achievable goals and expectations for your season.
- Willing to allow you to set your own goals and respect and support them.
- Willing to work with you to design and plan your season, including pre-competition, in-competition, and post-competition, to optimize performance and enhance health and well being.

Turn to Part 6 for more high performance recovery strategies.

By following the S's of smart training and adhering to the high performance training tips included in this book, you will be well on the way to making yourself a better player and athlete.

LEARNING SURVIVAL STRATEGIES TO MINIMIZE INJURIES IS FAR MORE PRODUCTIVE THAN LEARNING HOW TO TREAT THEM.

Successful athletes and coaches use sport-specific training and recovery programs that are scientifically based. They make effective use of mental training and ensure optimal health and nutrition.

It is vital that all players and coaches keep up-to-date with current research on off- and on-court training techniques and constantly strive to update their training and coaching practices.

References

Brukner, P. & Khan, K. (2002). Principles of Injury Prevention in Clinical Sports Medicine. Roseville: McGraw Hill Australia Pty Ltd. Page 5.

Wenger, H.A. 2003. Personal communication

Additional Reading

Balyi, I. & Hamilton, A. (2003). Chapter 2-Long-Term Athlete Development, Trainability and Physical Preparation of Tennis Players. In: M. Reid, A.Quinn and M. Crespo (eds). Strength and Conditioning for Tennis. London: ITF, Ltd.

Bloom, B. (1985). Developing Talent in Young People. New York: Ballantines.

Bollettieri, N. (1999). Nick Bollettieri Classic Tennis Handbook. New York: Tennis Week.

Bompa, Tudor (1995). From Childhood to Champion Athlete. Toronto: Veritas Publishing Inc.

Brody, H. (1987). Tennis Science for Tennis Players. Philadelphia: University of Pensylvania Press.

Coaching Association of Canada. National Coaching Certification Program (NCCP) Level 4/5 Coaches Certification.

Crespo, M., Reid, M., & Miley, D. (2003). Applied Sport Science for High Performance Tennis. Proceedings of the 13th ITF Worldide Coaches Workshop. Vilamoura, Portugal. London, England: International Tennis Federation.

Roetert, P. & Ellenbecker, T.S. (1998). USTA Complete conditioning for tennis. Champaign: Human Kinetics.

Salmels, J.H., Young, B.W., and Kallio, J. (1998). Within-career Transitions of the Athlete-Coach-Parent Triad. In: Wylleman, P. and Lavallee, D., (eds.). Career transitions in sport: A sourcebook for practitioners and researchers. Morgantown, VA: FIT Publications.

MY SPORTS MEDICINE AND SCIENCE TEAM

Medical:
Principal Physician _____

Tel:_____ Fax:_____

E-mail:_____

Principal Physical Therapist _____

Tel:_____ Fax:_____

E-mail:_____

Other Therapist_____

Tel:_____ Fax:_____

E-mail:_____

Principle Coach_____

Tel:_____ Fax:_____

E-mail:_____

Sport Psychologist/Mental Trainer_____

Tel:_____ Fax:_____

E-mail:_____

Sport Scientists and Others_____

Tel:_____ Fax:_____

E-mail:_____

PART ONE

Structured Training & Practice

Chapter One

The ABCs of Smart Training

Carl Petersen

When designing your training program, it is wise to follow the concepts outlined in the ABCs of smart training. Apply the ABCs of smart training during all off- and on-court training and all daily activities, including school and travel. Following the ABCs will increase training potential, improve skills, improve recovery time, and decrease injury potential.

A1–Athletic Stance and Alignment

Proper athletic stance means being prepared for the sports activity ahead. Think of keeping the knees soft (slightly bent), switch on your core (pelvic tension like a dimmer switch), and keep your shoulders relaxed and down and head neutral. Correct anatomical alignment must be attained and maintained to allow for proper force distribution upon the weight-bearing structures during activity. This can be facilitated by:

- Actively stretching muscles that are usually short and stiff (e.g., hamstrings, hip flexors, calves, and pectorals).

- Actively strengthening muscles that are usually long and weak (e.g., lower abdominals, upper back and posterior shoulder girdle muscles [infraspinatus], and hip external rotators [gluteal muscles]).

Proper alignment starts with excellent spinal alignment. To align your spine:

- Imagine someone pulling you by the top of your head, lengthening out your spine.

17

- The neck should be long and the shoulders relaxed, back, and down.

Checks on proper alignment include these:

- During movement emphasize correct knee alignment, with knees always tracking over the toes but not going past them.
- When doing lunges or split squats, keep the line of gravity through the pubic bone of the pelvis to avoid shear forces on the pelvic joints.

Ball squat. *Knees should track in line with the toes but never go past them.*

Ball split squat. *When doing split squats or lunges, ensure the line of gravity through pubic symphysis (bone).*

A2–ADAPTIVE TRAINING

High performance and superior levels of fitness are the result of many months or years of well-planned training. Adaptations occur to the body's systems when they are challenged by new stresses. If the workload is not high enough, no adaptation will occur. If the workload is too high, maladaptation occurs, possibly leading to over-training, overuse, and injury. The following are some principles of adaptive training:

- When designing a training program, one must respect the time frames for anatomical, physiological, and psychological adaptation to occur.

- Regular participation—at least 4–6 days per week—in a planned activity outside of tennis.

- Overload:
    - The training load must be high enough to tax the body's systems during a training session.
    - Overload encourages physical change and promotes adaptation.
    - To achieve overload, the duration of the activity must be long enough to produce a training effect and the intensity of the workouts must increase in a gradual and progressive manner.
    - A good rule of thumb is to increase intensity 10 percent per week.

- Regularly scheduling rest or recovery days (at least one per week):
    - Helps tissues such as muscle, tendon, ligament, and bone to adapt to the new stresses being placed on them through training and sports.
    - Helps prevent staleness or over-training.

Recovery. *Recovery and rest is an essential part of training.*

A3–AGILITY TRAINING AND ACCELERATION (QUICKNESS) DRILLS

Playing and training for tennis often find you off balance and in a uncontrolled environment such as wind, playing surfaces, and unpredictable opponents. Tennis requires stops and starts, lateral movements, backpedaling, crossover turns, and pivots. But with the decreased physical education in schools and lack of multi-sport involvement due to early sport specialization, many young players do not get the agility training needed. So, some form of agility and coordination training should be included as part of your daily sessions; you do not want to be an athlete who can play but cannot move. Points to remember when training for agility are these:

- Always start with an athletic stance.

- Agility and acceleration (quickness) drills must be structured so the muscles learn to fire quickly and in a coordinated manner.

- Quickness within two steps in all directions is key in tennis.

- Straight line sprinting may serve a conditioning purpose and helps fire the CNS (central nervous system), but it has little use in tennis.

- Agility and acceleration allow smaller players to be able to compete well and give larger players another weapon in their game.

- Agility can be gained by playing other sports and dynamic games that involve lateral movement and quick stops and starts, or by doing circuit drills that incorporate different exercises.

- Explosive first step side shuffle and crossover steps are essential to tennis quickness.

- You must give your body the opportunity to practice and play with changed and strengthened muscles.

See Chapter 4 for more ideas.

Agility cone slalom. *Use different exercises in a circuit fashion to improve agility.*

Step-ups. *Challenging the body in different ways will help develop agility and optimize performance.*

B1–BALANCED TRAINING

Balanced training means a correct ratio of time spent on the different components of fitness and performance: flexibility, stamina (aerobic and anaerobic), strength, speed, coordination, and tennis-specific skill exercises. All are important components of fitness and should be included in your program, depending on the phase of training you are in. Obviously, different activities have different demands and will require more emphasis on one type of training than another.

Example:

Each training week or cycle should include the proper amount of rest or alternative activity to allow for adequate adaptation to occur. Training-to-rest ratios vary depending upon the energy systems used, the event or sport, and the personality and training age of the athlete.

In general, training the different components of fitness can be done as follows:

• Suppleness (flexibility)	Daily (5–6 x per week)
• Stamina (aerobic)	Daily (5–6 x per week)
• Stamina (anaerobic)	Alternate days (2–3 x per week)
• Strength	Alternate days (2–3 x per week)
• Skill	Daily (4–5–6 x per week)
• Power	Alternate days (2 x per week)

Table 1.1. Frequency of exercise by type

B2–BALANCED BODY STRENGTHENING

Balanced training ensures that equal stress is put on the different parts of the body in different planes of movement. This achieves a good balance of stress for the body's upper and lower extremities and three-dimensional core cylinder. Work both sides equally to get a good balance between:

- Right and left sides.
- Flexor and extensor muscles.
- Medial and lateral rotators.
- Upper and lower body and core.

Planes of motion: Coronal, sagital, and transverse.

Split squat. Split squat with rotation and X-Band cords work the upper and lower body in different planes.

Example

Strength training should include exercises for all of the above areas. Try 2–3 upper body, 2–3 lower body, and 3–4 core exercises to ensure a good balance.

B3–BALANCE EXERCISES

Balance exercises are a fundamental component of functional mobility and dynamic activity and should be a part of everyone's training routine. Working on balance training is even more important as you increase strength and speed because you want to continually reset the balance clock and have the opportunity to practice and play with your newly adapted and strengthened muscles. Balance exercises:

Dynamic Edge Ski. Use a variety of equipment to optimize your balance training in different positions.

- Work on joint sense (proprioception).

- Reset the balance clock with a variety of exercises.

- Stimulate the complex interactions of the neuromuscular system when incorporated with closed chain and functional exercises.

- Are especially important after injury where there is any joint swelling and decreased proprioception.

- Should be included as part of the daily training plan as most activities depend on an element of coordinated balance in many planes of movement.

See Chapter 5 for more ideas.

B4–BEFORE AND AFTER: SEQUENCING YOUR TRAINING AND PRACTICE SESSIONS

- Follow a logical sequence from easy to hard training and simple to complex exercises.

Example:

> ▶ Continuous running before sprint training.

> ▶ General strength training exercises before hopping and bounding.

Small muscle group

- Properly sequencing your training and practice during the day is important to avoid them from interfering with each other.

- Correct sequencing also helps minimize central nervous system (CNS) fatigue so you will be better able to learn new skills.

Small movements

- Sequence your warm up, fitness training, and strength and practice sessions as shown in Table 1.2 to improve your ability to perform.

Large muscle group　　*Large movements*

	Warm-Up	Fitness Training	Strength Exercises	On-Court Training and Drills

START	• small muscles
	• small movements
	• controlled movement (static-conform)
		Anaerobic alactic (less than 15 sec)
		
		• CNS warm-up
		• agility drills
		• coordination
		• fast feet circuits
		• strength (max power)
		• technique
			Extremity strength
			
			• large muscles
			  - quadriceps
			  - hamstrings
			• hip extensors
			• multi-joint
			  - split squats
			  - lunges
			  - step ups
				Anaerobic alactic (less than 15 sec)
				
				• CNS warm-up
				• fast feet circuits
				• 4—5 ball drills
				• volleys
				• technique
				• short sprints
				• jumps

		Anaerobic lactic (15 sec to 2 min) • short intervals • hills/stairs • strength (endurance) • 10 ball drills • training High quality aerobic (2 min +) • long intervals (600m) • Fartlek routines		**Anaerobic lactic** (15 sec to 2 min) • 6—10 ball drills • catching tossed balls • rolling balls

END	• large muscles
	• large movements
	• dynamic movement
		Low quality aerobic (20 min +)
		
		• continuous (long, slow distance)
		• recovery work
			• Core strength
			  - back extensors
			  - abdominals
			• Small muscle groups
			  - hip rotators
			  - dorsiflexors
			• Single-joint exercise
			  - hamstring curls
			  - toe raises
				Recovery/Reps (2 min+)
				
				• serving practice
				• slow running
				• slow hitting

Table 1.2

C1–Consistent Training

Training should be consistent enough to force adaptations to the cardio-respiratory system (heart and lungs) and the musculo-skeletal system (soft tissue and bone). Table 1.1 gives guidelines for the necessary training consistency necessary to induce the desired adaptations. Consistent training means:

- Knowing what you are doing.
- Having confidence in your training program and plans.

- Having confidence in both on- and off-court training plans.
- Being able to justify what you are doing and why you are doing it.

Consistency doesn't mean "the same." You will continually individualize your program based on your needs and you will progress your training based on fitness gains, your goals, and feed-back from your coaches, therapists, and strength and conditioning coaches. Consistency is one antidote to the principle of reversibility: If you don't use it, you'll lose it. The training effect will be lost if training is stopped or spaced too far apart to trigger the adaptations.

C2–CORE CONTROL

You must train to improve the body's ability to stabilize the core and generate power outward to the limbs.

- Core musculature helps create movement at the spine and also exerts a stabilizing muscular force to maintain a neutral spine and pelvis.
- Use a variety of movements and training types to ensure a balanced approach to core training.
- Always switch on your core (low background tension—like a dimmer switch of the pelvic floor and lower abdominals) during all exercise and activity including tennis, training, and playing other sports.
- 3-Dimensional core stability is important to give you the strong platform to execute movements with the extremities.
- In health, there is a pre-anticipatory contraction, but with dysfunction, there is a timing delay or absence, so the muscle must be actively switched on by appropriate exercise.

Supine bridging. *This core exercise allows you to gain control of the pelvic floor and lower abdominal (transversus abdominus).*

- Remember, efficient movement needs optimal stabilization and requires intact bones, joints, and ligaments; efficient and coordinated muscle action; and appropriate neural responses.

See Chapter 6 for more core training ideas.

C3–Chain Exercises: Closed, Partially Closed, and Open

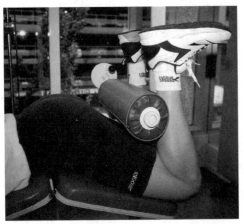

Leg curls. *Open chain exercise.*

To understand the concepts surrounding closed, partially closed, and open kinetic chain, view your body as a length of chain. Open kinetic chain exercise occurs when the end of the chain (arms or legs) is not fixed and does not support the weight of the body. Open kinetic chain exercises are best characterized as isolation movements—for instance, leg extension, leg curls, or bicep curls.

Closed kinetic chain exercise occurs when the hands or feet support the body weight. Closed kinetic chain is best referred to as *dynamic* and *functional* with the whole body working as an integrated unit. Examples of this would be a lunge or a squat.

Partially closed chain exercises would be any that partially support your body weight and require an integrated response from the muscles of the body. Examples of this would be a push-up position where the hands and feet partially bear the weight or any activity that loads resistance through the hands and arms and into the torso, as when using resistance bands, for example.

In all ground-based sports such as tennis, all of the body movements work within a kinetic chain linkage from the ground through the trunk. Understandably, then, problems most commonly arise with weak, tight hip flexors and weak gluteals. All three types and mixes of kinetic chain training should be utilized based on the needs of the individual and the demands of the sport. Exercises should be performed with the following points in mind:

- Exercises should be done in a controlled, coordinated, and functional manner.
- Exercises should work the hip in an extended position because it is the position of activity and function (see D2).

- Exercises like step-ups, split squats, and lunges can be made more functional by adding elastic tubing to partially close the upper core chain.

- Activation of the kinetic chain sling patterns from the legs through the hips and back to the shoulder restores the force-dependent motor activation pattern and normal biomechanical positions.

See Chapter 6 for more core training ideas.

Step-ups. *Train in a hip-extended position of function while partially closing and firing the upper core.*

D1–DIVERSITY IN DRILLS AND TRAINING

Training with diversity means using a variety of methods in your weekly program. For example, aerobic training may use a mix of running, cycling, swimming, or in-line skating to get the desired effect of aerobic fitness. Besides offering a greater range of non-weight-bearing alternatives for training, diverse training promotes development of fundamental skills. For example, core training may use a mix of floor, standing, ball, and cord exercises. Diversify training by:

- Analyzing the sport-specific movements and adding movement and challenging

Ball sit-downs. *Adding a variety of resistance and balance components increases the diversity of training.*

balance in ways that mimic the activity without introducing a high element of risk for injury.

- Altering exercises.
- Altering sequence of exercises.
- Changing the tempo to avoid drudgery and avoid over-training.
- Adding weights, balance equipment, balls, and stretch cords to increase the core component.
- Have specific training goals that make sense and have appropriate application to the sport.

D2–DYNAMIC HIP EXTENSION EXERCISES

- Hip-extended strength is the position of function for sports.
- The competitive posture shortens anterior muscles so athletes must have strength and stability into hip extension.
- Training should include exercises that promote both dynamic flexibility and strength.
- This type of exercise improves general fitness and helps you in your normal activities of daily living, such as lifting, stepping, carrying, pushing, or pulling.
- Utilize exercises that focus on connecting the core to the activity and that combine upper body, lower body, and core moves.

Hip extension. *This is crucial to optimal functional movement.*

D3–DECELERATION CONTROL

Tennis requires control during high-speed movements to allow you to quickly stop on a dime (decelerate) and then explode laterally or forward (accelerate) to get to a shot. Deceleration control occurs during:

- Quick stops.
- Direction changes.
- Follow through.

Muscles provide deceleration control by creating counter-force by lengthening (eccentric "contraction").

E1–EXERCISE AT A SLOW AND CONTROLLED TEMPO (SOMETIMES)

- Some exercises should be performed slowly.
- Controlled repetitions that take three to four seconds to complete help increase tension in the muscle fibers and build strength without too much stress on the soft tissues.
- Avoid using momentum to perform an exercise or doing exercises that are uncontrolled.
- Remember, training is not necessarily playing. Don't confuse the two when doing exercises.

DON'T JUST PLAY TO GET FIT, GET FIT TO PLAY™.

Deceleration. *Tennis requires control of high-speed movements.*

Standing hip abducton. *Slow tempo increases hip stability.*

E2–Excellent Form

While training, attention must be paid to form:

- Exercises should be functional and mimic sport and life's challenges.

- Always remember the importance of good form when doing an exercise.

- Correct form includes correct breathing, exhale on exertion (no breath holding), and always switch on your core (pelvic tension) prior to any exercise.

- Ensure quality of motion using good biomechanics as opposed to quantity with less precise form.

F1–Functional Training

Functional movement requires all the joints in the kinetic chain and the neurological system to work in concert in a coordinated and harmonious manner.

Tips for functional training

- Use multi-dimensional, multi-joint movement, not just isolated actions at one joint.

- Start by practicing parts of the movement, then combine the parts into movement drills, then practice and rehearse the movement drills, and then incorporate it into the activity or sport.

- Integrate multiple joint movements, linking the closed and partially closed kinetic chain.

- Functional training does not isolate muscles in a single plane of movement, but instead requires stabilization in three planes of motion during dynamic movement.

- Functional training must be dynamic in nature and require the participant to accelerate, decelerate, stop on a dime, change

Functional training. *Functional training develops powerful and coordinated multi-joint and multi-dimensional movement.*

directions, react to ground forces, and constantly adjust and react to different situations.

- Effective function and rehabilitation are best developed by using a variety of methods.

F2–FLEXIBLE PLANNING

- Remain flexible in your planning; training plans can be modified based on situation and circumstance.

- Be in control of your training plan, not a slave to it.

- When traveling, equipment and facilities will vary greatly. Be flexible and adaptable in your training routines. Take advantage of good facilities, including whirlpools and other recovery tools, when available, and have other routines you can do with minimal equipment.

F3–FUN

- Training and playing with different drills are, by their very nature, fun.

- Improvement is fun. Challenge yourself with hard training that makes use of natural movement patterns and allows you to improve and optimize performance.

- Remember that you play the game to compete and achieve success, but also to be with friends and have fun.

KEEP IT FUN: TRAINING SHOULD BE FUN AND STIMULATING, BOTH PHYSICALLY AND MENTALLY. IF IT'S NOT, WHY ARE YOU DOING IT?

Chapter Two

Dynamic Warm-Up and Cool-Down Guidelines

Carl Petersen

W hether you're getting ready for a match or trying to get the most out of your hitting or physical training sessions, following the advice below will help you perform well. You should do a sport- or activity-specific warm-up before every practice or playing session. To optimize your practice or training time and get the most for your time and energy, make sure that you are both physically and mentally prepared before stepping on the court, gym, or other training venue.

Slowly warming-up the body helps prevent injuries caused by going too hard and too fast with cold, unlubricated muscles and joints. Warm-ups vary depending on the type, duration, and intensity of activity you are going to do. It consists of a group of exercises performed immediately before the activity and provides a period of adjustment from rest to exercise. You must warm up to train, play, or stretch. Use any large muscle group activities like running, in-line skating, cycling, rowing, or skipping rope until a light sweat is achieved (Fig. 2.1, 2.2). This ensures that the temperature of the joints and soft tissues is increased. A good 10–15 minute warm-up will help optimize your training time. Warming up for 20–30 minutes will help contribute to your general tennis conditioning, especially early in the season.

ONE OF THE MAIN CONTRIBUTORS TO INJURY IN THE CLUB PLAYER IS THE COMPLETE ABSENCE OF ANY PRE-PLAY WARM-UP ROUTINE.

Fig. 2.1–2 *General warmup of large muscle groups with elliptical trainer and rope skipping.*

Proper warm-up prepares the muscles you will use in training and prepares the joints for movement and dynamic stability throughout a full range of motion. To warm up properly:

- Start slowly and increase the intensity and complexity of the warm-up.

- Use tennis-specific movements to help improve the relaxation-contraction coordination of the joints' prime movers and stabilizers. This will lead to more efficient movement and performance.

- Take extra time to perform a good warm-up on cold or windy days. A warm muscle is not only stronger, but its elastic properties are also increased (a two-degree increase of muscle temperature can increase a muscle's elastic properties by as much as 15–20 percent), allowing for better shock absorption.

- Warm up until you have a light glow (sweat).

YOU SHOULD DO A SPECIFIC DYNAMIC WARM-UP BEFORE EVERY TRAINING OR PRACTICE SESSION TO PREPARE YOURSELF BOTH MENTALLY AND PHYSICALLY.

Whatever warm-up method you use, your intensity should not be so hard that you are creating lactic acid in the muscles. So keep your heart rate low—about 110–130, depending on your age and maximum heart rate.

On the Borg Scale of Perceived Exertion you will be working between levels 3 and 5 (see Table 2.1).

Table 2.1. Dynamic Warm-up Intensity (Borg, 1982)		
Borg Scale of Perceived Exertion		**Talk Test Guidelines**
0	Nothing at all	Can very easily carry on a conversation.
1	Very easy	
2	Easy	
3	Moderate	You should be able to carry on a conversation.
4	Somewhat hard	
5	Hard	
6		Cannot talk continuously.
7	Very hard	
8		Cannot talk at all.
9		
10	Very, very heavy (maximal)	

ACTIVITY SPECIFIC WARM-UP IDEAS

Following are several activity-specific warm-ups that will give you some ideas to better prepare for the activity ahead.

Knee Warm-Up (joint lubrication)

Do these warm-up exercises before any weights or any exercise (running, jumps, sports) that involves knee flexion (bending). These exercises help lubricate the under surface of the knee cap (patella), so it slides smoothly and tracks properly.

Exercises

- Assisted squats 2 x 10 reps (Fig. 2.3).
- No-weight knee extensions 2 x 10 reps.

- Fire VMO (medial quadriceps) with 5 x 1/2 squats (double and single-leg squats (Fig. 2.5).
- Hip warm-up—leg swings front-to-back (Fig 2.6), side-to-side (Fig. 2.7), figure 8, donkey kicks (Fig. 2.8–9); 2 x 10 reps.

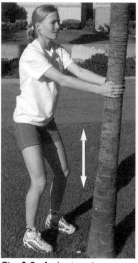

Fig. 2.3–4 *Assisted squats*   **Fig. 2.5** *Single leg squat*

Fig. 2.6 *Leg swings (front-to-back)*   **Fig. 2.7** *Leg swings (side-to-side)*

Fig. 2.8–9 *Donkey kicks (front and back)*

Warm-Up for Agility and Games

Before any exercise involving quick changes of direction, fast sprint-like movements, or lateral, front, and backwards movements, you want to make sure your low back, hips, ankles, and knees are warmed up. Try the following exercises to warm up the muscles and joints as well as to improve coordination and balance.

Exercises

- Aerobic activity x 8–10 minutes (run, skip rope, ride bike, row).
- Sprint drills x 20–30 meters:
    - Backward skips (toe reach).
    - Crossovers (with high knee drive) x 2 (Fig. 2.10).
    - High knees run (Fig. 2.11).
    - Side shuffles (8 reps / 8 reps.) (Fig. 2.12).
    4 Butt kicks (8 reps / 8 reps.) (Fig. 2.13).
- Dynamic flexibility x 10 reps:
    - Leg swings (front and back) (Fig. 2.6).
    - Leg swing figure 8s.
    - Hurdler's high knees (Fig. 2.14.16).
    - Standing torso twists (Fig. 2.17–18).
    - Crazy walks (heels, toes, inside foot) 1 x 2–5 meters each (Fig. 2.19–21).

Fig. 2.10 Crossovers

Fig. 2.11 High knee run

Fig. 2.12 Side shuffles

Fig. 2.13 Butt kicks

Fig. 2.14–16 *Hurdler's knees: straight, inside, outside*

Fig. 2.17–18 *Torso twists*

Fig. 2.19–21 *Crazy walks: heels, toes, inside of foot.*

Crazy walks, walking on heels, toes, and inside of feet will help improve balance and increase lower leg suppleness, strength, and ankle stability. Try going for 2 to 5 meters of each. The heel walks will strengthen the tibialis anterior muscle which is important to prevent tibial stress syndrome (shin splints).

Warm-Up for Strength (Weights)

Before doing a weight workout ensure you are well warmed-up with the following routine.

Exercises

- Aerobic activity x 10–12 minutes (treadmill run, skip rope, cycle, row).
- Knee warm-up (as above).

Fig. 2.22 *Wobble board (balance)*   **Fig. 2.23** *Physio ball balance*

- Balance and proprioception with wobble board (Fig. 2.22), rolled towel, physio balance ball (Fig. 2.23).
- Dynamic flexibility x 10 reps:
    ‣ Leg swings (front and back, side to side [Fig. 2.6–2.7] and figure 8s).
    ‣ Hurdlers high knees (Fig. 2.14–15).
    ‣ Donkey kicks (Fig. 2.8–2.9).

Warm-Up for Sprints

Before any exercise involving fast sprint-like movements, either on- or off-court, you want to make sure that your central nervous system (CNS) is firing properly in order to attain optimal performance and reaction time. A good speed warm-up will help trigger your CNS. Try the following dynamic warm-up.

Exercises

- Aerobic activity x 10 min. (run, skip rope, ride bike, row).

Fig. 2.24 Butt kicks

- Sprint drills x 20–30 meters:
    ‣ A march x 2.
    ‣ Skip with high knee drive x 2.
    ‣ Bounding (high) x 2.
    ‣ Butt kicks x 2 (Fig. 2.24).
- Dynamic flexibility x 10 reps:
    ‣ Donkey kicks x 2.
    ‣ Lying lower torso twists x 2 (Fig. 2.25–26).
    ‣ Thread the needle (Fig. 2.27–28).
    ‣ Supine bicycles x 2 (Fig. 2.29).

Fig. 2.25–26 Lying lower torso twists

Fig. 2.27–28 *Thread the needle (standing)*

Fig. 2.29 *Supine bicycles*

Fig. 2.30 *Running accel-erations*

Fig. 2.31 *Richochets (jumps in place)*

- Running accelerations—20–30 meters (Fig. 2.30):
  - ▸ Tempo runs at 60% x 2–3.
  - ▸ 0–70% (2 steps) x 2.
  - ▸ 0–80% (2 steps) x 2.
  - ▸ 0–85% (2 steps) x 2.
  - ▸ Fast run @ 85% x 2.
- Ricochets—jumps in place (Fig. 2.31):
  - ▸ Personal rhythm (PR) 2 x 20.
  - ▸ As fast as possible (AFAP) 2 x 20.

Warm-Up for Hopping and Bounding

Before any exercise involving jumps, hopping, and bounding movements, either on- or off-court, try the following dynamic muscle/tendon warm-up.

Exercises

- Aerobic activity x 10 min. (run, skip rope, ride bike, row).
- Sprint drills x 20–30 meters:
  - ▸ One side skips x 4 (2 per side).
  - ▸ Crossovers (cariokas) (as fast as possible) x 2 (Fig. 2.10).
  - ▸ High knees run x 2 (Fig. 2.11).
  - ▸ Side shuffles (tall) x 2 (Fig. 2.32).
- Dynamic flexibility x 10 reps:
  - ▸ Leg swings (figure 8s).
  - ▸ Lying lower torso twists x 2.
  - ▸ Alternating lunges x 2 (Fig. 2.33–34).
  - ▸ Sequential hops x 2 (Fig. 2.35–36).
- Accelerations (20 meters):
  - ▸ Tempo runs @ 50% x 2.
  - ▸ 0–65% (2 steps) x 1.
  - ▸ 0–75% (3 steps) x 2.
  - ▸ 0–85% (4 steps) x 2.
  - ▸ Tempo run @ 75% x 2.

Fig. 2.32 *Side shuffles*

Fig. 2.33–34 *Alternating lunges*

Fig. 2.35–36 *Hops and bounds*   **Fig. 2.37** *Progressive power jumps*

- Ricochets (jumps in place) (Fig. 2.31):
  - Personal rhythm (PR) 2 x 20.
  - As fast as possible 2 x 20.
- Progressive Power Jumps (Fig. 2.37):
  - 4/4/4 jumps @ 30/50/70% power.
  - 3/3/3 jumps @ 40/60/80% power.

Lower Body Warm-Up for Hitting Drills

Start with an easy jog around the court. As you jog add in the following exercises.

Exercises

- Coordination and general warmup:
  - High knees 2–4 x 5–10 meters (Fig. 2.38).
  - High heels 2–4 x 5–10 meters (Fig. 2.39).
  - Crossover steps 2–4 x 5–10 meters (Fig. 2.40).
  - Skipping 2–4 x 5–10 meters.
  - Side shuffle steps 2–4 x 5–10 meters.

Fig. 2.38 *High knees*   **Fig. 2.39** *High heels*   **Fig. 2.40** *Crossover steps*

Stop and hang onto the fence or net and further warm up the lower core with the following exercises that challenge your balance and warm up the hips and ankles.

- Balance and hip:
  - ▸ Leg swings (front and back; side-to-side) x 5–10 (Fig. 2.41–44).
  - ▸ Hurdler's high knees (inside, straight, and outside) x 5–10 (Fig. 2.45–47).
- Ankles:
  - ▸ Crazy walks (walking on heels, toes, and inside of feet) x 5 meters (Fig. 2.48–49).

Fig. 2.41–4 *Leg swings (front and back)*

Fig. 2.43–44 *Leg swings (side to side)*

Fig. 2.45–47 *Hurdler's knees—inside, straight, and outside*

Fig. 2.48 *Crazy walks on heels*

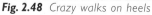

Fig. 2.49 *Crazy walks–inside inside of feet*

Upper Body Warm-up for Stroke Drills

Upper back, scapula, and shoulder warm-ups will improve function and control of your upper core, help initiate the correct muscle sequence firing, and lubricate the joint.

Exercises

- Shoulder and scapula:
  - ▸ Shoulder shrugs x 10–15.
  - ▸ Arm swings x 10–15 (Fig. 2.50).
  - ▸ Thread the needle x 10–15.
  - ▸ Dynamic pushups (narrow, medium, and wide hand position) 2 sets x 6 reps (Fig. 2.51–52).

Fig. 2.50 *Arm swings*

- Mid-scapular and post-rotator cuff with stretch cord 2 sets x 5–10 reps:
  - ▸ Rows (Fig. 2.53–54).
  - ▸ External rotations (Fig. 2.55–56).
  - ▸ Diagonals (Fig. 2.57–58).
  - ▸ Letter I, T, and W (Fig. 2.59–64).

Fig. 2.51–52 *Push-ups—wide and narrow*

Fig. 2.53–54 *Shoulder rows*

Fig. 2.55–56 *Shoulder external rotation*

Fig. 2.57–58 *Mid-back diagonal pulls*

Fig. 2.59–60 *Letter I*

Fig. 2.61–62 *Letter T*

Fig. 2.63–64 *Letter W*

Pre-Hit Conform Stretching

Dynamic warm-up is your best activity before playing. However, once you are warmed up, you can do some gentle conform stretches to maintain muscle length or to stretch out muscles that still feel tight (Fig. 2.65–69). These type of stretches are gentle moving stretches that are not aggressive enough to tear and weaken muscle fibers. Hold the stretches for 15–20 seconds at the point of tension only (*never pain*).

Fig. 2.65 *Quadriceps*

Fig. 2.66 *Hamstrings*

Fig. 2.67 *Iliotibial band*

Fig. 2.68 *Hip adductors*

Fig. 2.69a *Calf stretch (soleus)*   **Fig. 2.69b** *Calf stretch (gastrocnemius)*

Now you're ready
to step on the court.

On-Court Warm-Up

Work with your coach or hitting partner to develop an on-court warm-up strategy that works best for you. Warm-ups will vary depending on whether you're just out to hit, play a practice match, or play a tournament.

Hitting warm-up

- Suggested minimum on-court warm-up includes a sequence of 5–10 minutes of half-court tennis. Warm up the eye muscles by focusing on tracking the ball.

- Try for easy topspin with good contact and control. Get the racquet back early and groove the low to high stroke, focusing on contact and follow through.

- Play games like "preller" (bounce ball) or "slice ball" to get warmed up for lateral movement.

- Move back gradually and hit 20 forehands with minimal spin and medium pace.

- Next, hit 20–30 alternating backhands and forehands, increasing the spin, pace, and depth.

- Now it is time to come to the net and hit 10–15 volleys per side. Then hit some swinging vollys.

- Progress to some easy overheads. Try ten before hitting with any pace.

- Finally, try some easy serves. Start off concentrating on placement and rhythm using minimal spin or power for the first ten. Hit up the middle first and then swing out wider on the ad side, increasing upper body and hip rotation.

NOW YOU'RE READY TO PRACTICE OR PLAY.

COOL-DOWN AND RECOVERY WORKOUT

A gradual cool-down takes your body back to its resting state, helps clear lactic acid and other waste products from the muscles, and helps prevent "DOMS" (delayed onset muscle soreness) and "RMT" (residual muscle tension). For an adequate cool down, try 20–30 minutes of cycle spin (Fig. 2.71) at 75–80 RPM with heart a rate of 100–115 BPM or a water run (Fig. 2.70). On the Borg Scale of Perceived Exertion you will be working between levels 3 and 5 (Table 2.1). Follow this with an easy general stretch session.

See Chapter 31, High Performance Recovery Tips and Strategies, for other ideas.

Post-Hit Conform Stretching

Light stretching after training is important to minimize DOMS and reduce the potential for injury. Stretching exercises should be done as part of a regular post-training routine.

Instead of aggressively stretching, do a conform stretch, taking the stretch to the point of light tension and hold for 15–20 seconds. Be systematic, stretching all major muscle groups. This includes leg muscles of the quadriceps, hamstrings, calf, back, abductors, and adductors. Exhale on the initial stretch and then breathe normally.

GO EASY. NOW IS NOT THE TIME TO TRY TO AGGRESSIVELY
STRETCH TIGHT, TENSE, MUSCLES.

Fig. 2.70 *Water running*

Fig. 2.71 *Stationary cycle*

As well, stretches should be performed for the shoulders and elbows. Stretch the forearm extensors and flexors (Fig. 2.72–73), pectorals (Fig. 2.74), gluteals (Fig. 2.75) and hip flexors (Fig. 2.76). Stretch each muscle group to the point of tension, not pain.

See Chapter 3, Smart Stretching Guidelines, for more stretching ideas.

Fig. 2.72 *Forearm flexors*

Fig. 2.73 *Forearm extensors*

Fig. 2.74 *Pectoral Stretch*

Fig. 2.75 *Seated gluteals*

Fig. 2.76 *Hip flexor*

References

Borg, G. A. V. (1982). Psychophysical bases of percieved exertion. *Med. Sci. Sports Exerc.* 14(5), 377-381.

Additional Reading

Ellenbecker, T. & Roetert, P. (2001). The role of warm-up and stretching in tennis. In: M. Crespo, B. Pluim. & M. Reid. (Eds). *Tennis Medicine for Tennis Coaches.*

Chapter Three

Smart Stretching Guidelines

Carl Petersen

How often have you heard someone comment, "My hips are stiff and my back is sore. What should I do?" Well, the answer is stretch. Unfortunately, when time comes at a premium, the first thing to go is the most boring—stretching. But stretching is important, not only to aid recovery and keep the body moving well, but also to prevent injury. Normally, the muscles and tendon complexes will act as mini-shock absorbers for the joints. However, if they are short and stiff, the shock absorption capabilities are decreased, leading to stress on other areas.

Do conform, static, and facilitated stretches to optimize muscle and tendon length post training. Players should develop, with the aid of a physical trainer or physiotherapist, a static stretching routine that is performed consistently and comprises at least 12 exercises (Reque, 2003).

For some athletes, doing 12 different stretches may be too time consuming on a daily basis; therefore, choosing stretches that are multi-muscle and multi-joint can maximize stretching effectiveness while minimizing time spent. One way to do this is to stretch while on the phone or computer or when in the sauna or whirlpool.

Stretching should be done daily after a proper warm-up (achieve a light sweat) and during the cool-down period after on- or off-court training. If you're running late, stretch at home while text messaging or watching television.

Utilize a variety of stretching types to optimize your flexibility gains.

MANY SHORT STRETCHES THROUGHOUT THE DAY ARE BETTER THAN DOING NONE.

Five types of stretching are discussed in this chapter:

- Dynamic Stretching.
- Conform Stretching.
- Slow Static Stretching.
- Facilitated Partner Stretching.
- Myofascial Ball Stretching.

DYNAMIC STRETCHING

This utilizes moving stretches that are controlled and combine multiple joint movements in order to increase the limits of range of motion prior to dynamic activities. The following are some examples of dynamic stretching:

Dynamic stretches

- Shoulder and arm swings.
- Hip and leg swings (front and back).
- Hip and leg swings (side to side).
- High knees.
- High heels drills.
- Alternating lunges.
- Torso twists.
- Crossovers.

If tennis players have normal levels of flexibility, the warm-up routine should focus on dynamic stretching or general movements of gradually increased intensity.

High knees

Hip and leg swings (front and back)

Alternating lunges   **Torso twists**   **Crossovers**

Dynamic stretching used as a warm-up helps normalize joint mechanics, increases the dynamic range of motion (ROM), improves joint position sensors (proprioception), and improves the "relaxation-contraction" coordination. This type of stretching is appropriate prior to beginning any activity and must be included as part of the pre-tennis warm-up (see Chapter 2 for detailed tennis warm-up).

Conform Stretching (Pre-activity)

While research suggests that static stretching is not appropriate prior to activity, conform stretches are easy, controlled, low range of motion moving stretches that take the muscles and joints through a comfortable range of motion. They are not aggressive enough to tear or aggravate muscle fibers that are already shortened or injured due to hard exercise. Conform stretches are best done immediately before or after exercise and held only for 15–20 seconds as part of the gradual cool down (see Chapter 2 for pre-hit conform stretches).

Conform Stretching (Post-Training)

Continued movement and light stretching after training are important to minimize DOMS (delayed onset muscle soreness) and reduce the potential for injury. Muscle soreness is believed to be decreased with mild stretching exercises performed during the cool down period (Prentice, 1983). Stretching exercises should be done as part of a regular routine. Now is not the time to try to aggressively stretch tight, knotted muscles. Instead, take the stretch to easy tension and hold for 15–20 seconds (Petersen, 2004). Be systematic, stretching all major muscle groups. This includes leg muscles of the quadriceps, hamstrings, calf, back, abductors, and adductors. Exhale on the initial stretch and then breathe normally.

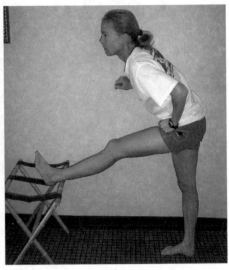

Iliotibial band & hip abductors Hamstring

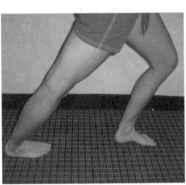

Calf   *Adductor*

Stretches should also be performed for the shoulders and elbows. Stretch the forearm extensors and flexors. Stretch each muscle group to the point of tension not pain.

Chest (pectoral) stretch can be done by placing an arm against a wall or secure object and stretching shoulder forward to feel a pull in the anterior chest.

Be patient when it comes to improving your flexibility because significant gains can only be realized after several months of work.

After training follow the high performance recovery tips and strategies in Chapter 31.

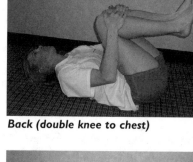

Back (double knee to chest)

Back (single knee to chest)

Low back and hip abductors

Pectoral

Whale tail (high gluteals)

SLOW, STATIC STRETCHING

Static stretching is best done as a separate training session after an appropriate warm-up. Hold
each static stretch for a minimum of 40 seconds
(it takes at least 20–30 seconds to overcome the
bias from the protective stretch reflex) and repeat
each stretch a minimum of two times.

A recent study showed that static stretches prior
to exercise did not prevent lower extremity overuse injuries, but additional static stretches after
training and before bed resulted in 50 percent
fewer injuries (Hartig and Henderson, 1999).

Cycle warm-up

Most static stretches are held for 30–60 seconds and repeated 2–3 times; however, more significant gains in flexibility will be made if the stretches are held
longer than one minute and repeated 3–4 times (most athletes told to stretch
for one minute do 30 seconds). Stretch the tightest areas first. Be progressive
in your stretching. Exhale as you stretch further into the range, and then
breathe normally as the stretch is held at the point of tightness.

The state of tension in other muscle groups should be assessed on a daily basis
and new stretches added to ensure that a good length-tension relationship is
maintained in all muscle groups responsible for on-court performance.

Hamstring

Quadriceps

Hip flexor

Hip adductors

Calf stretch (gastrocnemius)

Key Areas

- Focus on muscles that tend to be relatively short and stiff. This includes the pectorals, hip flexors, hamstrings, hip adductors, and calf muscles.

- Work with your physical therapist or strength and conditioning coach to determine which stretches are best for you.

FACILITATED PARTNER STRETCHING: HOLD-RELAX AND CONTRACT-RELAX

While static stretching has been the most widely researched, other stretching techniques such as PNF (proprioceptive neuromuscular facilitation), conform, and myofascial (or pressure point release) are all helpful. Facilitated partner stretches such as hold-relax and contract-relax PNF techniques have been shown to be more effective than just static stretching (Enoka, 1994). PNF techniques may be relaxing, as players can lie down and perform no work while being stretched passively. This can be an effective means of post-exercise relaxation (Reque, 2003).

Facilitated stretches make use of the "inverse myotatic reflex," where nerve receptors in the tendon are sensitive to isometric contraction and relax the muscle when it occurs. Two methods may be used:

- **Contract-Relax:** tighten the same (agonist) muscle, then stretch.
- **Hold-Relax:** tighten the opposite (antagonist) muscle, then stretch.

Use a partner you can trust who takes the muscle slowly to the point of tightness, applies appropriate resistance (approx. 25–30%) for 6–8 seconds, and then assists you to stretch further into the range. Go slowly and respect the signals your muscles are giving you.

Partner hamstring

Many traditional static stretches can also become facilitated stretches by using a towel, tree, wall, or your hands to apply resistance. This type of stretching will help increase range of motion and strengthen the muscle. Have your physical therapist or fitness coach help you with these.

PNF hamstring

PNF hip flexor

PNF adductor

PNF gluteals

MYOFASCIAL BALL STRETCHING

Physiotherapists, massage thera-pists, and other health professionals have been suggesting for years that patients use a tennis ball to release sore, tight muscles. Recently, in addition to using a tennis ball, small myofascial release balls are being used to stretch and soften tight mus-cles. These balls work not only to release trigger points in the muscle, but also to "smooth out" the myofascial system.

The effectiveness of massage or soft tissue techniques as an adjunct to stretching in order to facilitate flexi-bility has been demonstrated (Wittkorson-Moller et al., 1983). They have also been shown to pro-mote mood enhancement and feel-ings of well-being by reducing ten-

Myfascial ball release

sion, depression, anger, fatigue, anxiety, and confusion (Weinberg et al., 1988).

See Chapter 30, Soft Tissue Release (Muscle and Fasciae), for a full myofascial ball routine.

WHAT IF I AM TOO FLEXIBLE?

Normally you can never be too flexible. However, there are individuals who lack a certain amount of joint stability and may suffer from loose (subluxing) shoulders, loose ankles, or lumbar and pelvic malalignment syndromes. These individuals, usually females or males who have had a background in sports requiring extreme flexibility, such as gymnastics or dance, need to maintain a

Sissel disc bands

Dynamic Edge

Extreme balance board

Squats (balls and band)

balanced flexibility program, ensuring a good balance between the right and left sides and flexibility between the flexor and extensor muscles. They must also work hard on three-dimensional core strength to ensure the joints have equal support. This is most important for the scapulo-thoracic, lower back, pelvis, and hip areas. In addition, agility and balance drills must be done to ensure that the joint sense of position (proprioception) is working well and reprogrammed with your new muscle length.

TRAINING TIPS

- If a particular stretching exercise causes discomfort, try an alternative one or decrease the tension used.

- Include one stretch for each major muscle group targeted for the stretching session.

- If particular muscle groups are stiff, such as the hip flexors or iliotibial band, stretch them first and last.

- Allow a minimum of 10–15 minutes for dynamic stretching.

- A more comprehensive warm-up and static and facilitated partner stretching session will take from 30–60 minutes.

- If cycling is the training activity, be sure to stretch the lateral quadriceps and iliotibial band twice as much as you usually do.

Illiotibial band

RULES OF STRETCHING

- Do a warm-up prior to any type of stretching.

- Do a dynamic warm-up to prepare for any activity, including tennis.

- Do stretch dynamically before each and every training session.

- Do conform stretches after hard exercise.

Kneeling hip flexors

- Do establish optimal sport-specific range of motion prior to the competition season.

- Do self-monitor optimal range of motion regularly.

- Do utilize a separate time and routine for static stretching 4–6 times per week, waiting several hours after hard exercise to do them.

- Do use a myofascial ball to help stretch tight muscles, especially if traveling and no physiotherapists or trainers are available.

- Do take one day off from stretching per week.

- Use a combination of the different types of stretching to develop your own personal stretching routine.

References

Enoka, R.M. (1994). *Neuromechanical Basis of Kinesiology*. Champaign, IL: Human Kinetics.

Hartig, D.E., Henderson, J.M. (1999). Increasing hamstring flexibility decreases lower extremity injuries in military basic trainees. *Am. J. Sports Med.* 27(2): 173-176.

Petersen, C.W. (2004). Warm-Up, Stretching & Cool Down. In: *Fit to Ski*, CPC. Vancouver, Canada: Physio. Corp/Fit to Play Int. Inc. 36.

Prentice, W.E. (1983). A comparison of static and PNF stretching for improving hip joint flexibility. *Athletic Training*. 18(1): 56-59.

Reque, J. (2003). Flexibility. In: M. Reid, A. Quinn and M. Crespo (Eds). *Strength and Conditioning for Tennis*. London: ITF.

Weinberg, R., Jackson, A., & Kolodny, K. (1988). The realationship of massage and exercise to mood enhancement. *The Sport Psych*. 2: 202-211.

Witkorsson-Moller, M., Oberg, B., Ekstrand J., and Gillquist, J. (1983). Effects of warming up, massage and stretching on range of motion and muscle strength in the lower extremity. *Am. J. Sports Med.* 11(4): 249-252.

Additional Reading

Alter, M.J. (1996). *Science of Flexibility*. Champaign, IL: Human Kinetics

Anderson, B. (2000). *Stretching*. Bolinas, CA: Shelter Publications.

Thacker, SB, J. Gilchrist, D.F. Stroup and C.D. Kimsey. (2004). The impact of stretching on sports injury risk: A systematic review of the literature. *Med. Sci. Sports Exercise* 36(3): 371-378.

Chapter Four

Agility and Quickness Training

Carl Petersen,
Nina Nittinger, and Dan Haggart

Tennis requires quick movements that pass through many planes of motion and use numerous joints and muscles at the same time. Tennis movements include sprinting, side-to-side running, cutting, twisting, sliding, and quick stops and starts (Pluim & Safran, 2004a).

The drills in Chapters 4–6 will help improve athleticism, agility, balance, coordination, foot speed, lateral movement, and core stability necessary to perform all these movements. You will get to more balls sooner and be able get set up to hit the ball properly. Having good balance and a strong dynamic core improves stability on court, preventing injury and optimizing performance.

GETTING STARTED—DYNAMIC WARM-UP

Some form of warm-up should be done before doing any drills. Methodically warming the body's tissues helps prevent injuries that may be caused by going too hard, too fast, too soon with cold, unlubricated muscles and joints.

See Chapter 2 for more dynamic warm-up ideas.

One of the most important qualities to being a good player is natural speed. Some of the greatest tennis players are noted for their agility and speed on court. It's a matter of speed of court coverage, rather than just strokes. Strokes may fail when the

General warm-up

Beach cones   *Tree running*

body or racquet is in the wrong position relative to the ball. The key to good play is therefore speed and good fast footwork.

If you are genetically slow, there is not much chance you will ever be really fast. However, through fast feet training, you can improve your speed and tennis potential at any level—especially with young athletes. Sport scientist Dr. Istvan Balyi writes about the importance of developing the FUNdamentals in young athletes (ages 6–9). He describes them as the ABCs of athleticism—Agility, Balance, Coordination, and Speed—as well as the ABCs of athletics—Run, Jump, and Throw (Balyi, 2003).

Entire books have been written on agility and speed work for tennis and other sports, and we suggest you turn to them for additional ideas. The drills in this section were chosen because they mimic the type of specific quickness needed for tennis and will help you develop fast feet.

Create a menu of exercises using your imagination and make up an agility circuit that mimics your particular needs. Exercises can be varied depending on the setting and equipment available to you. Try doing 2 sets of 6–8 exercises for 10–15 seconds, with a 45–50 second rest in between. Change the venue for your training to keep it interesting. Use the track, beach, gym, or do your exercises beside the court.

Four types of agility and quickness drills are presented here:

1. Running drills.
2. Reaction drills.
3. Hopping and bounding drills.
4. Live ball drills (short court).

RUNNING DRILLS

Suicide Line Drills

Start on one side of the court, by the net (doubles sideline) and sprint to each line on the court and back. Concentrate on quick first steps and maintaining speed throughout. Do two sets per side. Make sure to touch each line and explode out of a crouched position.

Suicide line drills. *Add variety by doing either side shuffle, crossover, or sprint steps to lines.*

Cone Touch Drills

Set up three cones and move back and forth laterally to each cone for the prescribed period of time. Try:

- Side shuffles to cone.

- Kneel to touch cone.

- Circle around cone.

- Crossovers to cone.

Cone touch. *Varying the distance between cones adds variety and lets you work on acceleration and deceleration control.*

Cone Slalom Drill

Set up cones or half tennis balls in a slalom and do agility work running around the cones. Try:

- Straight slalom.

- Fast backpedal around cone.

- Stutter or split step at cones.

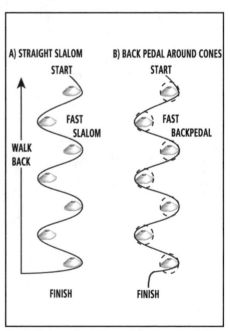

A) STRAIGHT SLALOM

START

FAST SLALOM

WALK BACK

FINISH

B) BACK PEDAL AROUND CONES

START

FAST BACKPEDAL

FINISH

Cone slalom. *Straight and fast backpedal around cones.*

Square Run Drill

Arrange five cones or half tennis balls as shown in the diagram approximately 10 feet (3–4 meters) apart. Start in the middle of the square and always facing in the same direction side shuffle step to the two front cones and back after circling them with short steps. Then proceed to the two back corner cones. Repeat 2–3 times.

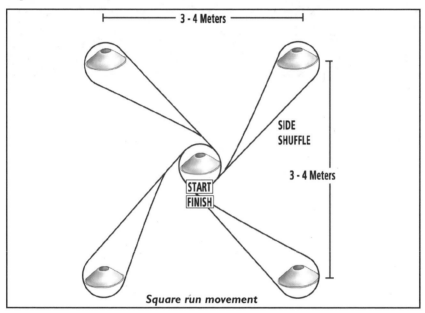

Square run movement

Tennis Pony Drill

With a harness around your waist attached to a heavy stretch cord, have a partner apply resistance while you start sprinting in place with good form (high knees and pumping arms). Now sprint forward 15–20 meters keeping a good sprint form (while your training partner runs behind applying resistance). Repeat 4–6 times with a rest of 30 seconds between sprints.

Pony drill. *This drill can be done incorporating lateral movements like side shuffles and skips as well.*

Training Notes and Precautions
• *When using resistance tubing, ensure it is of high quality.*
• *Inspect the tubing regularly for wear or weak spots.*
• *Ensure that it is either attached to something stable with all attachments secure and safe or held by a partner you trust.*
• *Use an appropriate waist belt or harness.*
• *You want the length of the tube to be such that there is a small amount of tension when you are closest to the attachment, but enough flexibility to allow you to get the full range of motion you are exercising in.*

Knee-ups Drill

Set up three lines of cones or pieces of tape a shown in the figure, and run each line as follows:.

Knee-ups

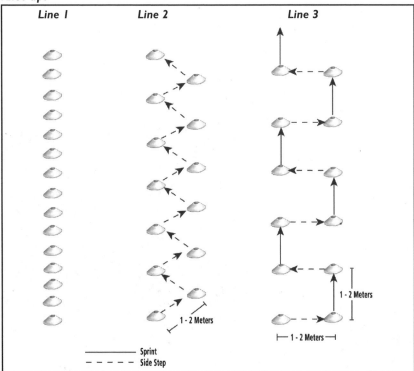

- Line 1: quick knees up.
- Line 2: side shuffle cone to cone.
- Line 3: side shuffle and front sprint all the way through the cones 3 times and repeat 3 times.

Anaerobic Shuttle (timed) (not shown)

Set up cones or lines 50 meters apart. Do a full sprint and then slow jog back. Do 5 sets of full forward and backward sprints with a return jog.

Next, do short shuttles with tired legs. Do these both forward and backward with five cones—1m, 2m, 3m, 4m, 5m.

Rest 3–5 minutes and repeat 1–3 times. Slowly increase the number of both 50-meter sprints and short shuttle sprints.

REACTION DRILLS

Hand Clap Direction Changes

Stand on the service T in a ready position with a training partner at the net. The partner claps hands and then points in the direction you must move to as quickly as possible. Split step on the clap, then, just like in a match, side step, backpedal, or sprint forward depending on the direction pointed. Start without a racquet in hand and then progress to carrying your racquet.

Start with 20–30 second drills and gradually build up the number of repetitions. Recovery time between reps should be the same as that between points.

Hand clap direction changes. *Vary the length of the movements by going 2, 4, or 6 steps.*

Resistance tubing can be added to increase the effort required in direction changes, acceleration, and deceleration. It can be held at the back or sides by a training partner (as in tennis pony drill).

Moving Ball Toss Drill (not shown)

- Partner stands about 6–8 feet away with 2 balls in hands.
- Partner holds arms out and lightly tosses 1 ball to right or left and takes 2 to 3 steps backward.
- Player must react and change direction depending on where ball is tossed, get it on one bounce, and toss it back.
- Drop 4–8 balls and repeat 3 times with a rest in between of 30 seconds.

Reaction Ball (Crazy Ball) Training

Using a "reaction ball" (a ball with bumps on the surface that make it bounce unpredictably), have a partner toss the ball while you are:

- Facing your partner (catch it on one bounce 2–3 times).
- Facing away from your partner (catch it on one bounce 2–3 times).

Crazy ball training

Shuttle Drill

Set up cones or half tennis balls in a slalom formation across the baseline. Put them about 2–3 feet in and 2–3 feet to the side. Run as fast as possible to the

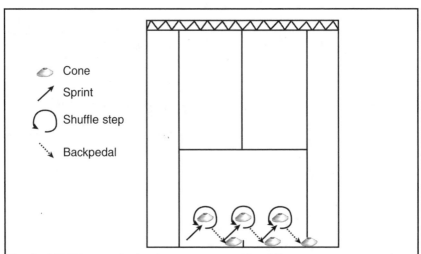

- Cone
- Sprint
- Shuffle step
- Backpedal

Shuttle drill. *This can also be done as a competitive drill among teammates where a set number of repetitions are timed.*

first cone, shuffle step around it, and backpedal to the next cone or half tennis ball on the baseline. Start with 5 or 6 cones and increase as stamina and foot speed do. Try 5–10 quick sets of approximately 10–15 seconds.

Towel-Ball Shuttle (adapted after Cook, 2003)

This can be done with two players competing or by yourself. Have 2–5 towels (rolled in a circle) to hold tennis balls. Spread them apart anywhere from 3–10 feet in a straight line and place a number balls at one or both ends, depending on whether you are doing the drill alone or with a partner.

Towel-ball shuttle

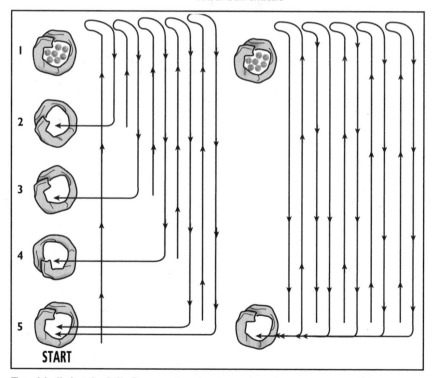

Towel-ball shuttle drill. *Five-towel and two-towel versions.*

Start at one end. The players must move laterally to the opposite end and pick up a ball from towel 1 and move it to towel 2 and move back to towel 1 and pick up another ball and move it to towel 3, etc. Time yourself or compete with a friend. Change sides and repeat the drill. You can work the anaerobic energy system by increasing the number of balls at the end towel and doing repeats of the drill for between 30–60 seconds.

You can change the drill by changing the number of towels to run back and forth or by using either a side shuffle or crossover step. Have the players work on hand coordination by having to use only one hand to pick up balls, either dominant or non-dominant. This drill can be done holding a racquet in one hand, or, for more external resistance, add a waist harness and elastic cord that a partner controls.

10-Ball Pickup

Place 10 balls on the court as shown in the diagram. Starting from the center, run out and pick up the balls and bring them back and place in a shallow bucket, box, or rolled towel. Try doing the exercise carrying a racquet and picking up balls with dominant and non-dominant hand.

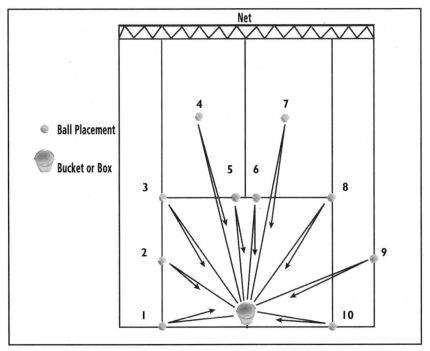

10-ball pickup drill

Get Up and Gos

- Start on the ground either supine (on your back), prone (on your front), or on right or left side. This can also be done standing facing forward or backwards.

- When your coach or training partner signals you, get up as quickly as possible and sprint forward between 10 and 20 meters.

- This can also be done carrying a medicine ball.

Medicine Ball Throw and Figure 8 Run

- Place two pylons or cones 2–3 meters apart.

- Start in middle of two cones and throw a medicine ball that is appropriate for your size either overhand, underhand (double), forehand, or backhand to your partner or coach.

- Now do repeated figure 8s, side shuffling around the cones, always facing forward.

- When your training partner or coach drops a tennis ball, you must sprint forward to catch the ball before it bounces twice.

- Vary the time you spend side shuffling around cones to mimic the time it takes to play a point. Also, try going a little longer on some to work on your anaerobic energy system.

START
POINT

10-20 m

Get up and gos

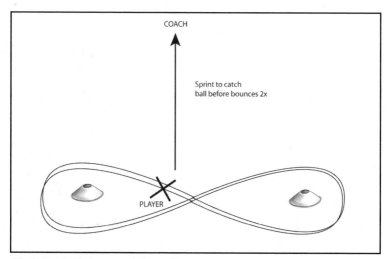

COACH

Sprint to catch
ball before bounces 2x

PLAYER

Medicine ball throw and figure 8s

Cone Drills

Spread cones or tennis ball cans at different points on the court or practice surface in a large M or W configuration. Holding your racquet, run to each cone, stop and swing, and then use short quick steps to move around the cone.

Cone drills. *Practicing like this emphasizes quickness in the first steps after a shot.*

HOPPING AND BOUNDING DRILLS

Progression of jumps should follow the rules of easy to hard and simple to complex. Start with multiple response jumps to develop power and power endurance.

Hexagonal Rail

Place tape or chalk lines in a hexagon design on your training surface. Starting in the middle, jump in and out of the hexagon, always facing in the same direction. Try doing double feet and single foot. Do 2x each direction both clockwise and counterclockwise.

Hexagonal rail

Line Hop Drills

Put chalk lines or lines of tape on the floor or court surface approximately 8 inches (20 cm) apart. You can use 3, 4, or 5 lines. Hop back and forth with control on one leg for the prescribed time, staying in a good athletic stance and keeping hips level.

3 lines	4 lines	5 lines
		___
	___	___
___	___	___
___	___	___
___	___	

Line hop drill

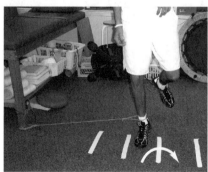 

Line hop with cords. *You can make this drill more challenging by placing some elastic tube around the ankle for resistance.*

Hop Training Notes and Precautions

Equipment Check—You need a pair of running shoes that have a non-slip sole, good shock absorption, strong medial arch support, and a strong heel counter. Consider wearing high tops (if ankle problems).

Surface Check—perform the jumps on a surface that is firm and forgiving like grass, dirt field, track, or sprung gym floor.

Special considerations should be given if you are heavy (decrease volume and amplitude of the jumps). As well, if you have spinal, knee, or foot alignment problems or a history of injuries, see your physician or physical therapist before commencing this program.

Rectangle Hops

This drill can be done in a gym or court setting. Make a rectangle on the court or floor with tape or chalk that is about the size of a piece of paper (30 x 20 cm or 12 x 8 inches). Always face in the same direction. Start by going around the rectangle once, staying in control. As your balance and strength increase, increase the number of times you go around, to a maximum of three. Adding outside resistance from cord around your ankle challenges your balance further.

Rectangle hops. *Hop in and out of the rectangle as indicated by the arrows. Try with and without elastic cord for extra resistance.*

Cone Hopping Drills

A) Continuous Hops

Arrange the flat collapsible cones or half tennis balls as shown in the diagram. Do continuous rhythm hops using (1) both feet, (2) single foot, (3) alternating right and left foot, or (4) alternating double and single (right or left) foot.

B) Hop and Split Hop (narrow-wide)

Arrange the flat collapsible cones or half tennis balls as shown in the diagram. The longer distance is three feet (1 meter) and the shorter distance is one foot. Get a good rhythm of normal, feet-together hopping when landing in the middle of the long section and doing a split step upon landing between the short distance cones. Do between 6–8 jumps per set and walk back to start.

C) Long-High Hops

Arrange the flat collapsible cones or half tennis balls as shown in the diagram. Alternate hopping long and hopping high with good body control and rhythm.

These are just a few hopping type drills that can be used to promote rhythm, coordination, power, and control. See suggested reading for other resources. Do between 6–8 jumps per set and walk back to start between.

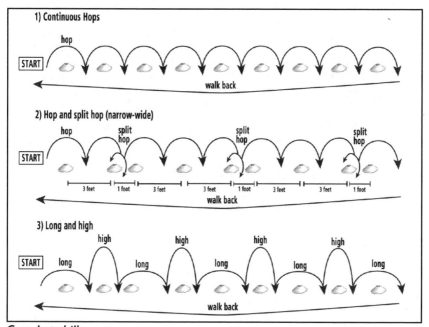

Cone hop drills

LIVE BALL DRILLS (SHORT COURT)

Following are some live ball mini-tennis drills that work on different components of agility. Speak to your coach for more ideas to incorporate as part of warm–up and to improve your fast feet.

Medicine Ball Throws and Catches

Start with a light medicine ball approximately 1–4 pounds (depending on your size).

Do 10–20 each of forehands, backhands, overhead, and underhand throws. You can also vary it by throwing with a bounce.

- Focus on correct form.
- Put this exercise in at the beginning of your workout before you are fatigued.

Deflated medicine ball. *If you use an inflatable medicine ball, you can change the bounce and focus of the drill with flatter bounces from a partially deflated ball.*

Backhand and forehand medicine ball toss. *Ensure you use correct fast footwork to set up for each throw and catch.*

Medicine Ball Short Court (not shown)

This is a competitive drill played on a short court to work on upper and lower core rotational strength and stability while mimicking forehand and backhand movements. Use a 2–6 pound rubber medicine ball that bounces. Play a set of games where the score starts at 4. Player A score goes up with each point won and down with each point lost and tries to get to 8; Player B's score goes down with each point won and up with each point lost and tries to get zero. You can work on agility and speed by playing a game where only forehand motion or backhand motion is used, forcing the players to move laterally to get into position.

Resistance tubing can be added (as in the tennis pony drill) to increase the effort required in acceleration and deceleration. It can be attached to a stable anchor at the back or sides or held by a partner. Four people work well with this drill, two playing and two holding. Then, switch for a rest break.

Up and Back Drill

Start on the service line and play short-court points. You must alternate hitting volleys and ground strokes from within the service area.

Up and back drill. *Emphasis is on fast up-and-back movement to get into proper position to hit the ball.*

Short-Court Reverse Drill

This is a great drill for lateral movement and footwork. Play short-court games with the following requirement—any ball landing in the deuce court must be hit with a backhand stroke, and any ball landing in the ad court must be hit with a forehand stroke (unless you're left handed then it is opposite). This drill emphasizes fast up-and-back movement to get into proper position to hit the ball.

Short court reverse drill.
Forehand from ad court.

Short court reverse drill.
Backhand from deuce court.

Slice Ball (not shown)

Play points to seven in the short court, using only slice and drop shots for touch. This is a great game for learning to slide when moving from hardcourt to clay court playing.

Preller (bounce ball)

This is a short-court drill to improve forward and lateral movement and anticipation. The ball MUST be hit before it bounces and MUST be hit down to bounce on your side before it crosses the net. Your opponent MUST do the same to return it. You can play points to seven. Resistance tubing can be added to increase the effort required in direction changes, acceleration, and deceleration. It can be held at the back or sides by a training partner.

Preller (bounce ball)

TIPS TO IMPROVE ON-COURT SPEED

Footwear

- Each surface—hard court, grass, sand (clay), carpet (synthetic), or dried cow dung (yes in some countries)—requires different construction and tread.

- The various surfaces foster different playing styles (e.g., serve and volley on grass and carpet, baseline play on clay, an all court/aggressive baseline game on hard court [Pluim & Safran, 2004b], and don't slip and fall in the dung).

- Ensure proper size, adequate toe box room, and the correct shoe for your foot (supinator or pronator).

- Shoes designed for another sport that have the wrong tread pattern do not optimize movement.

- Get professional advice (see Chapter 18 for some ideas).

Stay on the balls of your feet and constantly keep moving

- This keeps you in balance and ready to move quickly in all directions.

Widen your stance

- The pros stand poised in an athletic stance with their feet further apart than their shoulders, ready to drop and drive in order to move quickly for the next shot.

Stutter or split step when your opponent hits

- It doesn't matter where you are on court, always stutter or split step just before your opponent hits the ball.
- This allows you to move quickly in any direction.
- California based coach Ken Dehart calls this kind of movement "the mall shuffle"—it is as if you are trying to avoid running into someone in a crowded mall.

Always move faster than the ball

- Moving fast and preparing early for the oncoming ball gives you more time to get set up.
- The faster you move, the better you can prepare for the shot, adjust for the bounce, and decide what shot to hit in return.

Arc with smaller steps as you get near ball

- Use a path to the contact or hitting point that allows a small arc. Arcing behind the area where you want to contact the ball allows you to be moving forward at contact.

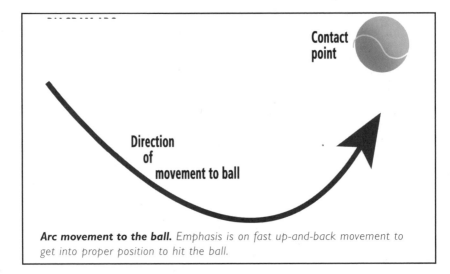

Arc movement to the ball. *Emphasis is on fast up-and-back movement to get into proper position to hit the ball.*

- Taking smaller steps as you get close to the contact point allows you to get into the right position to shift your weight forward as you hit.
- Avoid running straight toward the ball.

Hit and move

- Hit and keep moving, then recover if needed, then watch to see what happens, but keep the feet moving like a boxer.
- It is estimated that club players move their feet 4–6 times between shots whereas pros move them 10–12 times.
- The pros obviously are more likely to be in position for the next shot.

Gain time by hitting slower or with more looped topspin or slice

- Players believe that the faster they hit the ball, the less time their opponent will have to react.
- This may be true, but, unfortunately, opponents are able to return faster balls sooner, giving you less time, not more, unless of course you hit a winner or strong forcing shot.
- Be smart about the type of shots you return to allow yourself adequate time.

Run down every ball

- To improve your speed and fitness, even if a ball is wide or long, run it down and move to get into position to hit it.
- Running down wide, long, or short balls in practice will give you the confidence to go after them when you play.

You have time to hit the ball

- You have much more time than you think between the first and second bounce.
- The heavier or loopier the ball is hit, the longer the interval as it stays in the air longer.
- Never give up on a shot unless you're going to run into something.

Fit to Play™ training tips

- Try different exercises in each training session.
- Treat your "fast feet" training as part of your overall program to improve tennis.

- Try using other sports like soccer, ultimate Frisbee, or touch rugby to improve coordination.
- Try unfamiliar sports to improve your coordination and confidence.
- Do fast feet training 2–4 times per week. Always begin with a dynamic warm-up.
- End with a cool-down period of 5–10 minutes, followed by some easy flexibility exercises.
- Remember—warm-up to play, don't play to warm-up.

References

Balyi, I. & Hamilton, A. (2003). Chapter 2, Long-term athlete development, trainability and physical preperation of tennis players. In: M. Reid, A.Quinn and M. Crespo (Eds). *Strength and Conditioning for Tennis*. London: ITF 50-51

Cook, G. (2003). *Athletic Body in Balance*. Champaign, IL: Human Kinetics.

Pluim, B. & Safran, M. (2004a). *From Breakpoint to Advantage*. Vista, CA: Racquet Tech Publishing 33.

Pluim, B. & Safran, M. (2004b). *From Breakpoint to Advantage*. Vista, CA: Racquet Tech Publishing.

Additional Reading

Bourquin, O. (2003). Chapter 4, Coordination. In: M. Reid, A. Quinn and M. Crespo (Eds). *Strength and Conditioning for Tennis*. London: ITF 71-77.

Dinhoffer, J. (2003). *Tennis Practice Games*. Human Kinetics. Champaign, IL.

Kovacs, M. (2004). A comparison of work/rest intervals in men's professional tennis. *Medicine and Science in Tennis*. 9(3):10-11.

Moreau, X, Perotte, N, & Quetin, P. (2003). Chapter 9: speed and agility. In: M. Reid, A. Quinn, and M. Crespo (Eds). *Strength and Conditioning for Tennis*. London: ITF 149-163.

Chapter Five

Balance Training

Carl Petersen

B alance training is a fundamental component of functional mobility and dynamic sports activity and should be a part of everyone's daily fitness routine, whether destined for the professional tour or not. Top professionals look natural because they move naturally and have excellent balance.

Improving balance and joint proprioception will contribute to superior sports performance, enhance daily activity, and improve confidence with new activities. Your body will be able to react to unexpected events as well as stay protected during repetitive motions. Ultimately, balance training helps you to improve balance reactions in all of your joints and decrease your chance of injury.

Over the years, training devices have been designed and manufactured to try and mimic the balance, stability, strength, and energy systems required for sport specific training. These include The Dynamic Edge (Skier's Edge) and the Pro Fitter (Ski Fitter) that are both sport specific conditioning devices but also useful as rehabilitation tools. Other manufacturers have designed balance (proprioception) equipment such as the Reebok Core Board, Extreme Balance Board, Sissel Disc, foam mat (Airex®-Balance Pad), and Physio/Exercise Ball that were initially used in a rehab setting, but are now used for training.

Balance tools. *These can be as simple as walking and balancing on a log.*

If you have the opportunity, try them all and decide for yourself what suits your needs. You should also consider what environment and equipment would motivate you to train longer and more regularly. For some, training at home versus a gym may be more convenient.

WHAT'S IN IT FOR YOU?

Balance training adds variety to your workouts and helps prevent boredom. Train with a friend and vary the routine to keep it interesting and challenging. The key to a successful fitness program is motivation. By organizing your training and fitness program to include the equipment outlined below, you will not only improve your off- and on-court workouts but add some fun as well.

Rolled towel. When traveling and no balance equipment is available, try using a rolled towel. Stand on it for 5–30 seconds to challenge your balance.

Balance training benefits

- Improves balance, coordination, timing, and agility.
- Enhances dynamic core strength and stability.
- Maximizes dynamic functional leg strength and power.
- Improves motor skills and reaction skills.
- Develops effective upper and lower body strength.
- Improves cardiovascular endurance (depending on equipment used).
- Improves joint proprioception.
- Helps prevent repetitive strain injuries.
- Improves athletic performance.

BALANCE EQUIPMENT AND EXERCISES

The products presented below are designed to challenge and improve balance and sport-specific skills. When using this equipment or trying any of the exercises shown, you must accept full responsibility for the risk of injury to yourself and others. Please read and fully understand all instructions before using these products. Remember, the best protection from injury is common sense. Always start with the easiest exercises first, using a spotter, wall, or support poles to aid balance.

Wobble board (no touch). Try keeping the edges of the wobble board from touching the floor for 10–30 seconds.

Wobble board rotations. While in a squat and a split squat foot position, try making the edge of the board touch the floor all around for 5–10 circles in the clockwise and counter-clockwise direction.

Foam mat (Airex®-Balance Pad). Adopt different body positions while the unstable surface of a foam mat works your muscles. Stand on it to challenge your balance for 5–30 seconds. ▶

◀ **Sissel disc.** Adopt different body positions while the unstable surface of a sissel disc works your muscles. Stand on it to challenge your balance for 5–30 seconds.

Foam mat with elastic resistance. Challenge your lower core strength by doing cord resisted hip extension (cross country ski) exercise while on the foam mat. Do 5–15 repetitions, holding onto something to aid balance to begin.

Pro Fitter®. *Work on balance and hip abduction strength by standing on a Pro Fitter® with one foot and driving the resistance plates out to the side. Include the upper body by giving a diagonal pull on a stretch cord at the same time. Do 5–15 repetitions.*

Dynamic Edge®. *Use the Dynamic Edge® as a fun balance exercise. By varying how aggressive you work back-and-forth, or the time you work, you can get both strength and energy system benefits.*

Unstable surfaces. Though little research has been done to date, data suggests that using a variety of unstable rather than stable surfaces will activate the trunk (core) muscles more, especially on exercises that are unilateral (one-sided) in nature (Behm, 2005). This has been shown for shoulder press on a stability ball and with squat type exercises on unstable surfaces (Anderson & Behm, 2005).

Shoulder press on stability ball

Squats on unstable surface

Half foam roll. *Doing split squats on a half foam roll at the same time as doing a diagonal cord pull works on balance and upper body strength at the same time. Try doing 5–15 repetitions.*

Split squats (stable). *Start off doing split squats or lunges on a flat floor. As strength, stability, and balance improve, add external resistance from a stretch cord attached to something stable or held by a friend you trust. Try doing 5–15 repetitions.*

Split squats (unstable). *As stability increases, do the split squat onto a sissel disc or BOSU® balance trainer. Try doing 5–15 repetitions.*

93

Split squats (unstable with cord resistance). *Cord resistance can also come from the front as you do an arm extension exercise at the same time. Try doing 5–15 repetitions.*

Mini-tramp. *Challenge your balance while standing, or lightly hopping up-and-down, on a mini-tramp on one leg. Make it more difficult by tossing and catching a ball or light medicine ball at the same time or having someone throw you a ball. Try doing 5–15 repetitions.*

Figure of 8s on unstable surface. *Standing on Reebok Core Board, take a light weight and perform figure of 8s with extended arms. This will challenge your balance on the unstable base.*

Training Notes and Precautions

• *When using resistance tubing ensure it is of high quality.*

• *Inspect the tubing regularly for wear or weak spots.*

• *Ensure that it is either attached to something stable (and all attachments are secure and safe) or held by a partner you trust.*

• *Use an appropriate waist belt or harness.*

• *You want the length of the tube to be such that there is a small amount of tension when you are closest to the attachment, but enough flexibility to allow you to move through the range of motion for the exercise.*

Extreme Balance Board™. *Moving up and down from a high to a low tuck position while maintaining your balance works the core and legs as well as balance reactions. Stand on it to challenge your balance for 5–30 seconds.*

Training tips

• After strength training or straight ahead activities like cycling, running, or stair climbing, reset your joints' balance clock with balance exercises using any of the above equipment.

• Follow the guidelines of the manufacturer.

• Try to include 2–3 balance exercises per day in your workouts.

• Elastic tubing can be used with all the equipment to add an upper body or extra core component to training.

• Use your imagination and the equipment available to you to add another dimension to your workout.

• Using training equipment that mimics sport in a challenging but fun way encourages people to stick to it.

Equipment Information

Most of the equipment shown above can be purchased on the internet or from specialty sport and rehabilitation stores (Table 5.1).

Table 5.1

Equipment Resources

Equipment	Source
Rolled Towel	Locker Room
Mini Trampoline	Garage Sale
Wobble Boards	Gym or fitness supply store
Dynamic Edge or Skiers Edge	www.dynamicedge.com or www.skiersedge.com
Pro Fitter® or Ski Fitter	www.fitter1.com
Extreme Balance Board	www.extreme-balance-board.com
Bosu Ball	www.bosu.com
Sissel Disc	www.sissel.com
Airex® Balance Pad	www.fitter1.com
Reebok Core Board	www.reebok.com

References

Anderson, K. & Behm, D.G. (2005). Trunk muscle activity increases with unstable squat movements. *Can. J. Appl. Phys.* 30(1): 33-45.

Behm, D.G., A.M. Leonard, W.B. Young, W.A.C. Bonsey & S.N. MacKinnon. (2005). Trunk muscle EMG activity with unstable and unilateral exercises. *J. Strength Cond. Res.* 19(1): 193-201.

Chapter Six

Upper and Lower Core Training in 3-D

Carl Petersen, Martha Sirdevan, and Nina Nittinger

A re you tired of doing weights or bored with your gym workout? Looking for something to add to your training regime that is challenging and works the core and several muscle systems at once? Consider using a physio ball and stretch bands to keep you Fit to Play™ in three dimensions while at home or on the road. These exercises are versatile, practical, transportable, and affordable. Training with a physio ball and stretch bands strengthens the core (trunk) muscles in all directions of motion and ensures the exercises are functional.

Exercises like biceps and hamstring curls only involve a single joint and movement in one plane of motion. As well, using a treadmill, stationary bike, and step machine also works the body in only one plane of movement. Daily activity and training for tennis require the body to rotate around three different axes, in three planes of motion at the same time.

Upper and lower core strength training provides a stable three-dimensional power platform from which the extremities can

Single joint exercises. *Bicep and hamstring curls.*

work during multi-planar, multi-joint, and multi-muscle activities that involve acceleration and deceleration forces (Petersen, 2005).

As a tennis player, you need a strong core to maintain balance, stability, and alignment as you generate power. When moving laterally, the core muscles and hip stabilizers work to control movement. Many muscles attach to the "lower core" lumbo-pelvic-hip complex and spine and the "upper core" spine, ribs, and scapular region. When activated and recruited properly, the stability of the upper and lower core forms the foundation, platform, or base to all other movements. In tennis the soft tissues around the spine are always working dynamically in three dimensions (3-D) to protect from the forces of gravity and rotation.

Planes of motion

Core foundation. The core is the platform for all other movements.

Vleeming and Lee's integrated model of function has four components—three physical and one psychological (Lee, 2004; Panjabi, 1992):

- The passive support of form closure from the shape of the joint surfaces of the spinal column and pelvis.
- The active system of force closure from the muscle, tendon, and fascial tissue.
- The motor control, or balance, proprioception, and joint and muscle sense, from feedback along the neural control centers.
- The psychological component from emotions.

For tennis athletes to train and play well, they need control of all of these different yet interrelated stabilizing systems.

Pony back. *Kneeling on all fours, allow the back to arch down like an old pony. Exhale and arch back up to neutral. Hold for eight seconds and repeat eight times.*

Dr. Ben Kibler defines core stability as, *"the ability to control the trunk over the planted leg to allow optimum production, transfer, and control of force and motion to the terminal limbs"* (Kibler, 2005).

The first muscle to be recruited prior to any upper and/or lower body movements is the transversus abdominus (lower abdominals). Normally, it fires in a pre-anticipation of any movement, but with dysfunction there is a timing delay and studies have shown that without efficient and optimal recruitment, subsequent spinal dysfunction can occur (Richardson & Jull, 1995). Switching on your core or reconnecting the core with simple exercises that either close or partially close the kinetic chain for both upper and lower extremities helps increase the three-dimensional core stability and ensure optimal recruitment, timing, performance, and injury prevention.

3-D core. *Performing a squat while squeezing a ball between your knees and pulling a stretch cord apart combines the upper and lower core. The legs perform a closed kinetic chain squat as the stretch band partially closes the upper extremity kinetic chain to improve 3-dimensional core strength.*

Benefits of upper and lower core training in 3-D

- Improves posture, muscle strength, and endurance.

- Improves joint and muscle position sense (kinesthetic awareness), helping to center the joint and absorb stress.

- Improves stability in a functional hip-extended position.

- Improves ability to counter-rotate upper and lower torso and extremities.
- Improves dynamic balance and movement efficiency.
- Adds additional force vectors of resistance to traditional methods.
- Improves athletic performance.
- Helps the body to be able to react to unexpected events.
- Training on an unstable surface trains balance reactions and coordination at a subconscious level, facilitating these reactions to become automatic.

(Adapted after Petersen et al., 2004)

BEFORE YOU START

If using the ball mainly as an exercise tool, balance aid, or lying on it, start with a smaller ball that is less firm, and as your skill improves, you can use a larger, firmer ball. If planning to sit on the ball for prolonged periods, the hips and knees should be bent to 90 degrees with your feet flat on the floor.

Choosing the proper stretch band resistance is important. Visit a reputable sports training supply store to select the appropriate length and strength. Longer is always better as you can choke up or shorten it. Start with a lighter resistance than you think you need, as the stretch band provides continuous resistance and is often more difficult than you think.

Include a Dynamic Warm-up

Before starting this or any exercise routine, do some light core exercises to cue you to switch on your core and connect the upper and lower core muscles. This has also been described using the cue "fire the core and sustain" (McKechnie & Celebrini, 2002) (see Chapter 26 for more ideas). This gets the lower abdom-

Ball Precautions

- *For individuals new to exercise, see your physician.*
- *Check ball for flaws before each use.*
- *Avoid placing ball near heat or in direct sunlight.*
- *Avoid sharp objects and jewelry.*
- *Start gradually and get a feel for the ball before progressing.*

Stretch Band Precautions

- *When using resistance tubing, ensure it is of high quality.*
- *Avoid placing stretch bands near heat or in direct sunlight.*
- *Avoid sharp objects and jewellery*
- *Start gradually and get a feel for the resistance of the stretch band before progressing or increasing the tension.*
- *Regularly inspect stretch band for wear and tear and replace as appropriate.*
- *Inspect the tubing regularly for wear or weak spots.*
- *Ensure that it is either securely attached to something stable or held by a partner you trust.*

Dynamic warm-up examples. *Leg swings work on dynamic range of motion, balance, and core strength together.*

inal activated prior to starting the dynamic warm-up drills. See Chapter 2 on dynamic warm-up for more ideas, including leg swings (shown here).

LOWER EXTREMITY AND CORE EXERCISES

Ball Wall Squats

- Start with the ball against your lower back and the wall.
- Switch on your core at a low level, like a dimmer switch on a light.

Double leg squats. *Keep knee behind toes. Keep load through the heels and compress ball into wall.*

Single leg squat. *Ball at back.*

- Increase leg strength and stability by gradually increasing number of repetitions and depth of the squat.
- Start with 1–2 x 10 and increase to 2–3 x 20. Keep knees lined up over toes. Progress to single leg squats when able.

Single Leg Squat (ball at side)

- Start standing on one leg, leaning (60–70 degrees) against a ball placed at hip height.
- Lift inside foot and place behind ankle of opposite leg.
- Switch on your core (tension in the lower abdominals).
- Do a quarter squat, then drive up into extension using glutes and quads.

Single leg squat (ball at side). *Clasp hands behind back to decrease balance.*

Split Squats (ball at back)

- Stand in a split squat position with ball at back.
- Switch on your core.
- Keeping your back straight and your head up, load through the forward heel.
- Bend knees until your front thigh is parallel to the ground, ensuring that at the bottom of the movement your front knee does not pass your toes.
- Start with 1–2 x 10 and increase to 2–3 x 15.
- Keep knees lined up over toes.
- Strengthens core, front thigh, and buttocks.

Split squats (ball at back). *This exercise stretches the hip flexors and improves balance and strength at the same time.*

Dynamic Hip Hike (ball at back)

- Start by placing a physio ball at your mid-back against the wall in a split squat position, with one leg back and fire the core.

- Flex the hip so your knee comes up and across at waist height.

- Start with 1–2 x 10 and increase to 2–3 x 20. Keep knees lined up over toes.

- Strengthens core, front thigh, and buttocks.

Dynamic hip hike (ball at back). *Lower slowly keeping your core switched on.*

Standing Hip Abduction

- Stand holding onto something for balance with a light stretch cord looped around your ankle.

- Switch on your core and keep your foot pointed out at 45 degrees.

- Keeping hips level, abduct your leg out to the side 8 inches (20 cm) and hold for 2 seconds. Return slowly to the start position.

- Start off with 2 sets of 6 repetitions and progress as strength and ability allow to 3 sets of 10–12 repetitions.

Standing hip abduction. *You will feel it more in the buttock on the hip you are standing on.*

Side-lying Physio Ball Abduction

- Lie on your side with a physio ball between ankles.

- Switch on your core.

- Raise legs up into abduction and hold for 2–4 seconds.

- Start off with 2 sets of 6 repetitions and progress as strength and ability allow to 3 sets of 10–12 repetitions.

Side-lying physio ball abduction. *Raise both legs and ball, then lower.*

Bridging Hamstring Curls (Caution—hamstrings may cramp)

- This exercise strengthens the hamstring muscles while working on your core.

- Switch on your core.

- Start with bridging on the ball (raise bottom up only).

- Curl the ball toward you with both legs (with one leg after you get stronger—this is very difficult).

- Start off with 2 sets of 6 repetitions and progress as strength and ability allow to 3 sets of 10–12 repetitions).

Bridging hamstring curls. *As strength improves progress to curling the ball towards you with both legs, then ultimately with one leg.*

UPPER EXTREMITY AND CORE EXERCISES

For tennis players, and other athletes as well, the anterior muscles that internally rotate the shoulder (pectoralis major, anterior deltoid, subscapularis, and latissimus dorsi) are typically stronger than the external rotators (posterior deltoid, infraspinatus), especially on the dominant side. This can lead to poor posture habits, including forward head posture and a medially rotated shoulder. Over-development of the muscles on the front of the body coupled with the forward bent or flexed postures inherent in the ready position of most sports leads to this distinguishing posture (Ellenbecker, 1995).

Some form of posterior shoulder and mid-back strengthening should be included in everyone's workout. Here are several ways to ensure you target this often underused muscle group and help minimize potential shoulder problems. Choose 3 or 4 exercises.

Kneeling Ball Push-Ups

- Start off doing normal push ups off the knees on stable ground.

- Switch on your core to connect upper and lower body.

- Start with 2 sets of 6 repetitions and progress as you are able.

Kneeling ball push-ups. *As strength improves, try push-ups with your feet on the ground and your hands on the ball.*

Supermans

- Kneel on the ground with torso over a physio ball.

- Switch on your core.

- Raise arms up from the ground to 45 degrees only. Hold for 2 seconds, and repeat 10–15 times.

- Avoid raising too high and jamming your shoulder.

Supermans. *You should feel this in your lower trapezius (below shoulder blades).*

Batmans

- Train the mid-back muscles to improve posture.
- Lie over the ball and switch on your core to connect your upper and lower core.
- Raise arms up from the side of the ball to horizontal.
- Keep thumbs in line with ears and forearms horizontal to the ground. Hold for 2 seconds and repeat 10–15 times.

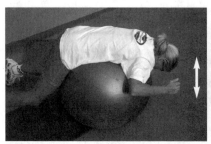

Batmans. *You should feel this between your shoulder blades.*

Prayer Holds

- Kneel with elbows on ball and hands clasped.
- Switch on your core and hold for 10 seconds while breathing normally.
- Don't let back arch. Stop if fatigue sets in.
- Repeat 2–3 sets of 5–10 repetitions.

Prayer hold. *Start going straight out, then progress to side-to-side and rotational movements.*

Prayer hold rotation. *Strengthens upper core, shoulders, and arms.*

Alphabet Protractions

- Stand with a stretch cord behind you.
- Switch on your core to connect upper and lower body.
- Drive the cord forward above the shoulder and write letters A–K.

Kneeling Single Arm Raise

- Kneel on a mat with a physio ball in front of you.
- Hold the ball with one hand and raise the opposite arm up keeping back flat.
- Hold for 4 seconds and repeat 10 times. Try 2–3 sets.

Standing External Rotations

- Stand with shoulders square, knees slightly bent and a tight tummy.
- Using a light stretch cord, pull it to the outside keeping your elbow at your side.

Alphabet protractions. *Write the letters A-K.*

Kneeling single arm raise

Standing external rotations. *As your strength improves, increase the range of motion and add more resistance.*

- Start with hand in front of your navel and finish at 45 degrees.
- Try 2–3 sets of 10–12 repetitions

Shoulder Blade (scapular) Retractions with Stretch Cord

- Switch on your core while standing with knees slightly bent.
- Pull a stretch cord to your chest and then pull apart and hold for 2 seconds.
- Do 10–15 repetitions and repeat 2–3 times.

Shoulder blade (scapular) retractions with stretch cord. Strengthens mid-back and posterior shoulder to improve posture.

Standing Two-Arm Row

- Switch on your core while standing with knees slightly bent and shoulders square.
- Keeping your shoulders down, exhale as you bring your elbows back until wrists meet armpits.
- Do 10–15 repetitions and repeat 2–3 times.

Remember that because these muscles are short and small, they fatigue easily; go lighter and easier than you think you should. Practice correct posture, keeping the shoulders relaxed and down with mild tension between the shoulder blades.

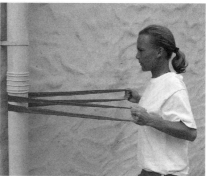

Standing two arm row. Works the mid-back and posterior shoulder.

COMBINED UPPER EXTREMITY, LOWER EXTREMITY AND CORE FOCUS

Kneeling Single Leg Raise

- Kneel on a mat with a physio ball in front of you.
- Hold the ball with both hands and raise up one leg at a time.
- Hold for 4 seconds and repeat 10 times. Try 2–3 sets.

Kneeling single leg raise. Do not raise the leg above horizontal to avoid jamming the spinal joints.

Squat with Back Extension

- Start with feet shoulder width apart and holding a physio ball out in front.
- Switch on your core to connect upper and lower body.
- Do a mini-squat while keeping knees over toes and raise the physio ball overhead.
- Hold for 4 seconds and repeat 10 times. Try 2–3 sets.
- Can also be done in a split squat position.

Squat with back extension. This exercise works the posterior core.

Front Step Ups with Diagonal Pattern

- Stand in front of a low to medium step (never past 70–80 degrees).
- Put one end of a stretch cord under your foot.
- Switch on your core.
- Step and touch your opposite toe to the step at the same time as you pull the cord in a diagonal pattern above your head.
- Start with 1–2 x 10 and increase to 2–3 x 20. Keep knees lined up over toes.

Front step ups with diagonal pattern. *Works the cross chain of muscle from glutes to opposite lats.*

Front Step Ups with Arm Drive

- Stand in front of a low to medium step (never past 70–80 degrees).
- Put one end of each stretch cord under your foot.
- Switch on your core to connect upper and lower body.
- Step and touch your opposite toe to the step at the same time as you pull the cords up into extension above your head.

Front step ups with arm drive. *Tension through the elastics helps partially close the kinetic chain and fire the functional slings of muscles.*

- Start with 1–2 x 10 and increase to 2–3 x 20. Keep knees over toes.

Front Step Ups with Shoulder External Rotation

- Stand in front of a low to medium step (never past 70–80 degrees).
- Put the stretch cord around both hands.
- Switch on your core.
- Step and touch your opposite toe to the step at the same time as you pull the cord into external rotation.
- Start with 1–2 x 10 and increase to 2–3 x 20. Keep knees lined up over toes.
- Can also be done in split squat position.

Front step ups with shoulder external rotation. Strengthens mid-back muscles at the same time as

Front Step Ups with Diagonal Pull

- Stand in front of a low to medium step (never past 70–80 degrees).
- Put the stretch cord around one hand.
- Switch on your core to connect upper and lower body.
- Start with 1–2 x 10 and increase to 2–3 x 20. Keep knees lined up over toes.
- Can also be done in split squat position.

Front step ups with diagonal pull. Step and touch your opposite toe to the step at the same time as you pull the cord in a diagonal pattern across your body.

Side Step Ups with Diagonal Pull

- Stand to the side of a low to medium step (never past 70–80 degrees).
- Put the stretch cord around one hand.
- Switch on your core.
- Start with 1–2 x 10 and increase to 2–3 x 15. Keep knees lined up over toes.
- Can also be done in split squat position.

Side step ups with diagonal pull. Do a side step up and touch your opposite toe to the step at the same time as you pull the cord in a diagonal pattern across your body.

Diagonal Hip Flexion and Ball Pull Downs

- Start by holding a physio ball at above head height against the wall.
- Start in a split squat position with one leg back and switch on your core.
- Squeeze the ball lightly and pull down to chest height.
- At the same time, flex the hip so your knee comes up and across at waist height.
- Raise ball slowly and lower leg slowly, keeping the core switched on.
- Start with 1–2 x 10 and increase to 2–3 x 20. Keep knees lined up over toes.

Diagonal hip flexion and ball pull downs. Strengthens core, shoulders, front thigh, and buttocks.

Circus Ponies (opposite arm and leg raises)

- Lie over the ball, balancing with hands and feet.
- Switch on your core.
- Raise opposite arm and leg to horizontal.
- Hold for 4 seconds and repeat 10 times. Try 2–3 sets with opposite and same side arm and leg extension.

Circus ponies (opposite arm and leg raises). Be careful not to raise the extremities above horizontal to avoid back hyperextension.

Prone Ball Bridges

- Lie over a physio ball with arms in a pushup position.
- Roll out until lower legs and feet are on the ball
- Switch on your core to connect upper and lower body.
- Start by holding in the bridge position.
- Hold for 4 seconds and repeat 5–10 times.

Prone ball bridges. As strength and stability improve, try pulling the ball toward you and back out slowly.

Ball Split Squats with Torso Rotation (ball at side)

- Stand in a split squat position with ball at hip height and bands around thighs.
- Switch on your core.
- Keeping your back straight and your head up, load through the forward heel.
- Bend until your front thigh is parallel to the floor, ensuring that at the bottom of the movement your front knee does not pass your toes.
- Your back leg should be almost straight and not touch the floor, while always exhaling on exertion.
- This exercise stretches the hip flexors and improves balance at the same time.
- Repeat 2–3 sets of 10–15 reps.
- Strengthens core, front thigh, and buttocks.

Ball split squats with torso rotation—ball on side (adapted after McKechnie & Celebrini, 2002)

Ball Sit Downs

- Sit on the ball slightly ahead of center.
- Have legs out in front, knees bent, and feet flat on the floor.
- Cross arms on chest and switch on your core.
- Slowly lean back to 45 degrees letting the ball roll to support your lower back.
- Start with 1–2 sets of 5–10 repetitions and progress to 2–3 sets of 15–20 reps.
- Strengthens core muscles as they lengthen.

Ball sit downs

Ball Sit Downs (squeeze ball or foam)

Doing ball sit down exercises on an unstable surface as opposed to a stable flat surface has been shown to increase muscle activity (Vera-Garcia et al., 2000). Adding external resistance with stretch bands, other balls, or weights should only serve to augment this effect.

- Sit on the ball slightly ahead of center.
- Have legs out in front, knees bent, and feet flat on the floor, and place a ball or rolled foam between knees.
- Cross arms on chest and switch on your core.
- Slowly lean back to 45 degrees, letting the ball roll to support your lower back.
- Start with 1–2 sets of 5–10 repetitions and progress to 2–3 sets of 15–20 reps.
- Strengthens core muscles as they lengthen.

Ball sit downs with foam and bands. *Adding stretch cords around your feet for resistance as you do the sit down adds to the core component.*

Seated Ball Rotations

- Sit on a mat, knees bent up, and a physio ball at your side.
- Switch on your core.
- Pick up the ball and rotate it from one side to the other side slowly.
- Can also be done using a weighted medicine ball.

Seated ball rotations. *Keep your lower abdominals fired as you rotate the ball back and forth.*

- Try doing a figure 8 over and under drill between the legs to stimulate increased 3-D core activity.
- Do 2 sets of 10–15 repetitions.

Ball Side Sit Ups

- Lie sideways on a physio ball with your legs split and against a wall.
- Switch on your core.
- Keep head neutral and raise up using lateral flexors and lower slowly to a count of 3 or 4 seconds.
- Start doing 2 sets of 6 and increase as strength improves to 3 sets of 12–15 repetitions.

Seated side sit ups

Data suggest that the trunk (core) stabilizers are more highly activated on an unstable surface (physio ball, etc.) and that using unilateral resistance exercises causes greater activation of the contra-lateral (opposite) side trunk stabilizers in a shoulder press (Behm et al., 2005).

116

Supine Physio Ball (weights)

- Lie back on a physio ball with it between your shoulder blades.
- Keep feet firmly planted and switch on your core.
- Try doing double and single arm bench press.
- Start 2 sets of 6 reps and increase to 3 sets of 15 per way.

Supine Physio Ball (weight plate or medicine ball)

- Lie back on a physio ball with it between your shoulder blades.
- Keep feet firmly planted and switch on your core.
- Try doing side to side movements, forward and back, and figure of 8s with either a weight plate or medicine ball.
- Start 2 sets of 6 reps and increase to 3 sets of 15 per way.

Supine ball with weights

Supine ball with weight plate

COOL-DOWN

You should include some conform stretches. Try stretching all muscle groups used in the strength routine. Be sure to key in on those that tend to get short and stiff like the hamstrings, hip flexors, calves, and pectoral muscles. Try holding each stretch for 15–20 seconds and repeat 2–3 times. Some stretches can be done with the physio ball. Use your imagination and the ball as a stretching partner.

See Chapter 3, Smart Stretching Guidelines, for suggestions.

CORE TRAINING GUIDELINES AND TIPS

Core Session Guidelines

- Each session, change the exercises to ensure you work different areas.
- Use other athletes as support during days when you have trouble making the effort to train. Interact and learn from each other.

- Do some form of upper and lower core training 3–4 times per week.
- Begin with a dynamic warm-up.
- End with cool-down period of 5–10 minutes followed by some easy flexibility exercises.
- Remember, always warm up to play, don't play to warm up.

Rules of Core Strength

- Always start all exercises by switching on your core (at a low level like a dimmer switch) to re-educate the lower abdominals and other muscles of the core to work in an anticipatory way. This also helps to connect the upper and lower core.
- A few non-fatiguing core exercises should be done prior to any training activity.
- This is especially important after a lay off, after an injury, or when you have been malaligned or have low back or hip pain and stiffness.
- Approach traditional sit-ups with caution as the elbow-knee movement places a lot of strain on the low back.
- Limit the number of traditional crunch type of exercises as they strengthen mainly the upper abdominals.
- Don't anchor your feet—this only encourages hip flexor strength which pulls on the low back.
- Avoid double leg lifts with the legs kept straight as these also put undue strain on the lower back.
- Slow it up—increased strength comes from increased tension on the muscle, therefore use slow controlled movements as your base work.
- The harder core workouts should be done at the end of strength workouts or after training so that the core muscles can adequately function as stabilizers during the strength exercises.
- You can do daily core work by switching on the core with all upper and lower body exercises.
- Rest intervals of 30–60 seconds between sets work best. Use this time to do some light stretching, balance drills, or work on a different muscle group.

A WELL DEVELOPED UPPER AND LOWER CORE STRENGTH WILL NOT MAKE AN AVERAGE ATHLETE ELITE; HOWEVER, POOR CORE STRENGTH AND STABILITY CAN MAKE AN ELITE ATHLETE POTENTIALLY VULNERABLE TO INJURY.

FIT TO PLAY™ GENERAL STRENGTH TRAINING TIPS

Upper Body

- When doing heavy flat bench press and pectoral work, ensure your mid-back and back (lats, trapezius, posterior deltoids, and erector spinae muscles) are worked as well.

- A 2-to-1 or 3-to-1 ratio of back and posterior shoulder exercises (pulling) to any front (pushing) exercises ensures a good balance.

- Avoid lateral raises (shoulder abduction) above 70–80 degrees. Doing repeated above shoulder lifts may increase the chance of developing impingement or rotator cuff problems.

- Avoid overhead lifts (military press) as they can cause impingement of the rotator cuff even in healthy shoulders.

Lower Body

- Avoid deep squats (only 80–90 degree bend).

- Avoid deep leg press greater than 80–90 degrees.

- Avoid step ups greater than 80–90 degrees.

- Avoid back hyperextensions—go to neutral only.

- Avoid fast intervals of less than 300 meters until ready (do sprint specific warm-up before beginning).

- Avoid hopping and bounding (plyometric) exercises until ready. Start doing them in the pool and ensure activity-specific warm-up.

Therapists and Coaches Must

- Assess and address alignment and posture.

- Assess functional strength.

- Train agility and balance regularly.

- Connect the core with closed and partially closed kinetic chain exercises.

- Choose exercises that add diversity and work on deceleration control.

- Know what you are doing.

- Educate, Educate, Educate.

- Have confidence in your program and training plans.

- Individualize program and progression for fitness/experience level.

- Be able to justify programs based on research and experience.

Prescribed Exercises Should Be

- Perceived to be relevant.
- Easily transferable and portable.
- Easy access to equipment.
- Relevant based on the sport.
- Multi-modal (upper and lower extremity and core).
- Relevant based on age of the athlete.
- Relevant based on phase of training.

References

Behm, D.G., A.M. Leonard, W.B. Yound, W.A.C. Bonsey, & S.N. MacKinnon (2005). Trunk muscle EMG actifity with unstable and unilateral exercises. *J. Strength Cond. Res.* 19(1): 193-201.

Ellenbecker, T.S. (1995). Rehabilitation of shoulder and elbow injuries in tennis players. *Clinics in Sports Medicine* 14(1): 87-109.

Kibler, B. (2005). Personal communication.

Lee, D. (2004). Principles of the integrated model of function and its application to the lumbopelvic-hip region. In: *The Pelvic Girdle* (3rd Ed). London: Churchill Livingstone.

McKechnie, A, Celebrini, R. (2002). Hard core strength: A practical application of core training for rehabilitation of the elite athlete. Course Notes. Vancouver, BC: April.

Panjabi, M. (1992). The stabilizing system of the spine. Part 1. Function, dysfunction, adaptation, and enhancement. *J. Spinal Disord.* 5(4): 383-9.

Petersen, C. (2005). Fit to play: practical tips for faster recovery (part 2). *Medicine & Science in Tennis* 10(2).

Petersen, C., Sirdevan, M., McKechnie, A. & Celebrini, R. (2004). Core connections 3-dimensional dynamic core training (balls & stretch bands). In: C. W. Petersen. *Fit to Ski: Practical Tips to Optimize Dryland Training and Ski Performance.* Vancouver: Fit to Play/CPC Physio. Corp 267-281.

Richardson, C.A., Jull, G.A. (1995). Muscle control-pain control. What exercise would you prescribe? *Manual Therapy* 1995; 1: 2-10.

Vera-Garcia, F., Grenier, S. & McGill, S. (2000). Abdominal muscle response during curl-ups on both stable and libile surfaces. *Physical Therapy* 2000, 80(6): 564-569.

Additional Reading

Bompa. T.O. (1993) *Power Training for Sport-Plyometrics for Maximum Power Development.* Oakville: Mosaic Press.

Compton, J. et al. (2003). *Ball Bearings: The Complete Illustrated guide of Ball Exercises.*

Victoria, Canada: Ball Bearings Book Company.

Ellenbecker, T.S., Davies, G.J. (2001). Closed Kinetic Chain Exercise: A Comprehensive Guide to Multiple Joint Exercise. Champaign, IL: Human Kinetics.

Kibler, W.B., Livingston, B. (2001). Closed chain rehabilitation for upper and lower extremities. *J. Am. Acad. Orthop. Surg.* 9: 412-421.

Knott, M., Voss, D.E. (1968). *Proprioceptive Neuromuscular Facilitation-Pattern & Techniques.* New York: Harper & Row.

Page, P., Ellenbecker, T. (2005). *Strength Band Training.* Champaign, IL: Human Kinetics.

Pearl, Bill. (1982). *Keys to the Inner Universe.* Phoenix, OR: Bill Pearl Enterprises, Physical Fitness Architects.

Verstegen, M. (2003). Chapter 7: Developing strength. In: M. Reid, A. Quinn and M. Crespo (Eds). *Strength and Conditioning for Tennis.* London: ITF 114-135.

Chapter Seven

Fast Eyes—
Visual Fitness

Dr. Donna Mockler and Dr. John Peroff

Your eyes are one of your most valuable assets. Vision plays a significant role in tennis and can be improved with a little training. Sight is our primary channel of information about the environment, accounting for almost 85 percent of the information sent to the brain. Yet, many athletes spend little time developing their visual skills. Since the average person uses less than half of their sight potential, it is one area open to much improvement.

In tennis, visual skills are critical because they are the first link in good eye-hand-foot coordination. Accurate visual/sensory input is required to feed the proper physical/motor response. It has been shown that better players can more accurately judge the speed of the ball and adjust the timing of their swing appropriately. Fine tuning visual skills provides the athlete with an opportunity to improve his or her game.

There is a big difference between good eyesight and good visual skills. Visual skills are the ability of the brain to accurately interpret information conveyed by the eye. They are learned skills and can be enhanced and improved just as with other forms of training. Without good vision, athletes are operating at well below their potential.

Balance, spatial judgment, spatial reaction, peripheral awareness, coordination, concentration, confidence, and visual fatigue all depend on an individual's visual skills. If you can't see the ball and judge its speed, direction, and position in space, your performance will be poor. Players who are able to maintain sight of the ball during its travel are less likely to misjudge its position and are in a better position to return it. Visual misjudgment is often the cause of missed shots or poor returns in athletes with well-developed physical and mental abilities. Optical illusions are a good example of how easy it is for the brain to misinterpret visual information. The ability to make accurate judgments and react instantaneously and correctly is greatly improved with sharpened visual skills. The faster you can process the image of the moving tennis ball, the more time you will have to react.

The average individual does not maximize the use of all his senses: taste, touch, smell, hearing, and vision. When one sense is compromised, the others compensate for that loss by becoming more sensitized. For example, we have all witnessed how a blind person's hearing and touch are much more acute than the average person's. Visual performance skills are learned. Accurate aiming and target localization, visual control, concentration, efficiency, and endurance can all be developed and improved.

Vision is critical to balance. Try balancing on one leg while shifting your gaze from side to side by moving your head. Now repeat the exercise keeping your head still and use only your eyes to look from side to side. Notice the difference in your balance. Often players are forced into an off-balance position. The eyes must be free to center on the task without movement of the head and neck. The head and neck muscles should not be used to direct the eyes. Proper training will free the eyes to move independently of the head and neck with a minimum of effort and greatly reduce the possibility of off-balance errors.

Poor visual skills also lead to poor concentration. Crowd situations, movement in the stands, sudden noise, and movement of an opposing player make it difficult to concentrate. Visual concentration is a learned and trainable skill. It is dependent upon a foundation of solid visual efficiency skills.

While improving visual skills cannot perform miracles or create ability, they can contribute to a marked improvement in mental and physical performance. Athletes need to be trained in visual skills just as they are trained in technique, power, and strength. Those individuals who understand and take time to improve their visual skills will have the edge over those who have yet to understand the importance of training the eyes and brain to perform better both on and off the court.

VISUAL SKILLS IMPORTANT FOR TENNIS

Visual Acuity

Both static (still) and dynamic (moving) visual acuity are important in the fast-moving sport of tennis. The target is in motion, the athlete is in motion, and the opponent is in motion.

Static Visual Acuity

Twenty/twenty is not enough. Athletes should have their vision corrected to 20/20 +, 20/15, 20/10 (beyond the 20/20 level whenever possible—keeping in mind that not everyone will be physiologically capable of seeing better than 20/20).

- If using sports frames with Rx lenses for tennis, ensure that the frames and lenses meet safety standards, do not impair peripheral vision, and do not slip and/or fog from body heat. The lenses should also provide ultraviolet protection. Adding tints to lenses can enhance contrast and your ability to see the ball.

- If wearing contact lenses, when possible use daily throw-away contact lenses. This will help to provide the clearest vision possible by keeping lenses free of defects from wear and tear.

- Dehydration of soft contact lenses can lead to sudden blur or fluctuating vision. Silicone based lenses can address issues of lens dehydration that may arise during prolonged matches. Dehydration concerns should be brought to the attention of your sports vision specialist.

- Laser refractive surgery and orthokeratology are other options which may be considered for visual correction when contact lens wear is contraindicated or unsuccessful.

> ▸ If no visual correction is needed, you should be diligent in the use of sunglasses to protect your eyes from the damaging effects of UV radiation on the sensitive tissues of the eye.

- Nutritionally, increasing the amount of Lutein (which is found in dark leafy green vegetables) in your diet is believed to play a role in protecting and preserving the macula, the "sweet spot" of the eye. This is the area of the retina which is responsible for our ability to see fine detail. Omega 3 oils from food (salmon, flax, walnuts, and dark leafy greens) or from supplements are also thought to help protect against ageing changes in the eye as well as prevent some dry eye conditions.

Dynamic Visual Acuity

This involves the ability to maintain clear vision while the athlete and/or the target is in motion.

Practical exercise

- While watching television, switch to the scrolling stock quotes and read out loud the numbers and letters on the screen. Try to do this task while running on the spot or doing dynamic exercises such as bouncing on a mini-trampoline.
- While walking or running, try to read small letters on signs, etc.

Contrast Sensitivity

This is the ability of the eyes to see detail under varying degrees of light intensity or brightness. Even though two athletes may each have 20/20 vision, one athlete may actually see more detail in certain lighting conditions than the other. The more sensitive the eye is to contrast, the clearer the image is at the back of the eye. Clearer images allow for faster processing of visual information and better reaction times. Uncorrected eye conditions such as nearsightedness and astigmatism, dry eyes, dehydrated contact lenses, as well as scratched sports lenses can all result in decreased sensitivity to contrast. Contrast sensitivity can be enhanced by the use of tinted lenses. Amber and yellow tints can enhance the visibility of the ball. Darker amber colored lenses are recommended for bright sunny conditions. On duller, flat lighting days consider yellow or light amber tinted lenses. Ensure that your sport lenses are kept in pristine condition as scratches may reduce lens performance.

Start wearing your sport lenses at least 30 minutes before the match in order to allow your eyes to adapt to the color shift.

Peripheral Awareness

Peripheral awareness plays a critical role in spatial judgment, allowing you to determine where you are in space, how you are moving through space, and how objects are moving towards or away from you in space. This visual skill relates to the ability to concentrate on the ball and know where the court lines are at all times.

Practical exercise

- While walking, look straight ahead and see how much detail you can pick out from your periphery.
- Place sticky letters to either side of a picture of a real sized tennis ball. See how far you can move the letters to either side of the tennis ball picture before they disappear.

Depth Perception

Depth perception is the ability to precisely judge the position of objects in space. Timing of the swing depends upon fine depth perception and relies on the ability of the brain to detect the subtle differences in information coming from each of the two eyes. Good depth perception is necessary for accurate shot placement, evaluating opponents' position on the court, and evaluating whether the ball is in play or not.

Practical exercise

- Take a string 3 meters (9.8 feet) long with 4 beads on it. Tie one end of the string to a fixed object. Hold the other end at the bridge of your nose. You should see two strings when you look at one of the beads about two meters away.
- Each of the two strings tells you where each eye is pointing. If the two

strings meet at a point in front of the bead, your eyes are telling you the tennis ball is closer than it really is; your swing will be early.

- If the two strings meet beyond the bead, your swing will be too late. Concentrate until the two strings meet at the bead and repeat the exercise.

VISION TRAINING

Beads on a String Exercise

Rapid automatic focus adjustment for all areas of visual space is essential for efficient visual function. This skill relates to the ease with which visual attention may be sustained and, equally as important, how it may be released from sustained fixation and attention.

Tennis players can use this exercise to train the equal use of both eyes at the same time. It will further develop your ability to shift two-eyed vision from one point in space to another point in space quickly and easily without tuning out the information from one eye. Both eyes are open and contributing. Start with a six foot piece of string with moveable buttons or beads of different colors on it. The beads should be spaced evenly along the string.

Fasten one end of the string to any convenient object at (or slightly below) normal eye level. Hold the other end of the string between your thumb and forefinger just below your nose. Stretch the string tightly so that it extends from your nose to its fastened end in a straight line.

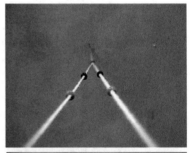

Make an X

- Look at a selected bead and you should see what looks like two strings emerging from the side of your head and meeting in a "V" or "X" at the selected bead.

- The other beads (in front of or behind the one that you are looking at) should also be seen as double. These are expected and desired responses.

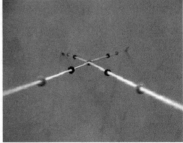

Beads on a String: V and X

Movable X

- As improvement occurs, place the beads at other spots on the string closer and farther away.

- As attention is shifted from one bead to another, the "X" should immediately be seen with the centre of the "X" exactly at the bead.

Bug Walk

Remove or push all beads to one end of the string. Look at the far end of the string and obtain the "V" response. Now visualize a bug walking slowing up the string toward you. As you slowly follow the bug, the "X" should move slowly up the string toward you. Work to move the "X" along the string slowly and smoothly until it reaches your nose and then back out to the other end again.

Variation of the Gaze

When all of the above procedures are easily accomplished, you should repeat all of them while moving your head to different positions—up, down, right, left—and still maintain the proper responses. Or, you may keep your head still while an assistant moves the string in different directions or in a circular path.

NOTE: If a letter is on your bead, make sure it is the near bead and make sure it is clear each time you look at the letter. You should slowly work the near bead to your nose each day.

Start near bead at 12 inches (30 cm). At three weeks the near bead should be kept single and clear at 10 inches (25 cm), while maintaining awareness of the other four beads.

It is also beneficial to perform the exercise in a sport-specific position. Adding a balance board or wobble board or kneeling on a physio ball can make it more challenging.

Vision training on a physio ball

CZSHONRVDK
NONSHRVOKS

HRNSZRVOKS
SZRHONSKCV

NDZCVSKOHR
CHRKCZOHRN

Chart A. *Common optometry chart.*
(Photocopy and laminate)

EXPCOFAGBL
HRAVTKMLPZ
CLKMEBPDGU
TZBSPCEROK
DEMOXNKAST
VOFTSABMXC
PKWRVEDSAN
NAHFDOGPUS
FBTXAPRXMO
OYEBRMCFTH

Chart B. *Common optometry chart.*
(Photocopy and laminate)

Speed of Focus/Accommodation

This involves the ability to rapidly and accurately adjust the focus of the eyes in order to see objects clearly at all distances. The purpose is to improve your ability to clearly focus on the tennis ball.

- Place chart B at 3 meters (9.8 feet). Hold chart A at finger tips in line with chart B. Read one letter from chart A, then switch to letter on chart B and focus back and forth, making sure the letter is clear each time before switching focus. This helps to train the eye muscles that allow you to follow the ball as it travels toward and away from you. After you have mastered this at three meters increase the separation of the charts up to four meters (13.1 feet).

- To vary the exercise read letters across, then up and down, then right to left and left to right. Repeat reading every second letter and then every third letter.

- This exercise is also good for concentration training. Always read the letters out loud to simulate the noise and distraction of the crowd.

Eye Movement and Tracking Ability

It is essential that both eyes point in the same direction and work together as a team (binocular vision) at all times. If not, concentration and depth perception are compromised. As the body tires during the match, the ability to maintain binocular vision diminishes and efficient processing of visual information is decreased.

There are two types of eye movements to consider:

- Pursuit eye movements are smooth movements which allow you to track or follow a visual target while either you or the target is in motion.

- Saccadic eye movements are quick movements of the eyes which allow you to shift focus from one point to another.

There is still some debate as to which eye movements are used during tennis; however, current literature suggests that smooth pursuit movements are used to follow the ball as long as possible as it approaches. It is believed that better players are able to track the ball for longer periods of time and are also able to pick up on the visual cues available during the initiation of the serve.

Efficient eye movements provide the foundation for fluid motor control of the arms, feet, and body.

Practical exercise

- Suspend a tennis ball on a string from the ceiling. Add 5 mm sticky letters to the ball. Set the tennis ball spinning in a circle around your body. Keep your body still and follow the ball with your eyes while attempting to keep the letters on the tennis ball clear.

- Take a tennis ball with letters on it and toss it in the air while walking (in a safe environment). Attempt to keep the letters clear.

- Bounce on a mini-trampoline and have a friend throw the tennis ball at you from different angles. Attempt to catch it while concentrating on the letters on the ball.

GENERAL FAST EYES TIPS

- Warm up your eye muscles at the beginning of each training session. Sit or stand comfortably, looking straight ahead at a wall—an empty wall with fewer visual distractions is better. Rotate your eyes in a clockwise direction, making large circles and stretching out towards the limits of your gaze. It is important that the movement be smooth with constant speed of movement. After 10 full rotations, repeat in a counterclockwise rotation.

- Maintaining focus and visual concentration is critical during vision training. Allowing focus to drift or fade compromises the neuromuscular changes.

- Athletes who learn to move their eyes instead of their heads have been shown to maintain better balance.

- Wear sunglasses at all times when training outdoors in order to protect your eyes from harmful UV rays.

- If able to wear sunglasses for practice or match play, ensure they have the correct UV protection and tint and are unbreakable or shatter proof.

Chapter Eight

Cross-Training— Water Training and Recovery Workouts

Martha Sirdevan and Carl Petersen

L ooking for a workout to keep you fit and take some of the stress off your sore joints and muscles? Try some water powered workouts. Whether you run in the pool, do pool exercises, or swim, the water offers many benefits to help keep you powered up and injury free, whether you're a professional athlete or hobby player.

Water workouts are a refreshing way to change your usual routine, and they are an easy way to transfer land-based workouts into a non-weight bearing environment (the water). This makes it a great way to diversify your exercise program while working in a safe exercise environment. As well, deep-water running has extensive benefits for injured athletes to enhance their performance and maintain their fitness while recovering from injury.

Water is denser than air, supplying three-dimensional resistance for strength movements that is 12 times greater than air. At the same time, water provides the buoyancy necessary to make cardio routines non-weight bearing (no pounding on your joints).

As you move through the water, you encounter more resistance than you do in air, thus strengthening your muscles and joints. Water workouts also work the core stabilizers. The faster you move, or the more you change your hand or arm positions to become less streamlined, the greater resistance your body will encounter, the harder you will work, and the more you will increase your strength. Meanwhile the muscles of your local stabilizers (inner core)—the multifidus and transverse abdominus—and the global stabilizers must work full time to maintain your balance and upright position.

Many athletes only turn to deep-water running when injury strikes. It would be best for all players to consider learning good water running technique and use it on a regular basis to promote recovery before being sidelined by an injury.

BENEFITS OF WATER WORKOUTS

- Water's buoyancy, pressure, and cooling effect (provided you're not running in the hot tub) result in a faster recovery time than for similar workouts on land.

- Healing is facilitated because circulation is increased through injured tissues and assists in the delivery of vital healing nutrients and removal of deleterious metabolites.

- Blood returns more quickly to your heart and your body cools more quickly.

- Water is an ideal environment to rehab after an injury.

- Water workouts help add variety to a fitness training routine. Water workouts are an excellent recovery method to use after training and matches.

- Water helps prevent the development of new secondary injuries which arise frequently during land-based, weight-bearing training with compromised biomechanics using weak and damaged tissues that are unable to bear their normal loads.

- Increasing water depth decreases loading on the joints. Working out in chest-deep water reduces weight bearing by 70 percent!

- Warmer water enhances muscle relaxation and decreases muscle spasm, tension, and guarding.

- You can improve range of motion and restore tissue flexibility and ease of movement by using floatation devices to increase your buoyancy.

- Buoyancy decreases compression on injured parts, and the warm water acts as a sensory input that helps block the pain receptors.

- Hydrostatic pressure increases with water depth and boosts venous return, aiding in reducing swelling (edema) that may be associated with injury in the lower limbs.

- Using hot and cold showers, contrast baths, and Jacuzzi jets plus a light swim will help increase circulation and decrease the effect of delayed onset muscle soreness (DOMS) and residual muscle tension (RMT).

WATER RUNNING

For your first time, use a flotation device around your waist. Anything that keeps your body afloat in an upright position works well. There are products that are specifically designed for deep-water running, but almost any floating device will suffice.

To get started, simply begin to run in the deep water. Your feet should not be able to touch the ground. The flotation device will allow you to comfortably have your head out of the water. Proper technique is essential. To get the maximal cross-over of training effect, your deep-water running form should be as close as possible to land running.

In order to *maintain* fitness, you will need to exercise with the same intensity, duration, and frequency as you would on land. To *gain* fitness, you must increase intensity, frequency, and duration.

Form and Technique in the Water

Imagine your own running gait. Keep your body in an upright position and avoid folding at the waist. Your body can be leaning forward approximately 5 degrees. Drive your knee forward to about a 45-degree angle. Your leg extends to allow your heel to plant first then your ankle flexes so that you simulate pushing off the ground with your toes as you drive your leg back behind you and the opposite leg begins the cycle once again. Make sure to pump your arms as if you were sawing wood.

Proper water running technique and correct body positioning are important. Getting some coaching on pool running is recommended to prevent you from acquiring bad habits during the learning process and to optimize the benefits of your workout.

Common form and technique mistakes to avoid

- Keep wrists straight and don't cup your hands as if doing the doggie paddle.

- Avoid a cycling motion with your lower extremities.
- Don't worry about moving through the water quickly.
- Resist the tendency to become more horizontal. As an easy check, you should be able to see your knees coming up in front of you.

Pool Running Tips

- Start slowly. Structure your program so that you gradually progress toward longer workouts. Before diving into hard workouts, you should be able to comfortably handle a steady 20–30 minute run in the water.
- Tailor your water running needs to your sports.
- Make it as pleasant as possible. Find a pool with a large deep end or diving tank that is available at convenient times and not crowded with swimmers. Music really helps pass the time as you work out.
- Find a partner. Arrange to meet and go for a run at the pool. Good conversation also helps pass the time.
- Keep time. Use a waterproof watch to time your runs and intervals, or find a pool with a large pace clock.
- As you get more comfortable with deep-water running, try doing portions of your workout without the flotation device. Continue to focus on form, and if you feel that you are sinking, put the flotation device back on.
- Stop if you feel chilled or fatigued.

WATER WORKOUTS

Workouts typically last for 40–60 minutes including the warm-up. Any longer than that and workouts can get a little boring. Similar to any other training session, warm up for 10 minutes at low level of exertion before increasing the tempo or starting an intense workout.

However, if it is your first time, a 20-minute workout should be hard enough. Start by warming up at an easy pace for 5 minutes. Then do hard running for 2–3 minutes followed by an easy run for 1 minute and repeat 3–4 times. Cool down with an easy run or treading water for 3 to 4 minutes.

Endurance Workouts

1. **Constant running at a consistent speed.** Deep-water run for as long as you would land run. The effort should be within your talk test range (able to say two sentences; if you can sing you're going too slow). Use

cadence as an indicator of your effort. Imagine your normal cadence on the land and transfer this to the pool.

2. Tempo runs. These are a great way to increase your endurance. Try 10 minutes of a normal pace followed by 10 minutes of an increased tempo. Keep the increased tempo to a pace that you can maintain and that is a step up from a regular jog pace. Finish up with 10 minutes of a regular jog pace again.

3. No floatation. Try a session where you don't use the floatation belt for a portion of the run.

Easy Water Running Intervals

Use a 2-to-1 or 3-to-1 ratio of hard running to easy running. For instance, do three minutes of hard running and one minute of recovery or easy running.

Your routine should include longer intervals of 1–3 minutes with rest periods of easy treading water or rest on the side of the pool for 1–2 minutes between.

Interval workout

1. Do 5 times 3 minutes with a 1–2 minute recovery between each.

2. Do jogs of 5 minutes, 4 minutes, 3 minutes, 2 minutes and 1 minute with a 1–2 minute recovery between.

3. Do 6 times 2 minutes with a 1–2 minute recovery between.

4. Do 10 times 1 minute with a 1 minute recovery between.

Fartlek Water Running (speed play)

Imagine running your favorite training run—including uphill, downhill, and flats—and duplicate it. Try to incorporate a variety of running into the fartlek session, just as you would on dry land. A combination of easy jog, steady-state running, sprinting, striding, and hill work will give you a hard workout while keeping the pool running interesting.

Sample Fartlek workout

1. Warm up with 10 minutes of easy deep-water jogging.

2. Do 5 x 20 seconds full out, with slow treading water for 1 minute between each.

3. Run at about 80% of your maximum pace for (30 / 45 / 60 / 75 / 90 / 75 / 60 / 45 / 30) seconds with a rest interval of approximately 50% of your run time.

4. Do fast runs of 1–2 sets of 3 x 60 seconds with a rest interval of 30 seconds.

5. Warm down with 10 minutes of easy water jogging.

Power and Resistance Training

1. Sprints and hops (shoulder to waist-deep water)

- Start with an easy jog for 5 minutes (talking pace).

- Do alternating leg walking lunges 2 x 10.

- Do ricochets (jumps in place):

    1) 2 x 20 jumps at easy rhythm, followed by,

    2) 2 x 20 jumps as fast as possible (minimize ground contact).

High knees   *Power jumps*

- Do progressive power jumps: 2 sets of 3 jumps @ 30%, 3 @ 50%, 3 @ 70%.

- Do power jumps (shoulder-deep water): 3 x 5–10

- Do high knees run (sprint drills in shallow end) 6 x 1–2 minutes with rest intervals of 30 seconds.

- Do a ladder run: 2 sets of 30/45/60/45/30 (rest interval same as work time).

- Run heeling (heels to butt) 4 x 10–30 seconds at 70–80% maximum.

- Cool-down—walk in the shallow end for 4 minutes.

2. Shoulder and torso strength (shoulder-depth water)

- Using tools such as fins, paddles, webbed gloves, or an old tennis racquet increases the surface area and resistance.

- Practice forehands and backhands with both dominant and non-dominant hand. Use a correct low-high swing and concentrate on technique. Try doing 2–3 sets of 15–20 strokes.

Fin forehand   **Fin backhand**

These are just a few examples of water running exercises. Regardless of fitness level, the water affords athletes a different three-dimensional playing field to train in or to recover in. Don't worry if you feel a little sluggish when you get back on land for a land workout, this feeling will disappear quickly. Consult a reputable physiotherapist or aquatics instructor who has experience working with athletes for more water workout ideas.

WATER WORKOUT TIPS FROM THE FIT TO PLAY™ TEAM

- Avoid hyper-extending (arching) your back while running.
- Your arm swing should be natural, just like running.
- Keep good posture.
- Fire the core by keeping the pelvic floor and lower abdominal muscles switched on.
- Breathe properly: exhale as you do the work. Breathe like you are running.
- Wear goggles to decrease irritation from pool chemicals.
- Try water workouts post-playing for an improved recovery.
- Finish each workout with an easy swim using a variety of strokes including, crawl, breast, back, and side stroke.

Treading Water

- An excellent activity for active rest.
- Use a small flotation device and use your arms paddling and legs kicking to stay afloat.
- Work between a 3–5 rate of perceived exertion (see Chapter 2).
- Try treading for up to 20 minutes at a time, occasionally hanging onto the pool edge for a short break or going to the shallow end to do some stretches.
- If your upper extremity is injured and you can only use your legs, try flippers.
- If your lower extremity is injured and you can only use hands, try hand paddles.

Additional Reading

Bates, A., Hanson, N. (1996). *Aquatic Exercise Therapy*. Philadelphia: WB Saunders Company.

Heller, L., Martin, K. (2005). WTA Tour: Aquatic Therapy for Tennis. *Tennis Medicine & Science* 8(1).

Huey, L., Forster, R. (1993). *The Complete Water Workout Book*. New York: Random House.

Wilder, R.P., Cole, A.J., Becker, B.E. (1998). Aquatic strategies for athletic rehabilitation. In: Kibler, W.B., Herring, S.A., Press, J.M., Lee P.A. (Eds). *Functional Rehabilitation of Sports and Musculoskeletal Injuries*. Gaithersburg: Aspen Publishers 109-126.

Chapter Nine

Stroke Fundamentals Training*

Tennis Canada

*We would like to thank Tennis Canada for allowing.us to use their document "Building the Foundation: Developing Great 'Tennis Habits' through an Improved Warm-up Routine" as the main resource for Chapter 9, "Stroke Fundamentals Training." We would also like to acknowledge the work of both **Wayne Elderton** and **Louis Cayer** in the development of this chapter.

INTRODUCTION

The scene is repeated all too often on courts around the world. Players who have gotten to a more competent level of play head out to "practice." What they do is a few non-specific drills and a lot of "hitting." Yes, they are active, yes, they are striking a tennis ball; however, to really improve, a strategy for improvement must be employed. Tennis players are notorious for wasting large amounts of time hitting with no purpose.

In the next two chapters, we will highlight three principles to boost your tennis improvement:

Realistic Practice. The scientific motor-learning principle is stated like this: "The transfer of learning between two situations is directly proportionate to the degree they are similar." If your practice doesn't resemble your competitive environment, you will be great at practicing and be unable to perform well in competition. This is the tennis player's constant complaint: "I can't do in a tournament what I do in practice." We will provide strategies and tips to help your skills transfer from practice to competition.

Correct Practice. This can be summed up in the phrase, "Practice makes permanent." What you repeat is what becomes the pattern you recreate in competition. If you practice four hours a day but repeat an incorrect or inefficient movement or psychological pattern, that is what will be ingrained. We will also provide strategies and tips to practice the correct skills.

Systematic Practice. The old saying about planning goes like this: "If you fail to plan, you plan to fail." Imagine trying to learn a skill (like piano) by randomly playing songs. It takes a disciplined path to progress a skill. Tennis is no different. When moving from recreational player to successful competitor, the secret is to be purposeful in what you do.

The on-court hitting warm-up is a critical part of any practice as it sets the tone for the entire practice. Preferably, it should not be viewed as a "warm-up" because the physical warm-up prepares the body for activity. It should rather be seen as fundamentals maintenance since this is the ideal time to develop and/or maintain fundamentals. Because players engage in the tennis specific warm-up every time they step on a court, the constant repetition will improve their basic skills tremendously. Remember, "practice makes permanent." Repeating bad habits will produce bad tennis.

Included here are a number of suggested drills as well as a checklist of the tactical, technical, physical, and psychological skills that can be developed when performing the routine.

PURPOSE OF THE WARM-UP

The first step is a general physical warm-up to prepare the body (described elsewhere in this book). Following that, it is time for the tennis specific warm-up (fundamentals maintenance). Typically, players waste this time by aimlessly exchanging the ball (often called "hitting"). They fool themselves into thinking this helps in some way. In contrast, top players develop excellent habits through constant repetition. They are "goal oriented" and use each time on the court to make a step towards improvement. By setting achievable and challenging goals, players can become goal oriented, learn to strive for excellence, and achieve tasks.

OUTCOME, PERFORMANCE, AND PROCESS GOALS

There are three types of goals that can be set. "Outcome" goals are ones that have to do with the final result of competition (e.g., a ranking, winning a tournament, beating an opponent, etc.). "Performance" goals have to do with the tactic a player is trying to achieve, what the ball does (its height, direction, distance, speed, and spin), or consistency (e.g., 10 in a row, etc). "Process" goals are the things a player does to achieve the performance and, hopefully (but by no means guaranteed), achieve the ultimate outcome. Process goals can be psychological (e.g., eyes focused on ball at impact), physical (e.g., feet moving), or technical (e.g., low-to-high racquet path).

"GLOBAL" GOALS

Players can set and practice process goals during the maintenance routine. For example, a good warm-up routine can include the following "global" elements: tactical, technical, psychological, and physical.

Tactical

Are you aware of the tactical purpose of the drill? Every shot should have a clear intention. Every drill should also re-create a situation of play.

Technical

The checklist elements for the technical goals vary with the shot (groundstrokes have different priorities than overheads, etc.); however, the following general priorities are typically true for all tennis shots:

Performance priorities

- Maintain your balance while moving to and performing the shot.
- Maintain appropriate timing and impact point in relation to the body.
- Use the arm and body together to create an "effortless" shot.
- Make recovery part of every shot.

Psychological

Ensure the player is displaying focus and intention on shots:

Tips for focusing

- Focus eyes on the ball (track ball from opponent's racquet to impact).
- Breathe out during contact to focus on timing the impact. This also enhances muscle relaxation.
- Maintain an attitude of "Never.make the same mistake twice."
- Maintain an attitude of "I will get to every ball."
- Focus effort and concentration by counting sets of 10, 20, etc., or by rallying for a specific time period (e.g., 30 seconds–2 minutes).

Physical

The following points ensure that players display the look of an athlete:

The athletic position

- Keep knees bent. Placing the feet more than shoulder width apart and around a 45 degree knee bend creates a lower "athletic height." This allows a player to spring off his legs.
- Stay on your toes with feet in constant motion.
- Relax your muscles (low muscle tension enhances overall coordination and specifically, coordination of impact point).

S.M.A.R.T. WARM-UP (ORGANIZING YOUR GOAL SETTING)

The warm-up is organized as a series of drills with all the same requirements as regular training drills. Just like training drills, warm-up drills should follow the be "S.M.A.R.T.E.R." guidelines:

- **Specific:** Each drill should have one specific element to focus on (players integrate skills better if they only have to process one thing at a time).
- **Measurable:** Provide a way to know whether or not you are achieving the goal. For measuring performance, determine a goal to be achieved in terms of quantity (give a consistency number) and quality (what is needed to achieve the number by including targets, specifying ball trajectory, etc.) For process goals, use body sensations (e.g., "turn your hips to face the net") or movements (e.g., "step with your feet wider than your shoulders") to measure achievement.
- **Agreed:** Ensure that you really believe and agree to commit to the goals set.
- **Realistic:** Ensure all skills are directly related to what really happens in match play.
- **Timed:** Set how long each drill will be (number of balls, time, etc.).
- **Evaluate:** Evaluate the performance (make it easy by measuring skills out of a possible score of 10).
- **Record:** Record the score based on your evaluation. For example, a performance goal might be recorded as, "Hit 7 out of 10 into the target area," and a process goal as, "Hit 5 out of 10 with a good impact point."

COMPETITIVE PLAYER FUNDAMENTALS MAINTENANCE ROUTINE

The following routine is only one of many possibilities. These drills were chosen because they cover many of the most common shots/tasks that players need to master at the competitive level. Use the checklists provided for each drill to ensure it is done with purpose and that you are accomplishing something that will improve your tennis.

Groundstrokes

Drill #1: Serviceline to serviceline "mini-tennis" rally.

Drill #2: Baseline to baseline neutral rally (down-the-line).

Drill #3: Baseline to baseline neutral rally (crosscourt).

Drill #4: Attacking forehand to defensive baseline groundstroke.

Drill #5: Baseline slice backhand.

Volleys

Drill #6: Mid-court volley to groundstroke.

Drill #7: At the net volley to groundstroke.

Overheads and Serve

Drill #8: Overhead smash to lobs.

Drill #9: Mixed overheads and volleys to lobs and groundstrokes.

Drill #10: Serve and return.

Quick or Extended Maintenance Routines

The routine can be organized as a "quick start" or extended "skill development" session and can be performed with two or four players on court.

- **"Quick start" version (15–20 minutes):** In this version, the idea is to have a thorough preparation for a practice match or training session. The time spent on each drill would be very short (1–2 minutes). Some drills could even be skipped or not done every session. Keep in mind that even though this is a quick version, the emphasis should still be on achieving goals and maintaining fundamentals. "Quick" doesn't mean purposeless and sloppy.
- **Extended "skill development" session (30–45 minutes):** The purpose of this session is to cycle through the warm-up skills with a view to

enhancing each skill or to focus on a particular one. For example, if the overheads are seen to be deficient, stop and spend more time on this drill. Once the skill is mastered, it is incorporated back into the warm-up routine for maintenance. This extended version would be more commonly used in the preparatory phase, especially at the beginning of the season.

GROUNDSTROKE DRILLS (1–5)

Drill #1: Serviceline to Serviceline

Purpose

This is a "scaled" down version of a rally to allow players to get their timing, rhythm, and feel and to ensure proper focus from the start.

Tactical goals

- Maintain a medium arced trajectory (1–1.5 racquet lengths over the net).
- Skill appropriate consistency (e.g., start with 10 in a row, 20, etc.).
- Depth: place a marker between the net and serviceline to help the player focus on making a rally shot.

Considerations

Since a mini-tennis rally is often seen as "easy," it is common to see players lazily exchanging purposeless shots rather than focusing on effective practice. The mini-tennis rally is the first part of an intentional technical warm-up. The following are things to look for during the drill:

- Footwork: Be activated and move feet to set-up for proper impact point right away.
- Breathing: Exhaling at impact will help synchronize a relaxed coordinated stroke,

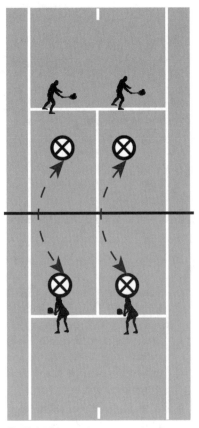

Drill 1. *Service line to service line.*

- Focus: Perform split-step and early preparation to judge the ball well.

- Symmetry: To ensure backhands and forehands get equal attention, place a marker in front of you. Balls to the right of the marker are hit with one stroke and balls to the left with the other.

Drill #2: Baseline to Baseline Rally (down-the-Line)

Purpose

The purpose of this drill is to practice a quality rally (neutral) ball. The ball must be rising when it reaches your partner who is positioned 4–6 feet behind the baseline. If the trajectory of the ball is dropping when it reaches your partner, it presents an attacking opportunity that opponents could capitalize on in a match. At first, the rising ball can be accomplished through high arcing balls. As the warm-up progresses, the balls should be hit with more speed. The ground-stroke rally shot is a critical foundation on which other groundstrokes (attacking, countering, etc.) can be built.

Tactical goals

- Maintain a "quality" rally that keeps the opponent neutral (a ball that is rising as it reaches the partner standing 4–6 feet behind the baseline). Any combination of speed, height, spin, or distance that achieves the task is acceptable (as long as it does not look like "attacking").

- Maintain a medium-arced trajectory.

- Maintain appropriate consistency (count how many sets of 10 quality rallies, etc.)

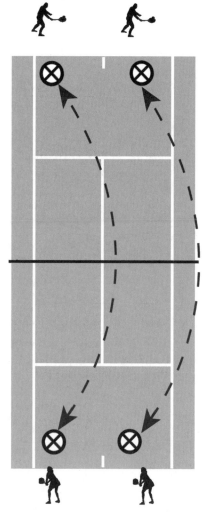

Drill 2. *Baseline to baseline (down the line).*

Considerations

The most common challenges in a groundstroke rally warm-up are inconsistency and hitting purposeless balls. Maintain focus and consistency by paying attention to the following elements:

Footwork

- Split step between every shot to balance and prepare to move in any direction.
- Track the ball and adjust movement laterally, forward, or back to avoid half-volleys, hitting above the shoulder, and letting the ball bounce twice.

Body Work

- Establish ground-up linkage (e.g., foot set-up, hip rotation, shoulder rotation, etc.). Players should engage their bodies and avoid using only their arms.
- Prepare the body by having shoulders and hips well turned on the preparation (e.g., on forehand, left arm should follow the racquet back).
- Look for the forehand to be "multi-segmented" with the hand being loose.

Racquet Work

- The racquet swing should be smooth and relaxed; it should be led by the butt of the racquet to ensure a "laid back" wrist and good "hitting zone" (time the racquet moves through the impact at the correct angle).
- Impact at a comfortable distance from the body.
- Concentrate on racquet acceleration through impact.
- If high-arced balls bounce above shoulder height and are difficult to handle from the normal rally position, either move forward to prevent the ball from bouncing over your shoulder (hitting on the rise), or move back and let the ball drop and impact it between your shoulder and waist level (hitting the ball on the decline).

Drill #3: Baseline to Baseline Rally (crosscourt)

Purpose

A crosscourt exchange is critical to keep opponents "pinned" in a corner. This drill will also help develop directional control while rallying. Balls that land in the center of the court "open up" the court, allowing an opponent to move you around.

Tactical goals

- Maintain all the goals listed in Drill #2 for the down-the-line rally.

- Place markers one step from the singles sideline and one step outside the doubles alley to identify where the crosscourt shot should pass through and the player's accompanying recovery position. Markers will help players place the ball at the appropriate diagonal angle.

Considerations

Control the direction of the ball well enough to keep the opponent in the corner. The crosscourt rally includes all the elements found in the down-the-line version (Drill #2). The key difference is the directional control and positioning for lateral recovery:

- Improve directional control by ensuring a proper "hitting zone" (extended distance the racquet is at the proper angle through the impact) .

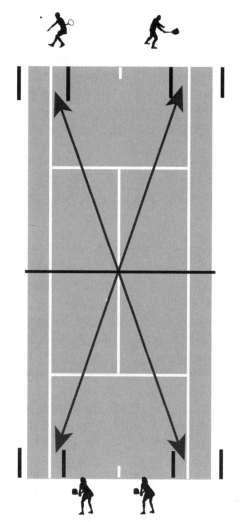

Drill 3. *Baseline to baseline (crosscourt).*

- Recover by moving to the location that bisects the angle of the opponent's shot. Recover just to the "inside" (more to the center of the court) of the markers closest to the center mark.

- In order to ensure proper focus in hitting and recovery, use markers to show where to recover to by the time the partner hits.

Drill #4: Attacking Forehand to Defensive Groundstroke

Purpose

This drill practices taking control of the point by attacking balls that are short-er and weaker with a strong forehand. The other side of the tactic is to prac-tice defending against these forehand attacks. At first, players can just practice the attack (with the partner stopping the ball). As the drill progresses, the defender can try to keep the ball going by consistently blocking the ball back.

Tactical goals

- Attacker: The trajectory of the ball needs to be leveled and still rising when it reaches the partner posi-tioned approximately 10 feet behind baseline.

- Defender: Place ball to three-quar-ter-court with a high arced trajec-tory so the attacker can take it inside the baseline at shoulder height.

Considerations

Attackers must balance power with consistency.

Attacker

- Have an intention of "forcing" and gaining advantage rather than hit-ting an outright winner.

- Move into the court and take the ball in front of the baseline.

- Prepare racquet at shoulder height to take the ball at shoulder height with a level swing.

- Use a neutral or semi-open stance as it will help "throw" the right side of the body (right-handers) at the ball to generate power and level out the swing.

- Focus on full shoulder rotation to level out the trajectory. Don't stroke with just the arm.

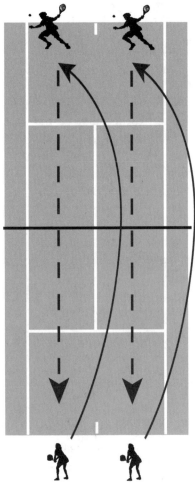

Drill 4. *Attacking forehand to defen-sive groundstroke.*

150

Defender

- Have a "get every ball back" attitude.

- Shorten preparation in order to time the reception of a power ball.

- Either block the ball back or hit a slower, high, rallying ball back to set-up your partner

Drill #5: Baseline Slice Backhand to Baseline Slice Backhand

Purpose

The backhand slice is important in order to defend, to approach the net, to handle low balls, to change the rhythm of a rally, or to maintain a rally when an opponent slices a ball to you. This is the situation we will prioritize here (how to maintain a rally by slicing back a ball that has been sliced to you). This drill will help get the feel for, and develop, basic slice technique.

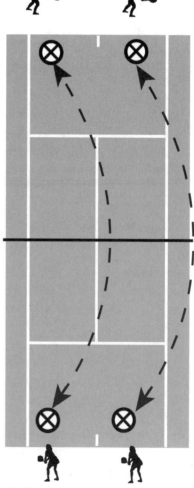

Tactical goals

- Maintain a "quality" rally that keeps the opponent neutral (a ball that is level as it reaches the partner standing 2–4 feet behind the baseline). This includes the shot's speed and depth.

- Maintain a medium arced trajectory and progress to lower trajectory with more power.

- Maintain appropriate consistency (e.g., count how many sets of 10 quality rallies).

Considerations

- Use a continental grip (volley grip; serve grip).

- Prepare racquet at about shoulder height with non-racquet

Drill 5. *Baseline slice backhand to baseline slice backhand.*

hand holding the throat of the racquet. The racquet should be in final position before the ball bounces.

- The racquet path should be high to low (or level when the ball is very low).

- Underspin and/or sidespin can be used.

- Some players will use more of a shoulder action ("follow-through" feeling) and others will use more of a forearm action ("hit" feeling). Both are acceptable; however, when learning, it is recommended to develop more of a follow through feeling for consistency.

Volley Drills (6–7)

Drill #6: Approach Volleys to Groundstrokes

Purpose
This drill maintains a cooperative first volley to groundstroke rally.

Tactical goals
Volleyer

- Practice the first volley received at mid-court (typically received lower than the height of the net) and respond with a three-quarter-court ball with a low-arced trajectory. The baseliner should not have to move inside the baseline to take the ball.

Groundstroker

- Keep the ball below shoulder level of volleyer so he cannot easily put the ball away in a match.

Considerations
Players should cooperate on these drills and match each other's pace. It shouldn't look like a player is attacking.

Volleyer

- Split step between every shot for balance and move forward on each volley.

- Set-up early with your hand. Ensure your shoulders turn (before the ball crosses the net).

- Step out by moving the foot closer to the ball first (e.g., move backhand side foot first on a backhand). Avoid a "crossover" step as the first step.

- On a low volley, use a wide base (feet wider than shoulders). Have the heel of the foot touch the ground first and roll "heel-to-toe" as your weight transfers forward.

- Engage the body by moving arm and body together and do not volley with just the arm.

- Many short racquet actions are acceptable; however, ensure that the impact point is not too far in front.

- Typically, players will receive low volleys, so it is important to have a "get down to the ball" athletic position.

- Recover back after the volley.

- Keep impact point close enough to use either a catching action or follow-through (shoulder action), depending on the speed and difficulty of the ball received.

Groundstroker

- Track the ball and adjust forward or back (no two-bounce or half-volleys).

- Practice full shoulder rotation to level out the ball's trajectory.

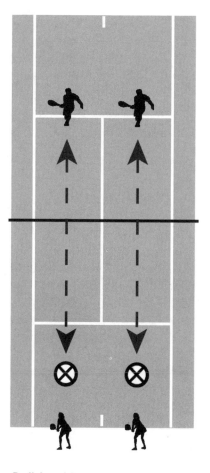

Drill 6 and 7. *Approach volleys to groundstrokes.*

Drill #7: Volleys to Groundstrokes

Purpose

This drill maintains a cooperative volley to groundstroke rally.

Tactical goals
Volleyer

- Practice the volley received at the net (position halfway between the net and serviceline) and send a three-quarter-court ball with a low-arced trajectory. The baseliner should not have to move inside the baseline to take the ball.

Groundstroker

- Keep the ball below shoulder level of volleyer so that in a real match situation they would not be able to easily put the ball away.

Considerations
Volleyer

- Recover back after the volley.
- Use "heel-to-toe" footwork action to transfer weight forward in a balanced manner.
- Use a "catching" action to control the ball.

Groundstroker

- Track the ball and adjust forward or back (no two-bounces or half-volleys)
- Setup and recover quickly.
- Practice full shoulder rotation to level out the ball's trajectory.

SERVE AND OVERHEAD DRILLS (8–10)

Drill #8: Overhead Smash to Lobs

Drill #9: Mixed Overheads and Volleys to Lobs and Groundstrokes

Purpose

The goal for the overhead is to handle a lob and smash it with control to the lobber. The lobber's goal is to be able to take an overhead and get it back with a controlled defensive lob.

Tactical Goals
Smasher

- Move back efficiently, execute the overhead, and recover.
- Use medium pace to promote appropriate consistency (count how many sets of 10 quality rallies, etc.)

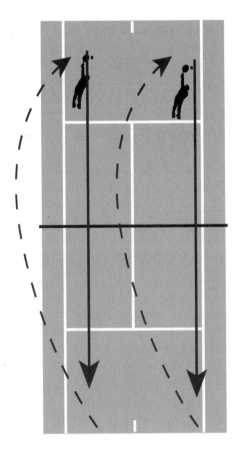

Drill 8. *Overhead smash to lobs.*

Lobber

- Maintain a high-arced trajectory that will help the ball land deeper than the serviceline.

Considerations
Smasher

- Position yourself at the serviceline to practice the overhead from where you will smash during matches (don't start close too the net).

- Your shoulders should be turned enough at preparation so that when the left hand is pointing up to track the ball, you should be looking on the outside of the shoulder, not on the "armpit" side.

- Use an athletic "throwing" action.

- Use forearm pronation.

- Minimize an "elbow pump" motion by ensuring the elbow remains level with the shoulders until the forward/upward movement begins.

- On mixed overheads and volleys, use quick footwork moving up and back.

Lobber

- Keep the ball high and landing past the serviceline (the lobber should be in a defensive position far behind the baseline).

- Use a short "blocking action" against hard smashes and a follow-through action for slower smashes.

- On mixed overheads and volleys, use drives; low, slow shots; and lobs to challenge the movement of the net player, all the while maintaining consistency.

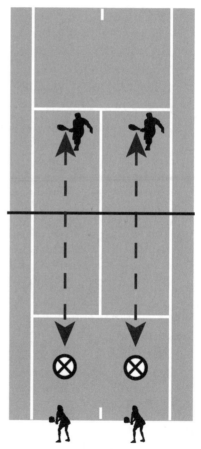

Drill 9. *Mixed overheads and volleys to lobs and groundstrokes.*

Drill #10: Serve and Return

Purpose

This drill provides practice to groove and improve the two most important shots in tennis—serve and return—by warming-up progressively, ensuring awareness of performance, and practicing variations.

Tactical goals
Server

- Serve with clear intentions.
- Practice variation of speed, spin, and placement.
- Ensure a high serve percentage.
- On the second serve, prevent the opponent from attacking by sending a neutral ball (a ball that is rising as it reaches the returner standing on the baseline). This includes the speed, spin, height, and depth of the shot.

Returner

- On the first serve return, your intention is to defend or neutralize.
- On the second serve return, your intention is to neutralize or attack.

Considerations
Serve

Ensure players warm up slowly to avoid injury. You can begin by warming-up either first or second serves.

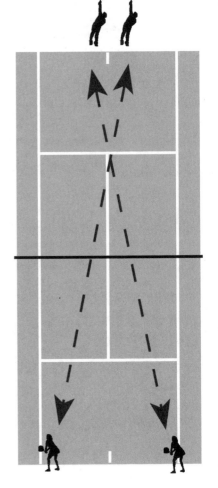

Drill 10. *Serve and return.*

After warming-up, ensure that the players have the focus and intensity of a match-like performance, including their usual routines before serving. You may alternate between first and second serves as well as simulating recovery following the serve. Check for:

- Upward "throwing" action on serve.
- Proper and consistent toss.
- Use each link of the body "uncoiling" from the ground up.

Return

- Take a position and practice an intention that you will normally do in a match.
- Split step before serve impact.
- Use "shuffle steps" to move sideways if time allows (otherwise "lunging" or "crossover" actions).
- Set up early with a wide base for balance.
- You may also consider practicing return from different positions to practice for change of tactics. You may consider including the appropriate recovery.

Chapter Ten

Tips for Tennis Training and Tactics

Josef Brabenec, Sr. and Nina Nittinger

WHAT ARE TACTICS?

Tactics are the implementation of the right technique and shot selection at the right time based on the game or match situation. For the player that means going through four processes.

The tactical process

1. Anticipate the flight and direction of the ball and your opponents position.
2. Evaluate your choices and solutions.
3. Make a decision for the best solution based on choices available.
4. Implement it.

The first three processes are the tactical part of the game. The fourth is the result of the first three. In tennis there is often the pressure of time and space. There are three different ways of thinking on court, depending on the time you have.

Under extreme pressure with minimal time, most decisions or actions are accomplished using *intuitive thinking*. This is the result of a lot of experience, and the player has responded to this situation many times before. *Operative thinking* is used when the player has enough time to evaluate between two or more choices. *Strategic thinking* is used when the player has plenty of time to create a strategy or game plan to win. This usually occurs between points or while changing ends. These three types of thinking, intuitive, operative, and strategic, are referred to as sport-specific intelligence.

There are four basic tactical goals and thoughts that all players should follow in a match.

Tactical thoughts and goals

1. How can I avoid my own mistakes?
2. How can I force my opponent to make mistakes?
3. How can I win direct points?
4. How can I avoid losing direct points to my opponent?

The remainder of this chapter provides many tips on how to practice in order to integrate tactical thinking into every situation and shot that may present itself during a match.

PRACTICE GOOD HABITS

Humans are creatures of habit. Good or bad, habits stay with us all our lives. There are some fundamental habits that a player should learn from the very beginning so they become second nature.

There are four habits we believe are more important than good strokes: the one bounce habit, position habit, no net habit, and regular breathing and time out habit.

One Bounce Habit

Beginner or tournament players should always hit the ball after the first bounce (volleys and overheads excluded) during warm-up or even when hitting against a wall.

One-bounce benefits

- It forces you to react faster and make faster decisions.
- It simulates the situation in match play. In a match you never stroke the ball after it bounces twice.

Position Habit

The player should stand not more than one step behind the baseline or right on the baseline (Andre Agassi's court position is a good example of this). This position will give you the following tactical advantages:

Proper position benefits

- You develop faster reflexes, earlier stroke preparation, and a faster game.
- You cut short an opponent's response time to your shot.
- You can respond more quickly to your opponent's shots.
- You are positioned to cut off your opponent's angled shots and get to drop shots more easily.

No Net Habit

This is an extremely important habit—always hit the ball long rather than into the net. More than 60 percent of all errors are balls hit into the net. "NOT A SINGLE BALL IN THE NET" should be the underlying theme in any practice session.

A player's neuro-muscular coordination while training is not inhibited to the same degree as it is in a match. The strokes you hit a foot long in practice will usually land in the court during a match. This is because your stroke is not as free flowing in a match because you are a little tighter and thinking of the outcome of a stroke (i.e., winning or losing a point).

Regular Breathing and Time Out Habit

During practice, as well as in a match, ensure that you are conscious of your regular breathing. You should learn to breathe out with every stroke, but not to the excess of a loud grunt that may disturb an opponent's stroke. Take two to three deep breaths every 15–20 seconds when training.

During practice, coaches should give their students short breaks of 20 seconds to recharge their mental batteries. This is to help concentration for the next drill. A young player should be taught to take this time in practice so that he gets used to taking it in a real match.

PRACTICE STROKES IN MATCH SITUATIONS

Certain situations repeat themselves more often than other situations in a match. These situations dictate both tactical and technical responses and should be practiced the most. There are five basic situations in tennis that are discussed below:

- You are serving (situations 1, 2, 3, 4, 9).
- You are returning (situations 1, 5, 6, 7).

- Both players are rallying at the baseline (situations 8, 10, 11, 13).
- You are the net player (situation 12).
- You are passing (situation 14).

Most important situations to practice

1. The most repeated situation is serving and returning—anytime you practice, spend 30% of your time on service and return.

2. A service followed by a forcing groundstroke, preferably a forehand.

3. A service followed by a solid first volley.

4. A service followed by an approach shot.

5. A deep return followed by another deep ground stroke. It is preferable to use cross-court shots because the court is nearly two meters longer and the ball travels over the lowest part of the net.

6. A return followed by a passing shot or a lob.

7. When facing second serves, move forward 2–3 steps to hit aggressive returns with the intention of gaining dominance in the point (run around a backhand to hit a powerful forehand or chip and charge followed by a volley).

8. Develop a forcing forehand allowing you to dominate points. Running around the backhand to hit an inside out forehand is an excellent and very efficient ploy.

9. During service practice, instead of power, emphasize precision of placement (depth) and effective use of a spin. The key is to get 70% of your first serves in.

10. Practice changing direction of your strokes from the baseline. Hit 2–3 deep shots cross-court and then down the line with authority. All down the line shots must be hit with total authority; consequently, they are more prone to error than cross-court strokes.

11. When you practice from your backcourt (the baseline), your position should be one step behind the baseline, no further. This is extremely important for young junior players.

12. An offensive net rusher should practice volleys in combination with an approach shot and develop a deadly overhead smash.

13. Practice changes of spin. Hit two strokes with topspin followed by a sliced backhand (a very effective combination).

14. Practice either passing or lobbing an approaching opponent in both easy and difficult situations.

Top male world players commit 1.5–1.9 errors for one winner; top female players commit 2–2.9 errors for one winner. The lesson for a club player is to play aggressively but in control of your shots.

PRACTICE REALISTIC COMPETITIVE SITUATIONS

It seems that today competition (tournaments) has been replaced by monotonous drilling sessions with stroke technique being perfected mostly in non-match situations. Repeated drill sessions, to the exclusion of all else, can progressively stifle competitive instinct, the desire to compete, or worse, the "know-how" to compete. All of these indispensable traits of a good tennis player can be suffocated by boredom, indifference, and "going-through-the-motions" training. Mind, effort, and intensity are absent, with the result that body motions are simply imitating movements of tennis. In such a training climate, it is nearly impossible to develop a true tennis competitor.

It is understandable that if there are 6–8 selected players in a tennis center, after a certain time, the results of the normal matches among them are predictable, and the players will lose the competitive edge. However, a creative coach should try to keep the competitive spirit of all players high in order to improve their tournament performance. This is one important objective of any coach's job.

Examples of Match Play Situations in Practice

- Play matches from 4:4 in each set in order to learn the final stages of a set. The round robin system is very efficient for this type of competition.
- Play tie-break matches. Again, the round robin system is best.
- Play matches where players use only one serve. This improves the second serve consistency.
- Play matches where the server always begins at 0:30. This provides the experience of the conversion of break-points for the returner and comeback effort for the server.
- Play sets (matches) where the server plays only serve and volley.

- Play sets where one of the players (or both) can take up to 3 points (maximum 2 points at a time) anytime during the set (e.g., at 15:30, take 2 points to make the score 40:30). This develops the tactical intelligence of the player.

- Play singles or doubles sets where both the players keep serving from the same side throughout the set (forehand or backhand court) and play all points only cross-court. This is excellent training for doubles.

- Play sets where the players should hit deeper than the service line. If they hit short they lose the point.

- Play sets where the server must finish the point before the fifth shot (or he loses the point).

- Play sets where a player wins two points when winning the point at the net.

- Play sets where a player loses 2 points when hitting the ball in the net.

- Organize team competitions—a tie consists of 2 singles and 1 doubles.

- Organize challenge matches or an intersquad tournament where all participants put some money in (prize money pressure).

- Organize placement, depth, and pace competition of individual strokes. This is very popular for the younger age categories. Have as many winners as possible.

- Play sets where the player loses 2 points when he commits a mistake on the first or second shot in a rally (returns missed from a powerful serve excluded).

- Play sets where a player wins a game if he wins 3 points in a row (series of three points in a row offers a high probability to win a game).

- Keep an active ladder where a player should play at least one match in two weeks.

- Organize tournaments with regular handicapping (+15, -15, etc.).

- Organize doubles tournaments.

- Regroup—challenge matches should be played once in 6–8 weeks.

In situations in which young players train in a tennis center 4–5 times weekly, or live in the center, it is extremely important to keep the competitive spirit "sharp" or else boredom, complacency, and indifference sets in. Coaches should try to organize these types of competitions on a regular basis as specific training or as a substitution for tournaments, if those are not available.

PRACTICE TACTICAL DECISIONS

What Is Correct Stroke Technique?

The *only* correct stroke techniques are ones which enable the player to achieve tactical objectives in competitive matches. The knowledge of *how* to correctly execute the stroke is not enough if the player lacks the ability to recognize *when* to use that particular stroke. This particular knowledge represents the mental strength of a player and is usually responsible for the final result of the match.

The following how and when scenarios should be built into practices in order to achieve the best tactical benefits.

When serving

- Having a high percentage (over 60%) of "forcing" first serves will reward the server with considerable tactical benefits because it puts constant pressure on the receiver.

- Left-handers should use their sliced serve from the backhand court as much as possible. It should be their bread and butter shot.

- Service placement wins points—power comes second.

- If a player does not serve like Sampras, Philippoussis, Krajicek, or Ivanisevic, he should only attempt a flat serve with maximal power about 20–25% of the time. Instead he should save his energy and use more variety of spin and placement.

- If a certain type of spin or placement bothers the receiver, use it on important points.

- Serve and volley must be seen by server as one unit (Edberg)—three-quarter speed, depth, spin, and placement are the keys to success. It can be used as permanent intimidation throughout a match or as a surprise move on important points. It is very effective when the server is not a typical net rusher (e.g., on game points in women's tennis) and also as a surprise move on second serve. The right-hander's topspin "kicker" from the backhand (ad) court is useful to open the court and force a weak return from a high backhand (as is the slice serve from the forehand court).

- Take time and program your serve before starting the service ritual.

When returning

- The initial waiting position depends on the serve or opponent, it can be on or behind the baseline.

- Against big first serves, focus on somehow getting the ball in play.

- Crosscourt returns are preferable to down the line shots because of easier court coverage of the server's second shot.

- Deep floating returns are effective against servers staying back.

- Against serve and volley players, chip short crosscourt or hit hard down the line.

- Automatically move forward 1–3 steps against second serves to send an "intimidation" message to the server.

- The correct mental attitude against the second serve should be, "This should be my point; I have the advantage."

- Be ready to run around your backhand to hit a forehand on weak serves.

- Second serves in women's tennis can often be attacked very aggressively (attempt put away shots). It is often the only short ball of the rally!

When rallying

- Each player should try to hit at least two or more consecutive shots in play.

- Modern tennis requires at least one stong weapon. If the forehand is your weapon, 60–70% of the court should be covered with it, and the backhand should be a solid support.

- 60–70% of the time, the player should use crosscourt shots for consistency, maneuvering, and angles for easier court coverage.

- Hitting down the line is much higher risk (shorter court, higher net, more difficult recovery). Hit down the line usually only after hitting a well-angled crosscourt shot *with the intention to put the ball away* (25–30% of the time).

- When the opponent hits deep (1 to 1.5 meters inside the baseline), the only correct response is to hit back deep.

- When the opponent hits a slower-paced ball directed to the receiver's backhand, run around whenever it is possible to hit an attacking forehand. Forehands from the backhand corner disguise the hitter's intended direction. Hit either inside out (crosscourt) or down the line. It also offers a higher possibility of hitting another forehand when the ball comes back.

- When the opponent hits shorter balls bouncing in the midcourt area, the receiver should consider the speed and bounce of the ball and then decide:

  ‣ When the bounce is lower (knee high), the player should opt for an approach shot (following the direction of the shot to the net). The key to a good approach shot is its depth. It is easier to cover the court behind an approach shot down the line. A crosscourt approach shot is only advisable when it forces the opponent into a long lateral run.

  ‣ When the bounce is higher (between hips and shoulder) go for a put away shot with a hard flattened drive.

  ‣ Depending on the opponent's position, a drop shot can be a good choice.

- When players exchange ground strokes from the backcourt, it is preferable to use a one-handed slice backhand (it is not so physically demand-

ing and saves energy). Use a one-hander also when reaching wide for a ball or when playing approach shots or volleys.

- The two-handed backhand has the advantage when returning the serve, passing, disguising a topspin lob, handling high bouncers to the backhand side, or simply hitting very hard shots.

- A simple tactical ploy is to hit three times to the backhand and then to change to the forehand; this often provokes an error.

- From the backcourt don't hit any balls into the net and try to stay somewhere between the baseline and one step behind it.

- In modern tennis, any shorter ball in the midcourt area requires an attacking response (attempt for a putaway shot or approach shot).

- Try not to commit unforced errors on the first two shots you play.

- The longer the rally, the less the advantage for the server.

- When a player hits down the line, the opponent's return will usually be hit away from him.

When volleying

- Think and execute aggressively.

- Block and punch the volleys from hard-hit passing shots. Swing at the floaters (namely from midcourt).

- The first volley is the most difficult—in most cases, place it deep.

- Use angle volleys when standing close to the net.

- With difficult shots, hit the volley down the line; volley crosscourt for putaways.

- Use the backhand volley when the passing shot goes right at the body.

When passing

- Try to make the opponent at the net hit a volley. The first volley is one of the most difficult shots to execute.

- Try to hit the passing shots down the line with good speed. Crosscourt passing shots require more touch, with topspin or slice and good angle.

- Blast the passing shot when hitting down the middle at the player at the net.

When lobbing

- Remember that a good lob can turn a defensive position into an offensive one.
- When the net player is looking into the sun, hit the ball high with back-spin.
- Use a topspin lob against players who tend to come very close to the net.
- Hit a sky high lob when completely out of position to gain time for recovery.
- Time is on the lobber's side because the slow ball gives the smasher additional time to think and perhaps choke.
- The best way to return a well-placed lob is with a lob.

When smashing

- Hit the ball hard. The smash is supposed to be the most destructive shot—keep it that way!

- From close range, "spike it" short with power and a high bounce—placement is not important.
- From a deep lob, hit the smash deep; good placement is important.
- When a lob goes over a right-hander's left shoulder (vice versa for left-handers), use a natural wrist pronation to place the smash inside out.
- Let the very high lobs bounce and then smash them.
- If a young player tends to favor the serve and volley, the smash must be mastered first.

When playing doubles

- Find a good partner.
- One player is always the leader in a doubles match but understand that DOUBLES is a TEAM game.
- The TEAM wins and loses together, nobody can win or lose doubles on his own.

- The most important shots are the FIRST SHOTS:

  THE SERVE

  ▸ Should have a lot of spin to give you more time to come to the net (the answer to a fast serve will be a fast return).

  ▸ Should be played 80% down the middle to avoid a return with angle for the opponent.

  ▸ Always communicate with your partner where your serve goes.

  ▸ If you serve down the middle your partner can cover the middle and cross to volley weak returns.

  THE RETURN

  ▸ Should be low crosscourt into the feet of attacking player.

  ▸ Has to be long if the player stays back.

  ▸ Has to be low down the middle or down the line (in case the net player can volley the ball it shouldn't be too high).

  ▸ A weak second serve has to be attacked and punished.

  ▸ Can also be a lob or chip and charge.

  THE SECOND SHOT

  ▸ First volley or

  ▸ Drive down the middle or

  ▸ Angled shot or

  ▸ Lob

- More than 75% of all points in doubles are decided within the first four shots of the point.

- The team that controls the net usually controls the outcome of the point.

- Avoid at any cost the position of USELESS player (NO MAN'S LAND)

- REMEMBER: Your partner is a key to successful doubles. There will not be any teamwork without a forgive and forget attitude.

- Do not try to emulate the shots of great players. Try to emulate their court position.

- The serving team typically wins nearly twice as many points as the receiving team. If the receiving team has an opportunity for a good second shot, the chances to win the point are even.

- Seven out of ten shots in doubles should go crosscourt or down the middle. The remaining three shots are divided between lobs and down the line shots.

- A player's position on the court must favor the coverage of the opponents shot down the middle—particularly the initial position of the server's or receiver's partner.

- The player at the net should watch only the opponents in front of them. Their moves and position will indicate the type and direction of their next shot.

- Observe and register your opponents' shots in the first 3–4 games. It will help you to anticipate their shots and moves in later stages of the match.

- The ability to anticipate makes the difference between a mediocre and a good doubles player.

- Players must be prepared to cover lobs over their heads. When the partner covers the lob, the lobbed player switches immediately to the other side.

- After hitting a good lob, both players move up to the net.

- As a receiver, do not forget to move 1–2 steps forward when a server misses the first serve; the same goes for a receiver's partner.

- If one player is pulled wide off the court, the partner has to move as well to cover the court.

- The objective of poaching is to make the receiver or the server with the first volley apprehensive and distracted.

- When poaching target the nearest opponent.

- When a player decides to poach, he must go all the way.

- When moving up to the net, a player must get at least two steps inside of the service box.

- When you are at the net and get a shoulder high or higher flat drive that is hit with reasonable pace, let it go because most of the time it will be long.

- In a friendly mixed doubles avoid hitting too hard against the weaker player. In a tournament match consider that player as just another opponent.

- Doubles is a black and white affair—either you are on the attack or you are on the defensive.

This chapter is meant for aspiring young players and recreational tournament and club players. Champions do not have to adhere to the above advice; they can improvise and hit certain shots anytime they feel like it—that's why they are champions.

Fit to Play™ Training & Practice Rules
Nina Nittinger

- Always warm up before training, practice, or play.
- No balls on court while playing or practicing.
- Take your water bottle and use it.
- Don't play when injured or sick.
- Learn from your mistakes.
- Play point by point.
- Never give up.
- Run every ball down.
- Don't look for excuses.
- Always cool down and do your post-training recovery work.

THE COURT IS YOUR WORKPLACE; PRACTICE LIKE IT MATTERS.

- Ensure your on-court time is efficient and effective.
- Refresh with a variety of practice partners. Different playing styles will stimulate your game.
- How you practice will have a huge effect on performance.
- Practice for doubles regularly.
- Practice using drills to build self-confidence.

Post-Match Practice
Every coach and player has different ideas about the importance of hitting after a match.

If you Win
- Cool down and do your post-training recovery work.
- Keep it simple. Try doing a short confidence-boosting session several hours later, but after a good warm-up.
- Do your pre-match preparation routine and ensure proper hydration and nutrition.
- Do any extra post-training recovery work you need (e.g., physiotherapy, massage, contrast baths, stretching, etc.).

If you Lose
- Cool down and do your post-training recovery work.

• Watch the match tape and do your mental training routines, including visualization techniques.

• Ensure proper hydration and nutrition.

• Do any extra post-training recovery work you need (e.g, physiotherapy, massage, contrast baths, stretching, etc.)

<u>If you get knocked out early in qualifying or the early rounds of a tournament, you have a chance to work on your game and fitness.</u>

• Listen to your body and your mind; trust your instincts about what you need physically, mentally, and emotionally.

• Know when to rest or take a day off.

• Communicate with your coach about the best time for you to practice.

• Avoid chasing tournaments. Instead, stick to your practice plan and work on improving fitness and improving match skills and tactics.

• Relax. You won't forget how to hit the ball if you take a day or two off.

Additional Reading

Bollettieri, N. (1999). *Nick Bollettieri Classic Tennis Handbook.* New York: Tennis Week.

Brabenec, J.(1997). *Improving Your Tennis-Double Your Fun by Playing Smart Doubles.* Vancouver, Canada: Tennisall Inc.

Cayer, Louis & International Tennis Federation (2004). *Doubles Tennis Tactics.* Champaign, IL: Human Kinetics.

Deutscher Tennis Bund (1995). *Tennis-Lehrplan, Band 1, Technik & Taktik.,* BLV Verlagsgesellschaft.

Deutscher Tennis Bund (1995). *Tennis-Lehrplan, Band 2, Technik & Taktik.* BLV Verlagsgesellschaft.

Ferrauti, A., Maier, P., Weber, K. (2002). *Tennis Training.* Meyer & Meyer.

Schonborn, R. (1998). *Tennis Techniktraining.* Meyer & Meyer.

PART TWO

Structured Yearly Planning & Periodization

Chapter Eleven

The Yearly Training Plan

Carl Petersen

M ost tennis players train and practice year round, implementing programs designed by their coaches or strength and conditioning specialists. Planning training schedules is an effective tool in reaching pre-determined objectives or goals. It allows you start on an effective training program with a clear idea of what it is you hope to accomplish. The plan gives direction to training; it is a guideline or template and must be continually revised to ensure optimum benefits and performance. Consider reviewing your overall plan at least each month throughout your training schedule.

HAVING A SPECIFIC WEEKLY, MONTHLY, AND YEARLY PLAN ALLOWS FOR ONGOING MODIFICATION AND REFINEMENT TO OPTIMIZE TENNIS PERFORMANCE.

The concept of periodization was first proposed by the Russian physiologist Leo Matveyev in the 1960s. It is the process of structuring your training and playing programs and schedule of competitions to provide optimum performance at the required times. This is done by dividing up the time available for training into smaller more manageable periods or blocks of training with specific objectives in each period. These blocks of time can be a weekly microcycle or longer blocks called mesocycles or macrocycles.

SETTING YOUR GOALS

- What are your physical goals for the next month?
- What are your physical goals for the next year?

- What do you want to achieve?
- Where do you want your world ranking to be?
- Which tournaments do you want to enter?
- Based on your current skill level and fitness level, what is a realistic goal for you?
- Do you have the potential to improve?
- Do you have time to improve in all areas, or do you need to focus on one or two?

Remember, you have control over the activities that lead towards reaching your goals, and proper planning and periodization are two such activities that will help you achieve them. Planning is a tool to reach pre-determined objectives.

By varying or cycling the specifics of training volume, intensity, and density you can achieve peak levels of conditioning at the proper time. Pre-planned variations in the program encourage physiological adaptations to more demanding training and, at the same time, avoid overstress or overtraining.

Periodizing the yearly training plan ensures proper exercise progressions and correct sequencing of energy system training. Proper planning and periodiza-

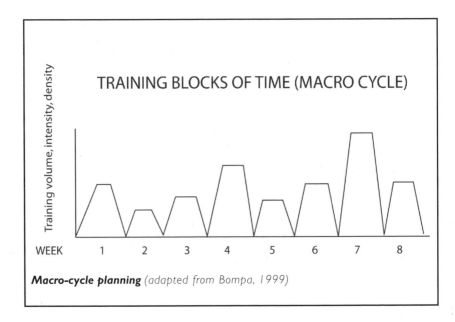

Macro-cycle planning (adapted from Bompa, 1999)

tion not only optimizes performance but also minimizes the risk of injury. Periodizing training allows for the anatomical adaptations to occur in the soft tissues and bone so that the possibility of overuse injuries or overstress is minimized.

One month blocks of time work well when setting up the periodization plan. This timetable allows a gradual increase in training volume over the first three weeks of the cycle followed by one week with decreased volume. The three-week build-up positively stresses the body, and the one week of decreased volume allows for general recovery and adaptation to the imposed physiological demands. This improves your overall conditioning and boosts confidence as you achieve your fitness and training goals.

THE YEARLY TRAINING PLAN

The yearly planning and periodization of your training season must include pre-competition preparation, in-competition maintenance, and post-competition rest and recovery breaks.

Ideally you should divide your yearly training plan into five phases:

Pre-Competition
- Phase A—Training for training.
- Phase B—Building the base.
- Phase C—Getting sport specific.

In-Competition
- Phase D—Tournament competition and maintenance.

Post-Competition
- Phase E—Rest and recovery.

The length of each phase will depend on the amount of time you can devote to training and how long your main competition period is. If you have a large block of time (greater than 3–4 weeks) between tournaments, it is possible to do a mini-recovery and pre-competition boost where you can build again on phases A, B, and C.

A good general guideline is to divide the pre-competition time available into equal thirds (phases A, B, and C). Design and build your program with the help of your coach, fitness coach, or therapist from the bottom up, moving one phase at a time from general activities with more volume and less intensity to more intense sport-specific conditioning. Using this system optimizes your physical skills and results in faster adaptations, decreased injury potential, and improved performance.

Example Training Plan

If you have 6 months to reach your fitness goal, then devote the first two months to Phase A, next two months to Phase B, and the last two months to Phase C. If you only have 6 weeks, you may want to devote the majority of that time to Phase A, with some Phase B and C training added in. Maintain your training level as you compete, and then in your next time block, focus on Phases B and C training prior to your next competition period. To design your plan, you must determine your strengths and weaknesses, as identified by structured physical and medical assessments (see Chapter 24). You must look at the entire picture for the year and plan your periodized training schedule accordingly.

GENERAL PERIODIZATION GUIDELINES

Phase A (Pre-Competition)—Training for Training

This is approximately the first one third of the program and comprises the period of general athletic preparation. The general objectives of this phase are to improve flexibility, stamina (general aerobic endurance conditioning), general strength endurance, and general technique and coordination. This period allows the anatomical changes in soft tissue and bone to take place as well as the physiological changes on the oxygen and energy transport system (heart and lungs).

Phase A training tips

- In the first phase there should be a high volume and low intensity in training.
- Get an Athlete Self-Screening Exam™ done and do some tennis specific fitness testing to determine your base fitness level. The USTA Fitness Testing Protocol is a good place to start, and many of the tests can be done on your own or administered by your coach, strength coach, or physiotherapist.
- On-court technique should focus on working on weaknesses, increasing the variety of strokes, and maintaining strengths.
- Use a variety of aerobic training methods, including running, cycling,

elliptical trainer, stair-climber, and other sport specific aerobic techniques and drills.

- Most of your aerobic training is of low to moderate intensity.

- Interval training is not done until the end of Phase A.

- Build up your aerobic sessions to a duration of 30–50 minutes at 60%–75% maximum heart rate for 4–6 sessions a week.

- 60%–70% of your time is devoted to aerobic endurance training plus on-court training.

- Strength training should focus on correct technique and multiple exercises.

Aerobic training

- Work on high reps (15–20) and lower resistance, including body-weight drills and ball and band exercises to build strength endurance.

- Improve posture and three-dimensional core strength.

- Build up the resistance gradually at about 10% per week, or as your strength improvement allows.

- Plan on strength training each body region approximately three times a week.

- A general whole-body strength workout is recommended, and it does not have to be sport-specific.

- As well, you should continue to work on hitting drills and on-court technique.

- Include fast feet and balance training during this time as well (see Chapters 4 and 5 for ideas).

- By sequencing your daily and weekly training, you can optimize skill development and training without having an interference of their training effects.

Phase B (Pre-Competition)—Building the Base

This is approximately the second third of the program. The general objective of this phase is to improve sport-specific stamina, including both anaerobic (alactic and lactic systems) and aerobic power. This is the stamina needed for energy supply and endurance, increasing maximum strength, and maintaining work capacity.

Phase B training tips

- Both on- and off-court training gets more specific.
- Coordination and fast feet drills get more important.
- Intensity increases and volume decreases.
- Include long and short intervals and fartlek (speed play).
- Use a variety of cross-training methods.
- Maintain your aerobic base by devoting about 40–50% of your off-court training time to moderate intensity aerobic endurance activities.
- Two or three of your aerobic sessions should incorporate interval training to mimic tennis demands.
- Initially start with 30 second to 120-second intervals of 2–5 repetitions at moderate intensity.
- Gradually increase the number and length of your intervals to improve aerobic capacity.

Strength training

- Avoid excessive speed workouts to avoid overtraining or injuries early in the season.
- Strength training will focus on further increases in general strength with lower repetitions.
- Focus more on strengthening exercises functionally pertinent to tennis.
- Try some sets with 12–15 reps and some with decreased reps of 6–10 to create overload and improve base strength.
- Choose exercises that connect the upper and lower core. Refer to Chapter 6 for more ideas.

Phase C (Pre-Competition)—Getting Sport Specific

This is approximately the final one-third of the pre-competition training program and comprises the period of sport-specific training and fitness. The general objectives of this phase are to maintain general aerobic and anaerobic stamina and strength, while at the same time increasing sport-specific strength, power, and speed and improving skills, agility, and total body coordination.

Phase C training tips

- Use shorter interval training using a variety of methods.

- Use fast feet, agility, coordination, and speed circuits and drills that mimic the time spent playing tennis. Findings in a recent study of men's tennis at the 2003 US Open were that 54% of total points were less than five seconds in duration, while 93% of total points lasted less than 15 seconds (Kovacs, 2004).

Agility (fast feet) training

- Do cross-training to avoid boredom and overuse.

- There is a decrease in total off-court training volume as your on-court training increases.

- Continue the interval training, but add higher-intensity and shorter intervals. Include some hill intervals for more resistance.

- Increase the speed of your functional exercises prior to adding more resistance.

- Strength training should include some functional exercises and focus on sport-specific needs of acceleration and deceleration.

- Add in some hopping and bounding exercises two times per week with at least two days between.

Hopping and bounding drills

- Include some form of balance training on a daily basis to give your body the opportunity to practice with changed muscle length and strength. Refer to Chapter 5 for more ideas.

Phase D—In-Competition Maintenance

The maintenance phase is the time during the competition or heavy sport specific activity period. The general objectives of this phase are to maintain all of the fitness components you have built up in the previous three phases, while allowing optimum performance and recovery between sessions. If you are particularly weak in one area, use a longer break between planned competitions to improve without sacrificing your on-court training.

Phase D training tips

Maintaining your gains

- Maintain your off-season conditioning gains.

- Now is not the time to attempt significant gains in strength and power.

- It is important to allow your body and central nervous system (CNS) adequate time to recover from fatigue following maintenance training.

- If you are tired (physically or mentally) due to fatigue of the CNS, either no skill development or even a loss of skill will take place during your on-court technical training sessions.

Energy system training

- During this time, there is less total volume of exercise.

- Continue to work on your basic aerobic endurance, and use non-weight bearing cross-training such as a pool run or cycling as a tool to aid recovery.

- Decrease the amount of interval training as you will get that on court and during matches.

- A light aerobic workout (long, slow, distance run or cycle-spin) should be done in the afternoon to remove lactic acid and to help achieve recovery. If training was minimal, an aerobic training can be carried out, but must be followed by a recovery work out (LSD, bike, pool run, etc.).

- Never do two anaerobic workouts in one day, (e.g., high volume and intensity of on-court training in the morning and hopping-bounding or sprinting in the afternoon).

- Alcohol within 6 hours of strength or anaerobic training may influence hormonal changes that will inhibit adaptation; therefore you will lose the effects of training. One beer, a single one, will do it. In other words, you wasted that training session. It's also a potent dehydrator, which is very detrimental to performance.

- If you perform high intensity training on a daily basis (e.g., 3–4 hours on court), you do NOT need a high volume for maintenance training! Instead, use recovery aerobic workouts followed by stretching and recovery techniques.

Strength training

- Maintain strength training, but with little attempt to increase strength.

- Eliminate low-rep sets.

- Heavy strength training is best done in the afternoon before a day off. The next day's aerobic training (light-medium-hard, depending on individual needs) will provide full central nervous system recovery.

- Do not do any heavy strength training with weights for at least 2–3 days before a match because it can interfere with the coordination you need on court. Instead stick to ball and band exercises as described in Chapter 6.

- Work on three-dimensional upper and lower core daily.

- Work on hamstring-quadriceps balance every third day. Though the quadriceps are working harder than the hamstrings when you play, the hamstrings are extremely important to protect the knee, specifically the ACL (anterior cruciate ligament).

- If your match was cancelled because of weather conditions, strength training, hopping-bounding, sprinting, or interval training can be performed. But do it in the morning, so you are well recovered either for that afternoon or the next days training.

Rest and recovery strategies

Facilitate full recovery by following the tips in Chapter 31, High Performance Recovery Tips and Strategies.

Phase D strength training

- Proper nutrition and hydration (see Chapters 13 and 14).

- Physiotherapy techniques including soft tissue work (massage).

- Sauna, whirlpool (in moderation), and hot/cold control.

- Mental relaxation and preparation.

- Light aerobic workout to help the removal of lactic acid.

- Proper dynamic warm-up before all training sessions.

- Thorough daily stretching.

- Experience and feedback gathered from years of traveling with teams suggests that every hour of sleep before midnight is worth two hours.

- If you stay out too late because of traveling or partying, you might feel that your system is not fully recovered (sleep lagged) even if you sleep in.

- Go to bed early and get up early.

Stretch to aid recovery

- If you need a short afternoon nap, take it (see Chapter 29 on Sleep Smarts for more information).

Phase E—Post-Competition Rest and Recovery

The transition between in-competition and pre-competition phases is the time between the end of your tournament season and the start of the next training cycle. The transition period needs to be individualized for each athlete. This time can be highly variable depending on the tournament schedule and may be affected as well by other factors. This is often the most underestimated phase. The main objective is rest, recovery, and recharging the physical, mental, and emotional batteries. The general objectives of this phase are recovery from the previous season, including injury rehabilitation, and maintenance of general strength and endurance. As well, it is a time to renew the playing hunger and desire. It is also a time to catch up on your social life, studies, and personal relationships.

Phase E training tips

- Recovery means giving your body the rest it needs (a few days to weeks) to adapt to the stresses you have put it through during an intense training season (Petersen & Norman, 1999).

- Use active rest activities to recover from a high-intensity or long-duration competitive season (Petersen & Norman, 1999).

- Perform other cross-training activities or sport skills that will help keep you fresh, improve overall athleticism, and prevent boredom in the training routine (Balyi, 1999).

- Recovery periods are days of lighter or no exercise. After big events, give yourself a few days of rest or minimal activity, then begin a period of 2–4 weeks of low- to moderate-intensity aerobic and strength workouts to maintain what you have gained. Try some cross-training or other sports to prevent burnout and to use your muscles differently.

 SETTING UP AN EFFECTIVE PLANNING AND PERIODIZATION PROGRAM FOR TENNIS CAN BE VERY DIFFICULT DUE TO FREQUENT TRAVEL AND A LONG COMPETITION PERIOD.

THE IN-COMPETITION PLAN

To ensure you perform well and play your best, you should further plan and divide your Phase D tournament schedule into three separate phases:

- Pre-competition (preparing for a tournament).
- In-competition maintenance (playing tournaments).
- Post-competition rest and active rest (recovery after a tournament).

Within each training and playing cycle, you need to include the S's of Smart Training:

- Structured training and practice.
- Structured tournament play and planning.
- Structured recovery and injury prevention.

The amount of time spent on each will depend on the purpose of the cycle. Try breaking your weeks into 3–6 week blocks or cycles.

A sample 6 week cycle

- 1 week pre-competition.
- 3 weeks in competition.
- 1 week rest and recovery.
- Followed by another 1 week of pre-competition.

A sample 4 week cycle

- 1 week pre-competition.
- 2 weeks in competition.
- 1 week rest and recovery.

Work with your coach and sport science and medicine support team to look at your proposed tournament schedule and repeat variations of these cycles throughout the competitive season. Remember, if you have a plan, you can always change it based on progress, schedule changes, and other unforeseen circumstances.

A sample 6 week cycle

Pre-competition	competition	competition	competition	rest & recovery	Pre-competition

A sample 4 week cycle

Pre-competition	competition	competition	rest & recovery

Tips to Optimize In-Competition Training and Playing

- Always include dynamic warm-ups, appropriate stretching, and cool-downs in your training and playing.

- Ensure sport-specific training in the pre-competition phase.

- Ensure general sports involvement and cross-training activities at all levels to ensure multi-skill development and to add fun. This is especially important with younger athletes.

- Regularly monitor signs of overstress. Note how you feel physically and mentally, including your mood and attitude to training and practice. Note your sleep and recovery cycles.

- You must schedule adequate rest and recovery breaks into your competitive plan for the year (one day rest for each 5-6 days playing or training).

- Set your priorities. It is extremely difficult to work on all of the fitness components at the same time and still effectively train technically on court. Choose one or two components to focus on and gradually build your in-competition training program over time.

- A smart training and playing plan allows you to be as flexible as required.

- When traveling, allow for jet lag concerns, climate changes, and other environmental concerns.

- Allow adequate time for practice and to adjust to court surfaces, altitude, and balls.

- Schedule your Team Tennis or exhibition and charity matches accordingly as they can all take their toll on your body physically, mentally, and emotionally.

- If you are playing both singles and doubles, you will need more rest and recovery.

- Avoid chasing tournaments. Instead, stick to your plan and work on improving fitness and improving match skills and tactics.

- Keep a daily logbook of training to aid in monitoring volume, intensity, and density of training loads and help recognize potential overstress or overtraining states (see Fit to Play™ Training Diary in Chapter 22).

- To ensure complete recovery from physical and mental stress of competition, adequate time should be allowed between the end of one season and the start of next. This period may last four to six weeks.

- In the intermediate time frame, it is important to introduce easy weeks into the training program. The aim of these easy weeks is to give the athlete time to recover and, therefore, diminish the risk of injury. During these easy weeks, the volume and intensity of training may be decreased and the opportunity may be taken to test the athlete's progress in the form of a time trial, mini-competition, or practice match.

- The optimal spacing of these easy weeks is probably every third or fourth week.

- In the short term, the training program must allow for adequate recovery between training sessions, as well as days of complete rest to enable total recovery. For example, an athlete whose training program involves weight training, aerobic and anaerobic training, as well as technique work might plan to combine aerobic work with a weight session and technique work with an anaerobic session.

PERIODIZING YOUR IN-COMPETITION PLAN WILL OPTIMIZE PERFORMANCE AND DECREASE INJURY POTENTIAL.

References

Balyi, I., & Hamilton, A. (1999). The FUNdamentals in long term preperation of tennis players. In: N. Bollettieri (Ed). *Nick Bollettieri Classic Tennis Handbook.* New York: Tennis Week 258-280.

Bompa, T. O., (1999). *Periodization: Theory and Methodology of Training,* 4th Edition. Champaign, IL: Human Kinetics.

Kovacs, M. (2004). A comparison of work/rest intervals in men's professional tennis. *Medicine and Science in Tennis* 9(3): 10-11.

Petersen, C. & Norman, D. (1999). Training concepts, conditioning goals, and program planning. In: D. Musnick et al. (Ed). *Conditioning for Outdoor Fitness* 119-120. Seattle: The Mountaineers.

Chapter Twelve

Tapering and Peaking for Major Tournaments

Carl Petersen

In order to optimize the chance of a superior performance, the physical, mental, technical, and nutritional factors of your final preparation must be carefully orchestrated. Achieving optimum taper and peak is particularly complex in tennis because of a multitude of factors, including frequent travel, different hotels, jet lag, weather and temperature extremes, altitude, foreign food, and environment. Other factors like postponements of matches, early round losses, doubles play, etc., make it even more complicated than in other sports. Therefore a disciplined, conscious effort is required from athletes and coaches to control the final preparation to optimize performance.

To achieve optimum taper and peak for major tournaments, athletes must use a standardized approach for the last few

IT IS UNREALISTIC TO TRY AND PEAK FOR ALL TOURNAMENTS WHEN YOU ARE STILL A DEVELOPING PLAYER. EVEN A WELL-PERIODIZED PROFESSIONAL PLAYER CAN ONLY HAVE A MAJOR PEAK A MAXIMUM 3-4 TIMES A YEAR.

days of training. If an athlete constantly improvises and changes routines, the factors contributing to a good or bad performance cannot be monitored and assessed, and a trial and error approach will characterize the final preparation. A systematic approach during the three to four days of activities preceding the start of a tournament is required. Such an approach will help achieve the player's desired physical and psychological states:

Physical characteristics of readiness

- Perfect health.
- Quick adaptability to training and playing situations.
- Good rate of recovery after training and playing.

Psychological characteristics of readiness

- Readiness for action.
- Quick and efficient adaptation to the stress of competition.
- High motivation.
- Tolerates frustration—before, during, and after competition.

ACHIEVING PEAK PERFORMANCE DURING A TOURNAMENT MEANS ACHIEVING A SUPERIOR BIOLOGICAL STATE—PHYSICALLY, EMOTIONALLY, AND PSYCHOLOGICALLY.

Pre-tournament guidelines

- Reduce volume of technical (on-court) training.
- Reduce volume and intensity of fitness maintenance.
- Get more rest.

- Higher intensity and specificity of on-court and match simulation training.
- Emphasize optimum hydration and nutrition.
- Achieve an injury and illness free state.
- Emphasize recovery and regeneration.

PRE-MATCH PREPARATION

It may take several years to develop the optimum tapering and peaking procedure for yourself, whereby the physical, mental, technical, and nutritional factors are properly integrated and sequenced. The work and refinement never seem to be over because after each match or practice, the procedure must be analyzed and upgraded based on your experience and the knowledge and experience of your coach and the sport medicine and science professionals you are working with.

HAVING A SPECIFIC PLAN ALLOWS FOR MODIFICATION AND REFINEMENT. NO PLAN, IS REPEATED GUESSWORK.

There are several things you can do in the days before a match to make sure you are optimally prepared:

Match preparation tips

- Anything you do during the last few days before a tournament must be in direct relationship with match preparation.
- Starting several days before your match, make practice as much match related as possible.
- Play points and practice real match situations.
- Work with your coach to develop a plan to optimize your on-court performance.
- When you do technical training, you must be sure that you feel comfortable on court the next day or, more importantly, for next day's match (i.e., fully recover for the next day's training).

DO NOT CARRY ANY FATIGUE INTO THE MATCH FROM THE PRE-MATCH WARM-UP OR YESTERDAY'S TRAINING SESSION.

- Don't work on your technique before a match if it makes you feel uncomfortable.

- Utilize recovery and regeneration techniques.

- During these days, off-court training must be used for enhancing recovery instead of gaining fitness.

- Maintain your dynamic flexibility training and stretching. This not only helps to gain flexibility, but also contributes to strength maintenance.

- Make sure that the regeneration techniques you are using (i.e., hot/cold, sauna, whirlpool, etc.) do not contribute to dehydration, but help the process of recovery.

 PAY ATTENTION TO PROPER PRE-MATCH NUTRITION AND HYDRATION.

When you have your taper and peak plan identified and refined, you have to develop alternatives for unforeseen situations such as rain, injury, or other delays in the match. Rain or delays can be extremely disconcerting for players.

Dealing with delays

- You don't have any control over the weather, so don't use it as an excuse.

- You need to know what makes you tick. Find out if you need people around you or if you prefer to be by yourself.

- Find out if you prefer to listen to music and relax or talk to your coach about match strategy.

- If you anticipate a short delay, try to stay active and warm by either hitting balls or doing exercises.

If you have a general plan and an "emergency" plan, nothing will interrupt your concentration and preparation for the match. It is a painstaking process to develop those routines, and it will take a while. Therefore you will have to start work on it as soon as possible.

FOR THE ELITE PLAYER, EVERY TOURNAMENT SHOULD COINCIDE WITH A MINOR PEAK.

The four-day match preparation diary and match-day preparation diary on the next two pages will help you design your own tapering and peaking plan. Photocopy the diary and make notes. Change your tournament peaking plans based on the analysis of your experience.

IMMEDIATE PRE-MATCH WARM-UP

You will want to create a pre-match warm-up routine. You will want to get your heart rate up (but avoid lactate build-up). Also, keep any hard effort to less than 5–10 seconds, with 30 seconds rest in between (100 percent recovery). The following guidelines will help you create your routine:

Start: _____ # minutes before the match starts.

Off-Court Warm-Up

- General dynamic warm-up.
- Upper core and shoulder warm-up.
- Lower core and leg warm-up.
- Ankle warm-up.
- Speed warm-up (central nervous system).
- Muscle/tendon warm-up.

Upper core shoulder warm-up

195

FOUR-DAY MATCH PREPARATION DIARY

(Photocopy and use one form for each day)

Number of Days Before a Tournament (circle):　　4　　3　　2　　1

- **On-Court Training**
- Quality　　＿＿＿＿＿＿＿＿＿＿＿＿＿＿＿＿
- Quantity　　＿＿＿＿＿＿＿＿＿＿＿＿＿＿＿＿
- Special Drills　　＿＿＿＿＿＿＿＿＿＿＿＿＿
- **Off-Court Training**
- Stretching (static and conform)
- Agility/Speed　　＿＿＿＿＿＿＿＿＿＿＿＿＿
- Aerobic　　＿＿＿＿＿＿＿＿＿＿＿＿＿＿＿
- Anaerobic　　＿＿＿＿＿＿＿＿＿＿＿＿＿＿
- Fartlek　　＿＿＿＿＿＿＿＿＿＿＿＿＿＿＿
- Core workout　　＿＿＿＿＿＿＿＿＿＿＿＿
- Upper body workout　　＿＿＿＿＿＿＿＿＿
- Lower body workout　　＿＿＿＿＿＿＿＿＿
- Recovery workout　　＿＿＿＿＿＿＿＿＿＿
- **Mental Preparation**
- Quantity　　＿＿＿＿＿＿＿＿＿＿＿＿＿＿
- Quality　　＿＿＿＿＿＿＿＿＿＿＿＿＿＿＿
- Content　　＿＿＿＿＿＿＿＿＿＿＿＿＿＿＿
- Tournament strategy (tactics)　　＿＿＿＿＿
- **Recovery & Regeneration**
- Sauna/Whirlpool　　＿＿＿＿＿＿＿＿＿＿
- Hot/Cold/Ice　　＿＿＿＿＿＿＿＿＿＿＿＿
- Soft tissue tech　　＿＿＿＿＿＿＿＿＿＿＿
- Physiotherapy　　＿＿＿＿＿＿＿＿＿＿＿＿
- Others　　＿＿＿＿＿＿＿＿＿＿＿＿＿＿＿

• **Nutrition**	Time	Content
• Breakfast	＿＿＿＿＿＿	＿＿＿＿
• Lunch	＿＿＿＿＿＿	＿＿＿＿
• Dinner	＿＿＿＿＿＿	＿＿＿＿
• Snacks	＿＿＿＿＿＿	＿＿＿＿

- **Hydration (fluid intake)—remember, dehydration is enemy #1!**
- Drink of pre-hydration　　＿＿＿＿＿＿＿＿＿
- Drink of hydration (during training)＿＿＿＿＿
- Fluid replacement (after training)　　＿＿＿＿
- **Preferred evening activities (circle)** Video　Movies　Reading　Music　Others

TOURNAMENT DAY PREPARATION
(Photocopy and use one form for each day)

- Wake up: _____ # of hours before the match

- Warm-up: _____ # of hours before the match

- Stretching
  - Individual: _____
  - PNF: _____

- What is your pre-match morning warm-up routine? (It must be identified and standardized.)

  _____

  _____

  _____

  _____

  _____

  _____

- Breakfast: _____ # of hours before the match
- Kind of snacks:_____

- On-court warm-up: _____ # of hours before the match
  _____ # minutes before the match
  - Type of warm-up:

  _____

  _____

  _____

- Match Strategy:

  - Tactical: _____

  _____

  - Physical: _____

  _____

  - Mental: _____

  _____

On-Court Warm-Up

- Short court.
- Groundstrokes (forehand and backhand).
- Volley and swinging volley.
- Overheads.
- Serves.
- Returns.
- Get ready for the match.
- Ensure you have everything you need, water, snack, tape, Band-aids, and cue cards.

 WHEN YOU GET OFF THE COURT, FOLLOW YOUR POST-TRAINING AND PLAY RECOVERY GUIDELINES!

This procedure must be sequenced with your pre-match psychological preparation.

If you qualify for the second round or doubles the same day, follow a simple between match routine:

Between same day matches

- Keep moving to help to remove lactic acid.
- Replace fluid.
- Stay away from fast carbohydrates (e.g., chocolate, French fries, etc.).
- Have a light snack.
- Keep stretching.

Start the same pre-match warm-up protocol as before the first round. At the end of the day, review and re-evaluate your activities and, if necessary, modify the plan accordingly.

PRINCIPLES OF FITNESS MAINTENANCE DURING COMPETITIVE SEASON

Organizing your individual playing and training schedule can be frustrating. Getting a good run to the finals or losing first round qualifying changes the way you need to plan and prepare for your next week. Finding practice partners, court times, and fitness facilities all enter the mix.

The following are suggested training sequences in the week leading up to a match. These guidelines are based on sound training and physiological principles. They take into account the importance of proper sequencing of daily and multiple-day training. You can individualize your plan to help you optimize your between playing and training activities.

7 Days Before Match

- **AM**

  ‣ Dynamic warm-up.

  ‣ HIT (tennis drills).

  ‣ Recovery cycle for 15 minutes (spin only, 80 RPM).

- **PM**

  ‣ Dynamic warm-up.

  ‣ HIT (tennis drills).

  ‣ Lower body and core strength.

  ‣ Post-training recovery routine and stretching x 30 minutes.

6 Days Before Match (or take the day off)

- **AM**

  ‣ Dynamic warm-up and agility drills: 2–3 x 6–8 exercises (10 seconds on, 50 seconds off).

  ‣ HIT (tennis drills).

  ‣ Recovery cycle for 15 minutes (spin only, 80 RPM).

- **PM**
  - ▸ Dynamic warm-up.
  - ▸ HIT (tennis drills).
  - ▸ Upper body strength.
  - ▸ Post-training recovery routine and stretching x 30 minutes.

5 Days Before Match

- **AM**
  - ▸ Dynamic warm-up.
  - ▸ HIT (tennis drills).
  - ▸ Intervals: run 3–5 x 300 meters or cycle 3–5 x 60 seconds.
- **PM**
  - ▸ Dynamic warm-up.
  - ▸ HIT (tennis drills).
  - ▸ Post-training recovery routine and stretching x 30 minutes.

4 Days Before Match

- **AM**
  - ▸ Dynamic warm-up.
  - ▸ HIT (tennis drills).
  - ▸ Recovery cycle for 15 minutes (spin only, 80 RPM).
- **PM**
  - ▸ Dynamic warm-up.
  - ▸ HIT (tennis drills).
  - ▸ Lower body and core strength.
  - ▸ Post-training recovery routine and stretching x 30–50 minutes.

3 Days Before Match (or take the day off)

- **AM**
  - ▸ Dynamic warm-up and agility drills 2–3 x 6–8 exercises (10 seconds on, 50 seconds off).
  - ▸ HIT (tennis drills).
  - ▸ Recovery cycle for 15 minutes (spin only, 80 RPM).

- **PM**

  ‣ Dynamic warm-up.

  ‣ HIT (tennis drills).

  ‣ Upper body strength.

  ‣ Post-training recovery.

2 Days Before Match

- **AM**

  ‣ Dynamic warm-up and HIT (tennis drills).

  ‣ Intervals: run 3–5 x 200 meters or cycle 3–5 x 45 seconds.

  ‣ Recovery cycle for 15 minutes (spin only, 80 RPM).

- **PM**

  ‣ Dynamic warm-up and HIT (tennis drills).

  ‣ Post-training recovery routine and stretching x 30 minutes.

1 Day Before Match

- **AM**

  ‣ Dynamic warm-up and agility drills: 1–2 x 6 exercises (10 seconds on/50 seconds off).

  ‣ HIT (tennis drills).

  ‣ Recovery cycle for 15 minutes (spin only, 80 RPM).

- **PM**

  ‣ Dynamic warm-up and HIT (tennis drills/match play).

  ‣ Post-training recovery and stretching x 30 minutes.

Day 0: Tournament Day

If a Morning Match

- **AM**

  ‣ Pre-match routine.

  ‣ Easy HIT—tournament or match play.

  ‣ Post-training recovery routine.

- **PM**

  ‣ Light aerobic and stretching x 30 minutes.

If an Afternoon Match

- **AM**

    ▸ Dynamic warm-up and agility drills: 1–2 x 6 exercises (10 seconds on, 50 seconds off).

    ▸ Pre-match HIT.

    ▸ Recovery cycle for 15 minutes (spin only, 80 RPM).

- **PM**

    ▸ Pre-match routine.

    ▸ Tournament or match play.

    ▸ Post-training recovery routine and stretching.

HAVE RESPECT FOR YOURSELF.
HAVE RESPECT FOR YOUR OPPONENTS.
HAVE RESPECT FOR YOUR COACHES AND SUPPORT TEAM.
HAVE RESPECT FOR THE GAME.

Your on-court training is to a certain extent dictated by weather conditions. Specific prescribed fitness maintenance cannot be provided accurately as conditions for training, facilities, and training hours are constantly changing. However, if certain principles of periodized annual training are properly applied, optimum maintenance of fitness can be achieved. The principles are simple but interrelated, and the interplay between them is necessary to provide optimum loading and recovery. Your coach, therapist, and fitness coach at the tournament site will help you apply the principles and help provide training facilities and equipment. You are, however, the person ultimately responsible for your program.

One of the most important training principles is that the training effect from the fitness maintenance program will not take place immediately after the workout. For example, the endurance or strength training you did today will not have an immediate effect on your fitness level, but it will affect your fitness status 4–6 weeks down the road! A delicate balance is required to fulfill the needs for optimum fitness maintenance as well as take care of full recovery. Nobody knows your body better than you, therefore a conscious effort can help you to discover and fulfill your own needs for fitness and recovery. Your coach and physiotherapist/fitness coach can help you find the balance, but your input is very important and needed to ensure that your performance and recovery needs are met.

Additional Reading

Balyi, I., Way, R. (1995). Long-term planning of athlete development. The training to train phase. *B.C. Coach* 2-10.

Balyi, I. & Hamilton, A. (1998). Long term athlete development–soccer. A British Columbia approach. *B.C. Coaches Perspective* 2(4): 8-13.

Balyi, I. & Hamilton, A. (2003). Chapter 2: Long-term athlete development, trainability and physical preperation of tennis players. In: M. Reid, A. Quinn and M. Crespo (Eds). *Strength and Conditioning for Tennis*. London: ITF 50-51.

Berger, R., D. Harre & I. Ritter (1982). Principles of athletic training. In: Harre, D. (Ed). *Principles of Sports Training*. Berlin: Sportverlag.

Bompa, T. O. (1993). *Periodization of Strength: The New Wave in Strength Training*. Toronto, Canada: Veritas.

Coaches Association of Canada (1990). National Coaching Certification Program. Level 3. *Theory Coaching Manual, 1990*. Gloucester, ON, Canada.

Dick, F. (1990). *Sports Training Principles*. London: A & B. Black.

Matvyev, L. P. (1991). Modern procedures for the construction of macrocycles. *Modern Athlete & Coach* 30 (1): 32-34.

Tennis Canada & Parent, A. (2006). *Long-Term Physical Development Program*. Toronto, Canada: Tennis Canada.

WTA Tour (2004). Physically Speaking, The Off-Season Year End Essentials. November.

WTA Tour (2005). Physically Speaking, In-Season Schedule for Success. November.

WTA Tour (2005). Physically Speaking, The Colors of Success. October.

PART THREE

Structured Environment

Chapter Thirteen

Tennis Nutrition

Patricia Chuey and Carl Petersen

PERFORMANCE EATING

Tennis is both an aerobic and an anaerobic sport. During training, tennis players are required to run in a sprint-like fashion for bouts of 3–30 seconds. During match play, most points last only 5–15 seconds (Kovacs, 2004). Depending on the drills, training sessions may last from 1–3 hours and be repeated twice a day. Tournaments require similar daily demands and may last for three days to two weeks, depending on the tournament and whether you play in the qualifying rounds.

A PROPER DIET WILL ENSURE THAT THE ATHLETE HAS THE ENERGY SOURCES AVAILABLE TO PEFORM AT A HIGH LEVEL.

ENERGY SOURCES

The primary energy source for muscle and nerve cells while doing this type of anaerobic (fast work, less than two minutes) is glycogen. Glycogen comes from eating simple and complex carbohydrates (CHO) (i.e., fruits, vegetables, grains, pasta, bread, and cereals). Simple and complex CHOs are classified by the number of sugar units present in their chemical structure. The five most common simple sugars are glucose, fructose, maltose, lactose, and sucrose. Dietary carbohydrate is the primary source for the body to manufacture glucose (Coyle, 1995). The four most common sources of complex CHOs are rice, wheat, corn, and potatoes.

Carbohydrate foods are given a "speed rating" (glycemic index) of fast, moderate, or slow, depending on how quickly they affect blood sugar levels. Table 13.1 lists the "speed ratings" of a variety of foods, particularly simple and complex CHO sources. These are all compared to a glucose drink, which is set as a standard of 100%. Foods rated from 70–100 or more are considered "fast," from 50–69 are "moderate," and below 50 are "slow." Glucose, maltose, and foods derived from corn and potatoes give faster blood sugar responses than porridge, for example, as shown in the table.

How Foods Affect Performance

An awareness of the glycemic index of carbohydrate (CHO) foods is important for athletes. The type of CHO eaten prior to or during exercise is of significance to tennis players because eating fast CHOs as part of the pre-activity meal may cause a large shift in the blood sugar, which in turn can have a negative effect on skill development or performance due to fatigue and inability to concentrate. Fast CHOs can go as far as doubling the resting blood sugar level within one hour of eating. This response triggers a compensation reaction, resulting in a drop in blood sugar to below the resting level within 1–3 hours after eating. This "rebound" effect can often occur just as play is starting or in the middle of a match.

Symptoms of rebound

- Headaches.
- Lack of energy.
- Inability to concentrate.
- General irritability.

Table 13.1. Food Speed Ratings (Glycemic Index)

FAST (speed rating)				
100–110%	100%	90–99%	80–90%	70–79%
maltose	glucose**	carrots	Cornflakes	bread (whole meal)
		parsnips	potatoes (instant)	white bread
		lucozade	honey	millet
			Puffed Wheat	white rice
				Weetabix
				potatoes (new)
				broad beans

MODERATE-SLOW (speed rating)					
60–69%	50–59%	40–49%	30–39%	20–29%	10–19%
brown rice	spaghetti (white)	spaghetti (whole meal)	butter-beans	kidney beans	soya beans
shredded wheat	All Bran	porridge oats	blackeye peas	lentils	peanuts
Ryvita	digestive biscuits	sweet potatoes	chick peas	fructose	
bananas	yams	sponge cake	apple	sausages	
raisins	sucrose	custard	ice cream		
Mars bar	sweet corn	tinned beans	skim milk		
Muesli	pastry		yogurt		
short-bread			whole milk		
			tomato soup		

Obviously, these symptoms are not conducive to skill development or performance. In light of this information, it makes sense to recommend a pre-competition meal of slow CHOs, such as fresh fruits, vegetables, grains, cereals, breads, pasta, and beans, together with lean protein.

CONTROLLING THE BLOOD GLUCOSE RESPONSE

Unfortunately, situations occur in which slow CHO sources are not available or are not prepared in a suitable form. In this case, the effect of the fast CHOs can be reduced by eating raw, lightly cooked or unprocessed forms. For instance, a raw apple will have less risk than would applesauce. All fast CHOs should be taken with fiber-rich foods which assist in slowing the blood glucose response.

Essentially, the key for tennis players is to choose meals and snacks as outlined below.

CHO guidelines
- Before and during activity—foods containing slow and moderate CHOs.
- After activity—a combination of fast and slow CHOs.
- Pre-sleep snack—fast CHOs.

REPLACING GLYCOGEN STORES

Since glycogen stores take 24–48 hours to replenish, they must be replaced daily, using slow and moderate carbohydrates (Costill & Hargreaves, 1992). To aid in glycogen storage, water should be consumed along with this CHO. It takes three grams of water to store one gram of glycogen.

IT IS BEST TO REPLENISH CHOS WITHIN 20–40 MINUTES FOLLOWING EXERCISE; THIS WAY IT TAKES ONLY 12–16 HOURS TO RELOAD YOUR MUSCLES.

However, after workouts there may be very little appetite or opportunity. Using a liquid CHO allows for glycogen replacement and also promotes hydration. Using a CHO supplement mixed with water or skim milk immediately following strenuous activity will help replenish glycogen stores. This is particularly important in order to help prevent fatigue when traveling a long distance, playing matches day after day, or playing at high altitude.

ABCS OF TENNIS NUTRITION

A proper diet and nutritional knowledge are essential elements of training that should not be ignored until the night prior to a tournament. There are a few simple steps one can take to maximize nutritional preparation for tennis training and tournament play. The following ABCs of meal planning have been adapted from guidelines specified by sport scientist Dr. Istvan Balyi.

Step A: Advance Planning

Planning for a balanced diet should be an ongoing and daily part of training. This establishes a routine which can be followed prior to heavy training sessions or major tournaments. All meals should include a good mix of protein and carbohydrates.

ROUGHLY 1/3 OF EACH MEAL PLATE SHOULD CONTAIN PROTEIN AND THE REMAINING 2/3 OR MORE SHOULD BE CARBOHYDRATE.

Protein helps to build muscle tissues and cells that may be damaged with exercise. Carbohydrates ensure adequate energy stores in the muscle tissue. Choose lean protein foods wherever possible and drink plenty of water. (Carrying a water bottle and using it will assist in this matter.)

In addition to ensuring the body stays hydrated, water helps to modify the appetite and may help the body metabolize stored fat. Studies have shown that a decrease in water intake may cause fat deposits to increase, while an increase in water intake may actually reduce fat deposits. To ensure adequate hydration, it is also vital to avoid alcohol within six hours of strength or anaerobic training. Alcohol may cause hormonal changes that can inhibit the adaptive process, resulting in a loss of the effects of the training session. If you do use alcohol, be sure to drink twice the amount of water to promote hydration. If you crave the taste of alcohol, try alcohol-free beer or wine. Ideally, stick to caffeine-free beverages, such as fruit juices or herbal teas.

A further advanced planning suggestion is to eat in the early evening and avoid overeating because it puts stress on the digestive system and may not allow for adequate relaxation and sleep.

Meal A suggestion (pre-match dinner)

- Skinless baked chicken, fish, or lean beef.
- Rice pilaf or pasta (light tomato/vegetable sauces).
- Steamed vegetables.
- Fresh green salad.
- Whole wheat bread.
- Dessert: fresh fruit/oatmeal cookies.
- Beverages: skim milk, fruit juice, herbal tea.

Step B: Breakfast Before Activity

The pre-activity meal should be eaten at least 2–3 hours prior to training and should consist mainly of complex carbohydrates (e.g., hot or cold cereal, grains, breads, muffins, waffles, fresh fruits, and juices). Avoid high fat foods (e.g., bacon, eggs, sausage, fried foods). Eat foods high in fiber with a moderate-slow glycemic index. Once again, include adequate fluid.

Meal B suggestion (breakfast)

- 1–2 glasses fresh fruit juice.
- Shredded wheat cereal with banana and skim milk.
- Bran muffin.
- Beverage: water, herbal tea, decaf coffee.

Step C: Competition Food

Eat light and ensure low fat carbohydrate choices from the slow-moderate groups. Avoid overeating. Drink water more frequently and in small quantities. Try to eat this meal 2–3 hours before being called on court.

Meal C suggestion (pre-match)

- Broth-based soups (chicken or vegetable).
- Crackers, bread, or rolls.
- Beverage: water, skim milk, or fruit juice.
- Whole wheat bread sandwich with chicken, roast beef or peanut butter and jelly.
- Beverage: water.

Step D: Replenishing Carbohydrates

Be sure to plan for post-competition or training replenishment of carbohydrates and fluid. This helps prepare the body for the next day's activities. Obviously, if playing in a tournament day after day, you will need to maintain your consistent balanced diet.

Meal D suggestion (post-match)

- Pasta with tomato and meat sauce.
- Fresh green salad.
- Whole wheat bread or rolls.
- Dessert: fresh fruit, homemade low fat cookies.
- Beverage: water, fruit juices.

Post-exercise carbohydrate supplements

(*approximately 50–70 grams CHO*)

- 3 oz. cereal (raisin bran) + 1/2 cup skim milk + 1 banana.
- 1 cup yogurt.
- 1/2 cup raisins.
- Medium-sized potato.
- Sports drink or bars containing 50–70 grams of CHO.

General Nutritional Training Tips

- Start the day with complex carbohydrates like hot or cold cereal, oatmeal, oat bran, or other. They are high in fiber and you can easily add protein with milk, yogurt, or soy milk.
- Eat plenty of fruits and vegetables. Try for 5–6 servings per day (portion size is a tennis ball). They provide an excellent source of carbohydrates as well as antioxidants.

- Eat lean protein from a variety of sources, but be sure to include a fish source several times per week. Beans and legumes are also a good source of daily protein. Make a salad out of chick peas, red and white kidney beans, lentils, and black beans.

- Commit to establishing a regular habit of eating and drinking immediately after training or playing.

TIPS FOR NUTRITION WHEN TRAVELING

Finding proper nutrition on the road can be difficult. Regardless of whether you are training or competing, you need to consume high carbohydrate, low fat food to optimize performance. A little thought and planning will help ensure you get good nutrition away from home.

Domestic Travel

- Always pack your water bottle and use it.
- Pack a high carbohydrate, low fat nutrition basket for the road.
- Supplement fast food meals with raw vegetables and fruits.
- Avoid deep fried foods, cream sauces, and gravy.
- Remove visible fat (e.g., chicken skin).
- Choose pizzas with thick crust and vegetable and fruit toppings.
- Choose chicken, fish, or hamburgers with vegetables and condiments. Avoid cheese, bacon, or sauce toppings.

  (Adapted from the SNAC Card "Checklist for the Traveling Athlete and Coach," produced by the Sport Nutrition Advisory Committee of the Sport Medicine and Science Council of Canada.)

International Travel

- Always pack your water bottle and use or drink only bottled water.
- Pack a high carbohydrate, low fat nutrition basket for the road.
- Pre-order your airline food (airlines often have various menus to choose from).
- Avoid washed uncooked vegetables and peeled and washed fruits, especially in developing countries.
- Purchase fruits that have skins you can peel off.
- Wash vegetables in bottled water or cook them.
- Avoid eating from roadside vendors or at the beach.

Sample High Carbohydrate Low Fat Snacks

(no refrigeration necessary)

- Whole grain breads, muffins, and cereals.
- Hot cereals like porridge (just add boiling water).
- Rice cakes and breads.
- Bagels, pita breads, raisin breads.
- Tuna or salmon in water.
- Jams and jellies.
- Juice packs.
- Fresh fruits and vegetables.
- Dried fruits (raisins, cranberries, apricots).
- Plain cookies like digestives or graham crackers.

Two months before heading off for tournaments take a detailed look at your diet. Does it provide the vitamins, minerals, proteins, fat, and carbohydrates that your body needs to perform? Follow Canada's Food Guide to Healthy Eating (www.hc-sc.gc.ca/fn-an/food-guide-aliment/index_e.html) or the USDA's food pyramid (www.mypyramid.gov) on the next two pages by consuming a variety of foods each day. It is also recommended to talk to a dietitian.

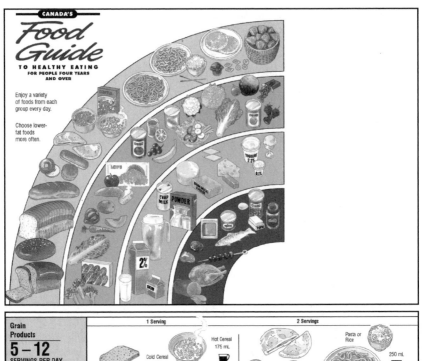

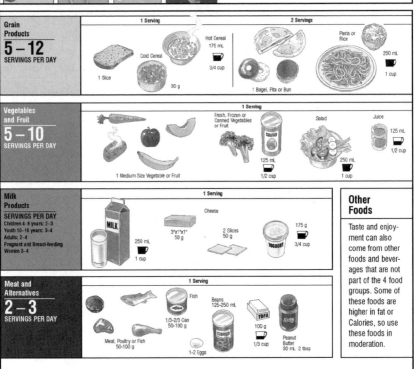

Canada's Food Guide to Healthy Eating

Food Guide Pyramid

A Guide to Daily Food Choices

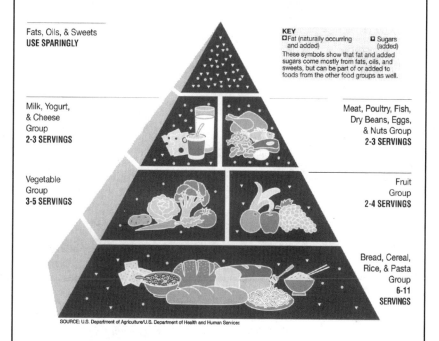

Fats, Oils, & Sweets
USE SPARINGLY

KEY
□ Fat (naturally occurring and added)   ◪ Sugars (added)
These symbols show that fat and added sugars come mostly from fats, oils, and sweets, but can be part of or added to foods from the other food groups as well.

Milk, Yogurt, & Cheese Group
2-3 SERVINGS

Meat, Poultry, Fish, Dry Beans, Eggs, & Nuts Group
2-3 SERVINGS

Vegetable Group
3-5 SERVINGS

Fruit Group
2-4 SERVINGS

Bread, Cereal, Rice, & Pasta Group
6-11 SERVINGS

SOURCE: U.S. Department of Agriculture/U.S. Department of Health and Human Services

Use the Food Guide Pyramid to help you eat better every day. . .the Dietary Guidelines way. Start with plenty of Breads, Cereals, Rice, and Pasta; Vegetables; and Fruits. Add two to three servings from the Milk group and two to three servings from the Meat group.

Each of these food groups provides some, but not all, of the nutrients you need. No one food group is more important than another — for good health you need them all. Go easy on fats, oils, and sweets, the foods in the small tip of the Pyramid.

To order a copy of "The Food Guide Pyramid" booklet, send a $1.00 check or money order made out to the Superintendent of Documents to: Consumer Information Center, Department 159-Y, Pueblo, Colorado 81009.

U.S. Department of Agriculture, Human Nutrition Information Service, August 1992, Leaflet No. 572

USDA Food Guide Pyramid

Sport Nutrition Supplements
Dallas Parsons, RD/Sport Dietitian

In the competitive spirit of sport, it is inevitable that supplementation is often part of an athlete's training diet. Sport nutrition products can be used as a convenient method to provide the body with fuel before, during, and after training, but for the most part, nutrition should come from whole grains, fruits, vegetables, lean protein, and low fat dairy. Under the existing regulatory environment, there is no accurate way to identify all of the constituents of every ingredient found in supplement preparations. Consequently there is no way to guarantee the safety and purity of these products. Talk to your sport dietitian before using nutritional supplements.

Sports Nutrition Supplements		
Product	**Possible Uses**	**Comments**
Sports bars	Before, during and after training	Should have carb to protein ratio of 4:1 and < 3g fat/100 cal
Protein bars	After training or as snack	Provide between 12–35g protein/bar; common protein sources are whey and soy
Sports drinks	Before, during, and after training	Should have 4–8% carbohydrate solution and include sodium; may also have calcium and magnesium
Energy gels or fruit chews	Before, during, and after training	Supply quick energy; electrolyte content varies
Protein powders	After training or part of a meal or snack, for weight gain, or travel	Check whether also supplies carbs; may be artificially sweetened
Meal replacement drinks	Before or after training	Quickly digested and provide fluids, good for a "nervous" stomach before competition
Vitamins and minerals	Daily	Individual requirements should be assessed by a dietitian or physician

Eating and Drinking for Recovery

Dallas Parsons, RD/Sport Dietitian

Why is eating and drinking after training important?

During training or competition, your body loses fluids and uses a lot of muscle glycogen. Carbohydrates and water are what the body needs to replenish. If an athlete is dehydrated and glycogen-depleted, his/her body cannot recover and perform well during subsequent training.

When should I eat for optimal recovery?

It is recommended that athletes consume food and fluids within 30 minutes of completing exercise because blood flow to the muscles is greater and muscle cells are more insulin-sensitive. At this time the body is able to maximize its ability to replace glycogen; this is especially important when athletes train more than once a day.

What should I eat?

Athletes should consume carbohydrate-rich foods that they enjoy and emphasize fluid replacement. It doesn't matter whether you prefer liquids or solid foods. Foods with a high glycemic index can be absorbed more quickly and recent studies have shown that including some protein (as little as 10 grams) after exercise may enhance glycogen resynthesis by aiding the stimulation of insulin. After resistance training, protein may also help stimulate muscle growth due to the release of insulin and growth hormone.

How much should I eat?

It is recommended that athletes consume 1.0—1.5 grams of carbohydrate per kilogram (2.2 pounds) of body weight immediately after exercise and then follow that with an additional 1.5—2.0 grams of carbohydrate per kilogram at a meal or snack within two hours.

Take home message

- Commit to establishing a regular habit of eating and drinking immediately after training.
- Choose carbohydrate-rich foods that you like and drink plenty of fluids.
- Include 10—18 grams protein in your recovery snack to maximize glycogen uptake.

Eating and Drinking for Recovery—continued

Recovery Meal
Example: A 130lb (130 x 0.45 = 58.5kg) athlete

Timing	Food & Amount	Carb (g)	Protein (g)	Fluids (ml)
Within 30 minutes post-workout (goal 59–88g carb)	500 ml Gatorade 250 ml water Cliff Bar	28 0 44	0 0 10	500 ml 250 ml
	Totals	**72 g**	**10 g**	**750 ml**

One hour later at a meal (goal 88–118 g carb)	Deli turkey 6" sub sandwich with
	    1 tbsp light mayo
	    1 slice cheese
	pretzels (70 g bag)
	water (500 ml)
		40
		1
		2
		57
		0
			16
			0
			3
			6
			0
				500 ml

	Totals	**100 g**	**25 g**	**500 ml**

Top 10 Recovery Foods for Athletes

Food	Serving Size	Calories (kcal)	Carbs (g)	Protein (g)	Fat (g)
1. 1% chocolate milk	2 cups	320	54	16	6
2. Low fat (1% milk fat) fruit yogurt	175 g	150	26	6	2
3. Peanut butter & honey sandwich	1	430	73	13	14
4. Cinnamon raisin bagel	1 small (71 g)	200	39	7	1.7
5. Sports drinks	varies	varies	varies	0	0
6. High carb energy bars	1 bar	varies	varies	varies	varies
7. Dried fruit bars	1 bar	varies	varies	varies	varies
8. Bananas	1 large (118g)	109	28	1.2	0.6
9. Low fat granola cereal	3/4 cup (40 g)	120	28	8	1
10. Meal replacement drink	1 can (227 ml)	240	41	10	4

Top 10 Nutritional Issues for Athletes
Patricia Chuey MSc., RDN.

1. Healthy Eating

Good nutrition means eating a variety of foods. Many people get stuck in a routine of eating the same five to ten staple foods over and over again: pasta, bananas, bagels, chicken, carrot sticks, and lettuce salad. However, we need to mix things up a little.

Remember the 80—20 rule: Eat well at least 80 percent of the time but leave some room for soul nourishment and pure pleasure. If you're going to ingest foods or drinks that offer little nutritional value such as coffee, beer, jelly beans, pop, sugary cakes and so on, make the indulgence worthwhile. If the food offers no nutritional value, at least aim to get maximum psychological pleasure out of it. (Maximum 20% of the time.)

2. Energy Management

Eat 3 meals a day with the largest portion being vegetables or fruit, but also ensure you add some lean protein. A minimum of 3 of the 4 food groups is ideal. This ensures you get adequate protein and enough carbohydrate to fuel your muscles and brain.

Eat 2 or 3 healthy snacks each day. Don't allow more than 4 hours to pass in a day without eating.

3. Hydration

Stay well hydrated: Drink water with all meals, snacks, and anything sweet or salty. Drink in a 1:1 ratio with caffeine, alcohol, or pop. You'll know you are well hydrated when you urinate every 1—2 hours during the day and your urine is clear or pale in color.

Drink water before, during, and after exercise!

4. Pre-exercise Eating

Eat a "smart" dinner the night before: lots of vegetables; whole grains; and some lean red meat, poultry, fish, or tofu.

Have a high carbohydrate evening snack to top up muscle glycogen stores, especially if you can't eat breakfast. Some examples include: fruit, a bagel with jam, popcorn, or cinnamon toast.

Top 10 Nutritional Issues continued

In the morning aim for a breakfast with mostly carbohydrates but also a bit of protein for staying power. Keep this meal low in fat and moderate in fiber. The more time you have between eating and exercise, the larger the quantity you can eat.

5. Recovery

Focus on rehydration: drink at least another 2—4 cups of water.

Eat or drink carbohydrate foods and a little protein within the first 30 minutes of finishing a hard workout or activity (e.g., peanut butter and jam sandwich, fruit and yogurt, bagel with turkey slices, cereal and milk, or a typical lunch meal).

If you drink caffeine, alcohol, or pop, drink extra water.

6. Eating on the Road

Fast food is still, for the most part, much too high in fat, very high in sodium, and often served in gargantuan portions. Instead, look for meals with large portions of vegetables or fruit.

Pack high quality, healthy snacks to take with you on the road. Don't use a trip as an excuse to blow your healthy eating plan.

Be aware that mood swings, stress, frustration, and other emotions may change eating habits.

7. Weight Management

Do not obsess about weight!

Pay attention to hunger and satiety cues. Tune into meal volume, timing, and spacing.

Don't approach every meal like it's your last opportunity ever to eat. Rate your fullness on a scale of 1—10, where 1 is starving and 10 is over-full. Try to stop at level 5. This is the point where you feel psychologically and physiologically satisfied, but not stuffed.

8. Supplementation

Supplements are not replacements for food. Don't be fooled by advertising hype.

Top 10 Nutritional Issues continued

Sport drinks, bars, and gels have a role to play. Realize, though, that they are generally designed for use during prolonged exercise.

The main benefit of sport drinks is that their flavors, bright colors, and jazzy packaging remind athletes to drink more fluids when exercising.

Taking a daily multivitamin and mineral tablet is a good insurance policy for meeting all your micronutrient needs. Choose a reputable brand, or talk to your dietitian about how to select one that is right for you.

9. Vegetarianism

If you are a vegetarian, you need to replace the meat portion of your diet with a variety of healthy meat alternatives such as beans, lentils, chickpeas, tofu and other soy products, nuts, nut butters, seeds, eggs, dairy, and fish (if you eat them).

If you eliminate dairy products as well, you need to consider calcium and vitamin D, and when you eliminate all foods of animal origin, vitamin B12 also needs special monitoring.

10. Food Safety and Quality Concerns

Although organic food may not necessarily offer higher nutritional value, certified organic foods will reduce your intake of pesticides and other chemicals. In this regard, extra cost is still worth it.

Organic or not, washing all produce is still critical to minimizing food poisoning.

For more information see Patricia Chuey's book, *The 80–20 Cookbook—Eating for Energy without Deprivation."*

Doping and Ergogenic Aids

Dr. Bernard Lalonde, MD

The sport of tennis has not been immune to the world of malappropriate use of ergogenic aids, otherwise known as doping. Fortunately the sport of tennis is such that the use of ergogenic aids is rare, and several organizations are endeavoring to see that it stays that way, including the ATP, WTA, World Antidoping Agency (WADA), Canadian Centre for Ethics in Sport (CCES), Tennis Canada, and the USTA. What most, if not all, athletes want is a level playing field. They want to know that there are not cheaters in their midst. They want to be sure that the winners at the end of the day have not used illegal substances to their advantage.

The list of substances that are banned is a continuously evolving one. WADA has published a list that most countries and international and national organizations have become signatory to. It is the duty of each athlete to familiarize himself/herself with the contents of all substances he/she puts in his/her body. At the end of the day, the athlete pays the price for being caught with an illegal substance in his or her body, not the therapist, doctor, trainer, guru, etc.

The vast majority of doping charges in tennis have been so-called "inadvertent doping." That s when an athlete takes a substance that he/she thinks contains no illegal substances. These are not infrequently found in over-the-counter products, so-called nutritional products. Increasingly the prudent athlete stays away from these supplements, as it is frequently impossible to know from batch to batch what contaminants they may contain.

The following organizations have excellent web sites that are continuously being updated. Tennis players should familiarize themselves with these sites and educate themselves with their content.

Resources

World Anti Doping Agency www.wada-ama.org/en/tl.asp

Canadian Centre for Ethics in Sport w w w.cces.ca

The successful athlete is one who pays attention to good preparation in all phases of his or her training. This *Fit to Play Tennis* book contains the essentials of these principles as laid out in the introduction "Making Yourself a Better Player and Athlete." Ergogenic help is found in the right balance of appropriate foodstuffs, hydration, and proper training both on and off court. Look no further. The answer is within you.

References

Costill, D.L., Hargreaves, M. (1992). Carbohydrate nutrition and fatigue. *Sports Med.* 13(2):86-92.

Coyle, E.F. (1995). Substrate utilization during exercise in active people. *Am. J. Clin. Nutr.* 61: S968-S979.

Kovacs, M. (2004). A comparison of work/rest intervals in men's professional tennis. *Medicine and Science in Tennis* 9(3): 10-11.

Tarnopolsky, M. (2000). Protein and amino acid needs for training and bulking up. In: L. Burke & V. Deakin (Eds). *Clinical Sports Nutrition (2nd edition)* 90-123. Roseville, Australia: McGraw Hill Book Company Ltd.

Additional Reading

Bar-Or, O. (2001). Nutritional considerations for the child athlete. *Canadian Journal of Applied Physiology.* 26(Suppl.): 186-191.

Burke, L. (2000). Nutrition for recovery after competition and training, In: Burke, L., Deakin, V. (Eds). *Clinical Sports Nutrition (2nd edition)* 396-427. Roseville, Australia: McGraw Hill Book Company Ltd.

Chuey, P., Steele, D. (2004). *The 80-20 Cookbook: Eating for Energy Without Deprivation.* Vancouver. (Details on the book and ordering information is available at www.eatingforenergy.com.)

Clark, N. (2003). *Sport Nutrition Guidebook (3rd edition.).* Champaign, IL: Human Kinetics.

World Anti Doping Agency: www.wada-ama.org/en/tl.asp.

Canadian Centre for Ethics in Sport: www.cces.ca.

Chapter Fourteen

Hydration For Tennis

Patricia Chuey and Carl Petersen

As the summer sun beats down during a long match and you start to feel thirsty and fatigued, you should be very concerned about your hydration. According to Dr. Michael Bergeron, any water deficit can have a negative effect on a player's performance. He states that as a player becomes dehydrated, the heart must work harder, body temperature increases, strength and endurance decrease, fatigue occurs faster, and even mental capacity (e.g., shot selection and concentration) is reduced. The following is a review of the importance of hydration during exercise and hydration protocols for tennis.

WHY HYDRATE?

- In a normal day, even without exercise, the body loses more than 2 liters (about 2.1 quarts) of water.

- Most of this water is lost as sweat or through breathing.

- Sweat loss rate is individual with not all players sweating the same amount in similar conditions. Some players can sweat up to three to four liters/hour while playing.

- During exercise, eighty percent of the energy produced by exercising muscle converts into heat and the muscles generate about ten times the heat they would at rest. This increases fluid needs by up to 2 extra liters (quarts).

- In tennis you often play multiple matches in the heat, thus increasing the risk of fluid loss and potential heat stress.

- Indoors you still sweat a lot, and in a dry environment you still sweat a lot but won't feel it.

Dr. M. Bergeron suggests the following is true:

- Many players begin play or training somewhat dehydrated.
- The more dehydrated a player is at the beginning of a match the more likely body temperature will rise during play—especially if the match goes long.
- Adolescent boys can sweat as much as three liters (over 100 ounces) per hour.
- Players tend to begin the second match or training session significantly more dehydrated then prior to their first match or practice.
- Problems related to fluid-electrolyte deficits occur more often during the second match of the day, especially with little recovery time between matches.

Thirst is a delayed response. By the time you feel thirsty, you are already slightly dehydrated. It is therefore critical to supply your exercising body with the water it needs, even before you think you need it:

Hydration tips
- Drink before thirst.
- Carry your water bottle and use it.

HYDRATION BEFORE, DURING, AND AFTER TRAINING OR PLAYING

Before Exercise

Two to three cups of water or other hydrating fluids consumed 2–3 hours prior to exercise is recommended. In addition to water, hydrating fluids include real fruit juices (without added sugar), low fat milk, soya milk, and weak herbal tea. Consuming this fluid well in advance of the match will allow the kidneys to process it in time. Additionally, drinking 1–2 cups of fluid, as tolerated, 5–10 minutes before a match begins is also recommended.

228

Consuming sugar within an hour of exercise causes a release of insulin in the body. Insulin causes the muscles to take sugar from the blood. When you start exercising, blood sugar may be lower than it should be, decreasing your energy and performance. Once you start to exercise, other hormones let the sugar from the drink stay in your blood.

Recent research has shown that caffeinated beverages such as coffee do not have as much of a dehydrating effect as once thought. If you normally drink a moderate amount of caffeine before exercise, this should not be a problem as long as your main source of fluid comes from beverages such as water, juice, and diluted sports drinks. Caffeine can actually have the effect of reducing the perception of fatigue during exercise. Note that in high doses, caffeine is considered a banned substance.

SPORTS DRINKS CONTAINING GREATER THAN 8% SUGAR ARE NOT RECOMMENDED FOR USE BEFORE EXERCISE.

During Exercise

In activity lasting less than 60 minutes, little benefit is derived from drinking any other beverage than water. Cold water will cause slightly enhanced absorption and better hydration than warm water. If you are adequately hydrated, large sips of water are better absorbed than small sips. However, if you are moderately dehydrated, water will remain in the stomach and can cause sloshing. The key is to prevent dehydration by taking about 1/2 cup (100–200 ml) of cool water every 15 minutes during exercise.

After the one hour mark in prolonged activity, a sport drink with a 4–8% glucose solution is beneficial. These drinks supply both fluid and carbohydrate which can enhance energy. Once started, it is recommended to continue drinking the sport drink in combination with water at regular intervals until completion of the exercise session. Most sports drinks provide 200–300 mg of sodium per 500 ml to improve palatability and rehydration. Additional electrolyte replacement is not necessary in activity lasting less than four hours.

After Exercise

Adequate recovery from exercise is the most commonly overlooked aspect of sport nutrition. The three steps are:

- Rehydration.
- Replace muscle fuel (glycogen).
- Replace electrolytes.

Rehydration. The first priority immediately after a hard workout should be rehydration. Consume 1 liter (4 cups) of fluid for each kilogram of weight lost. If not monitoring weight, aim to consume at least 2–3 cups of water. Following strenuous exercise in the heat, you may need as long as 24–48 hours to replace water loss. If you will be celebrating and drinking alcohol after exercise, be sure to drink at least one large glass of water before that first beer!

Replace glycogen. Beyond hydration, the second priority in enhanced recovery is replacing used muscle glycogen by consuming carbohydrate rich foods or beverages. Aim to consume 50–100 grams of carbohydrate in the first 30–60 minutes after exercise and include 10–20 grams of protein to promote faster recovery. For example, have a bagel with jam or natural peanut butter, a banana plus a yogurt or orange juice, and a couple of high-quality cookies such as Fig Newtons or homemade oatmeal raisin cookies (see Top 10 Recovery Foods in Chapter 13 for more ideas.)

Commercial recovery drinks supplying close to 50 grams of carbohydrate or more would also be acceptable. If using commercial recovery drinks, choose one with a 3–1 ratio of carbohydrate to protein. This combination has shown to produce ideal levels of insulin that cause the muscles to store the maximum amount of glycogen. Small amounts of protein taken with carbohydrates before, during, and after hard training are also recommended to help minimize muscle protein breakdown as a result of heavy workloads (Tarnoplosky, 2000). Beyond the first hour of recovery, aim to consume 100 grams of carbohydrate every 2–4 hours for the next 24 hours.

Replace electrolytes. Electrolyte replacement, if necessary, is the third step in recovery from exercise. Replacing sodium and potassium is generally only a concern in activity lasting more than four hours. Since most diets are already very high in sodium, the most practical way of replacing lost electrolytes is to return to consuming a normal balanced diet as soon as possible after exercise. If you sweat excessively, it is okay to add a small amount of salt to your food or to rehydrate with a sports drink. Salt pills should be avoided as they are too concentrated and can irritate the stomach lining, causing vomiting and diarrhea, which can be a serious addition to dehydration problems.

SPORT DRINK SMARTS

- Sports drinks with a carbohydrate content greater than 8 percent are NOT recommended for use during exercises but could be consumed following a workout or competition.

- During exercise stick to 4–8% carbohydrate solutions with some protein in them.

- Avoid sports drinks that are too concentrated as they can cause cramps and or diarrhea.

- Stick to the manufacturer's recommendations.

- Experiment with sport drinks in practice situations prior to using them in competition.

- Remember that nervousness slows digestion and absorption and an adjustment may have to be allowed for.

- The amount of electrolytes you lose during exercise is somewhat genetic and also depends on your sweating rate.

- A small amount of salt in the sports drink may be beneficial to offset losses through sweat. But, you must ensure you get adequate salt intake in the evening meal.

READ THE LABELS OF ALL SPORTS DRINKS YOU INTEND TO USE.

HYDRATION TIPS AND FACTS

- Significant dehydration (greater than 5% body weight) can impede heat loss, cardiovascular function, and performance.

- You are well-hydrated for a match if your urine is relatively clear, dilute, and a good volume. If you're going to the bathroom every 45 minutes, you may have drank too much.

- Drinking 500 ml (2 cups) of water in the half hour before a match and 100–200 ml during the change of ends in matches is recommended.

- A properly formulated sports drink may have advantages over water in extended matches due to offering energy, electrolytes, and better taste.

- Drink cooler fluids (around 5 degrees Celsius, 41 degrees Fahrenheit) as they are emptied faster from the stomach than body temperature fluids.

- Sports drinks should have a concentration of no more than 7–8% carbohydrate as any more than this can reduce the rate of emptying from the stomach.

- In most situations, drinking water during a match will suffice. Prolonged match-play may require addition of CHO and/or electrolytes (speak to your dietitian if any concerns).

- Sometimes it is a good idea to weigh oneself before and after playing, with the weight lost roughly equivalent to how much fluid has been lost and needs replacing. A rule of thumb is one liter (4 cups) per kilogram (2.2 pounds) lost.

- To prevent a state of chronic dehydration when training in hot weather, a player should keep a record of his or her early morning weight (taken before breakfast and urination). Any deficiencies should be corrected daily with liberal amounts of tomato juice, orange juice, and water.

- Eat complex carbohydrates to ensure your muscles have the fuel needed for intense training and play in hot conditions. Carbohydrates are burned fast in hot conditions and help store more water.

EXCESSIVE WATER (ONLY) CONSUMPTION, COMBINED WITH AN EXTENSIVE SODIUM DEFICIT, CAN LEAD TO HYPOANATREMIA (LOW BLOOD SODIUM)—A POTENTIALLY LIFE-THREATENING CONDITION.

References

Bergeron, M.F. (2002). Playing tennis in the heat: Can young players handle it? *ACSM-Current Comment,* Aug.

Tarnopolsky, M. (2000). Protein and amino acid needs for training and bulking up. In: Burke, L., Deakin, V. (Eds). *Clinical Sports Nutrition (2nd Ed)* 90-123. Roseville, Australia: McGraw Hill Book Company Ltd. ●

Additional Reading

American College of Sports Medicine (1996). Position stand on exercise and fluid replacement. *Medicine and Science in Sports and Exercise* 28(1): i-vii.

Parsons, D. (2004). Sports drinks and athletic performance. *Sport Med BC. Best Practices Quarterly* 20(1): 1, 3.

Chapter Fifteen

Playing and Training in the Heat

Dr. Tim Wood

Exercise in the heat, including playing tennis, can be potentially harmful and even life threatening to the individual. As a tennis player, you can be susceptible to heat illnesses because of the relative intensity and length of your on- and off-court activities. This chapter provides a brief overview of what happens to players in these circumstances and then gives simple practical advice on how to play tennis in the heat and how to avoid significant complications.

When playing tennis in a warm environment, the body gains heat through metabolic processes which allow the muscles to contract and move the player around the court, as well as from solar radiation, and conduction and convection from objects warmer than the body—for example, the court surface.

EXCESSIVE HEAT BUILDUP CAN DO TREMENDOUS DAMAGE TO YOUR BODY AND, IN EXTREME CASES, CAN BE FATAL.

Evaporation of sweat provides the major physiological defense against overheating in humans. Heat is transferred to the environment as the water is vaporized from the surface of the skin. This cools the skin and in turn cools the warm blood which has been shunted from the interior of the body to the surface. Sweating commences soon after the start of any exercise, and the rate of sweating increases directly with the ambient temperature.

The amount of sweat vaporized depends on a number of factors including the surface area exposed to the environment, the temperature and humidity of the ambient air, and convective air currents around the body, such as the wind. However, humidity is the most important factor. On days of high humidity, there is already a high water content in the air, and this makes it more difficult to evaporate sweat. For this reason, playing in a hot and humid environment presents the greatest challenge to an individual to maintain the core or internal body temperature below 40 degrees Celsius (104 degrees

Fahrenheit). Humans can only survive core temperatures above 41 degrees Celsius for short periods, and the body (in essence the brain) must limit the rise (e.g., stop exercising) before this core temperature is reached.

TIPS TO PREVENT HEAT ILLNESS IN TENNIS

Each of us has a specific tolerance to heat exposure that may vary depending on our fitness level, acclimatization, general health, state of exhaustion, recent diet, liquid and electrolyte consumption.

Fitness

- Less fit individuals are at greater risk of heat illness.
- It is important to perform adequate conditioning and fitness training prior to undertaking any practice or competition in a hot and humid environment.
- The athlete must have trained appropriately and be conditioned for the planned activity.
- Initially you must exercise cautiously in the heat at only 60–70 percent maximum effort.

Acclimatization

- Certain physiological changes occur when an individual practices or plays in hot and humid conditions regularly. In particular, sweating occurs at an earlier onset and in an increased amount with less sodium (salt) content. Overall these changes produce a more efficient heat loss.

- Individuals who are traveling from a cold to warm environment should allow at least seven to ten days to acclimatize.

- Initially, training sessions should be light and of a short duration (15 to 20 minutes), and at least two to four hours of daily heat exposure is required.

- The effectiveness of heat acclimatization will be reduced if the player is tapering (reducing the amount of training and practice) prior to the tournament.

- There is some affect on heat acclimatization in the rested state, but it may be necessary to perform relatively intensive training and practice to maximize acclimatization.

- If the tournament is in a hot and humid environment, consideration must be given for both the heat and humidity.

- Air conditioning also affects acclimatization. To maximize acclimatization, try to stay exposed to the environmental conditions 24 hours a day.

- If the only exposure you have to hot conditions is during training and practice and you return to an air-conditioned environment, the effectiveness of acclimatization is reduced.

- Air conditioning should be restricted to night time for sleeping and adequate recovery.

TRAINING IN A HOT, DRY ENVIRONMENT PROVIDES ONLY PARTIAL ACCLIMATIZATION FOR A HOT, HUMID ENVIRONMENT.

Wear Appropriate Clothing

- Clothing should be loose fitting to allow circulation of air between the shirt and body and be light colored to reflect the radiant solar heat.

- The material should be able to absorb moisture readily such as cotton or linen.

- From a physiological point of view, changing into a dry shirt will slow heat loss until the shirt becomes wet through.

Alter Playing and Training

- If possible, practice and competition times should be moved to avoid the hottest part of the day, which is typically between 11.00 AM and 3.00 PM. However, often the temperature will continue to rise until 5 PM and this should be taken into account.

Drink Appropriate Fluids Before, During, and after Playing

- Some players can sweat up to four liters/hour (4.23 quarts) but are only able to absorb a maximum of one to one and a half liters/hour of fluid.
- Significant dehydration (greater than 5 percent body weight) can impede heat loss, cardiovascular function, and performance.
- One easy way to check whether an individual has drunk enough before playing is that the urine should be relatively clear, dilute, and a good volume.
- It is recommended that 500 ml of water is drunk in the half hour before a match and 100 to 200 ml at the change of ends during competition.
- Drink cooler fluids (around 5 degrees Celsius, 41 degrees Fahrenheit) as they are emptied faster from the stomach than body temperature fluids.
- Sports drinks should have a concentration of no more than 7–8% carbohydrate as any more than this can reduce the rate of fluid emptying from the stomach.
- A small amount of salt in the sports drink may be beneficial to offset losses through sweat.
- In most situations drinking water during a match will suffice.
- Sometimes it is a good idea to weigh oneself before and after playing, with the weight lost roughly equivalent to how much fluid has been lost and needs replacing. A rule of thumb is half a liter (half quart) per pound lost.
- To prevent a state of chronic dehydration when training in hot weather, the player should keep a record of their early morning weight (taken before breakfast and urination). Any deficit should be corrected each day with enough fluid, predominately water.
- Eat complex carbohydrates to ensure your muscles have the fuel needed for intense training and matches in hot conditions.

General Health Concerns

- Younger and older tennis players may be at more risk and extra precautions should be taken when organizing competitions for these age groups.

- Due to age-related physiological changes if you are younger than 15 years and older than 40 years, you may be more susceptible to heat injuries.

- Obesity is a significant risk factor for heat stress. Therefore over-weight individuals need to take extra precautions if exercising in a hot and humid environment.

- Players should not play tennis or exercise when they are unwell, particularly when they have a fever or are suffering from a gastrointestinal illness, which may mean that they start playing mildly dehydrated.

- Certain medications may also increase the risk of an individual suffering from a heat illness, and a player should discuss this with his local doctor before undertaking any exercise in the heat.

Dealing With Heat Illness

If a player appears to be affected by the heat and experiences any light head-edness, headaches, dizziness, or feels "wobbly" in the legs, then this may be a sign that he is having difficulty in coping with playing in the heat.

- The player should stop exercising immediately and be removed to a cool area.

- The legs should be elevated.

Elevate the legs

- The player should commence drinking cool fluids.

- Recovery is often swift with no complications, but the player should not return to the court for that day.

- A medical assessment may be recommended if the symptoms do not subside quickly or other problems emerge.

GENERAL HYDRATION TIPS FROM THE FIT TO PLAY™ TEAM

- Get used to drinking additional fluids prior to entering competitions in hot and humid climates.

- Avoid alcohol, especially when traveling on a plane, due to the double dehydration affect of alcohol and the dry cabin environment.

- If you anticipate a long match, weigh yourself before and after to establish how much fluid has been lost.

- When first practicing or competing in a hot and humid environment, reduce the number, intensity, and duration of training sessions and build up gradually over several days.

- Train in the morning or evening when the temperature is cooler and seek shade between training sessions.

- Wear appropriate clothing. In hot and humid conditions, players should wear a minimal amount of loose-fitting, perforated, light-colored clothing.

- Use a towel filled with ice and tied at each end to put around your neck at changeovers or during breaks.

- Wear a hat while on court to decrease exposure to the sun.

- Wear sunscreen on court to reduce the risk of a sunburn.

Apply ice wrapped in a towel

Wear a hat and sunglasses

In summary players, coaches, parents, sport medicine and science personnel, and tennis officials and umpires should be aware of the potentially catastrophic consequences of playing in the heat. Steps should be taken to minimize the risk of heat illness to players (and officials). The above advice contains simple measures to achieve this.

Additional Reading

American College of Sports Medicine (1996). Position stand on heat and cold illnesses during distance running. *Medicine and Science in Sports and Exercise* 28(12): i-x.

Bergeron, M.F. (2003). Heat cramps: fluid and electrolyte challenges during tennis in the heat. *Journal of Science and Medicine in Sport* 6(1): 19-27.

McArdle, W.D., Katch, F.I., Katch, V.L. (1996). *Exercise Physiology: Energy, Nutrition and Human Performance (Fourth Edition)*. Philadelphia, PA: Lea and Febiger.

Pearce, A.J., (2005). Heat strain in tennis: A selected review of the literature (part 1). *Medicine & Science in Tennis* 10(2): 14-16.

Sports Medicine Australia revised heat guidelines at www.sma.org.au.

Wenger, C.B. (1988). Human Heat Acclimatization. In: *Human Performance Physiology and Environmental Medicine at Terrestrial Extremes*. Pandolf, K.B., Sawka, M.N., and Gonzalez, R.R. (Eds) 153-197. Indianapolis, IN: Benchmark Press.

Chapter Sixteen

Playing and Training at Altitude

Carl Petersen

Many athletes have experienced first hand playing tournaments or training at altitude in Switzerland, Mexico, Colombia, USA, etc. As well, some athletes may use high mountain hiking or altitude training camps to help boost their aerobic systems during the pre-competition period. Exercising and competing at higher altitudes can have enormous performance consequences. Within a few hundred meters of altitude gain you can quickly suffer from:

- Headache.
- Nausea.
- Dizziness.
- Fatigue.
- Shortness of breath.
- Various other symptoms.

Acute mountain sickness (AMS) effects can vary widely in the general population, and the severity depends on the elevation, the rate at which you reach the new, higher elevation, and your individual susceptibility. But contrary to what many think, factors like age and physical condition do not correlate with susceptibility to altitude sickness. Some of us simply get it—and some get it more severely than others.

In general, high altitude leads to an inability of your body to do physical work. The higher the altitude, the greater the decrease. Performance at altitude is impaired in sports where aerobic power is a factor and where recovery that uses the aerobic system is important.

Because water content in the atmosphere decreases with altitude, high air is extremely dry. As well, in your body's efforts to get enough oxygen, you breathe through the mouth, thus increasing water loss and losing the heat-conserving mechanism of the nose. To worsen matters, an early sign of AMS is loss of thirst and appetite, which also increases the chance of dehydration.

THE BODY'S ADAPTIVE CHANGES

When your body is subjected to a low oxygen (hypoxic) environment, adaptive processes attempt to facilitate the intake, transport, and utilization of oxygen. The adaptive responses occur in overlapping phases.

The immediate phase relates to getting air into the lungs. As you go up in altitude, the oxygen in the air you breathe decreases and ultimately less oxygen gets to the muscles. Your body hyperventilates to provide you with sufficient oxygen, and the lower oxygen level in the muscles stimulates increased heart rate to deliver more blood. Exercising at altitude in turn increases the oxygen demand and stimulates both increased rate and depth of respiration.

HIGH ALTITUDE PULMONARY EDEMA

The first symptoms are initially the same as for the milder symptoms of acute mountain sickness.

First Symptoms

- Difficulty in sleeping.
- Early morning waking arousal.
- Slight headache.
- Mild dyspnea (difficulty breathing) on exertion.
- Stacked breathing (Cheyne-Stokes respiration).
- Night waking with an irritating or frightening sense of suffocation as the respiratory drive switches back and forth from carbon dioxide to oxygen stimulation.

Progressive Symptoms

- A dry cough.
- Pain in the chest.
- Giddiness.
- Confusion and overwhelming lethargy (trying to sleep immediately after stopping any exercise).

Full-blown pulmonary edema may be present with rales (rasping or gurgling lung sounds from the edema). The face and extremities may be blue (cyanotic) and there may be severe pain on breathing.

Treatment

Mild high altitude sickness is usually self-limited and symptoms decrease over two to five days. Treatment is symptomatic; aspirin may be the drug of choice (speak to your physician). Providing a warm environment with plenty of liquids and easily digestible carbohydrates eases acclimatization. There is no reason to administer bottled oxygen to an otherwise healthy person who has early symptoms. In fact, it may delay acclimatization. Pulmonary edema on the other hand requires prompt medical attention. The person must descend, if possible, and be given oxygen. He or she should stay in a seated position to lower the diaphragm and improve ventilation.

Preventative Tips

- Stay in good physical condition, especially aerobic (building an aerobic base prior to going to altitude gives you a higher reserve to acclimatize faster).
- If exercising heavily, try to decrease the intensity of your aerobic workouts. The training formula is a decrease of 12% for each 900 meters (2,953 feet) above 900 meters.
- Anaerobic and strength activities are minimally affected, so if you must do extra exercise, hit the gym not the road.
- Go easy the first couple of days and gradually increase your exercise loads over the next few days.
- Expect that your recovery time after each point will be increased.
- Keep moving to help clear out some of the excess lactic acid in the muscles by keeping the blood flowing after points, and at changeovers bounce legs up and down to keep circulation clearing the metabolites (waste products).

- Minimize caffeinated beverages and alcohol since they can dehydrate the body.
- Drink up to 12 glasses of water per day.
- Eat foods high in carbohydrates on the day before travel to altitude and for two days after to increase carbon dioxide production.
- Try for a diet of 70% carbohydrates, 20% protein, and 10% fat.
- If you wake with a suffocating feeling, try sleeping sitting propped up with pillows.
- If you know high altitudes really bother you, consider sticking closer to home and playing at sea level.

HIGH PERFORMANCE TRAINING TIPS FOR PLAYING AT ALTITUDE

- Arrive as early as possible before competition.
- Previous exposure to altitude may make acclimatization faster.
- Extra fluid intake is necessary, ensure you stay well hydrated (urine should be relatively clear).
- Do light exercise only on the first two days. No high intensity, and get lots of rest.
- Get extra sleep on the first few days. Best to go to bed early rather than sleep in.
- Do mentally stimulating activities to avoid boredom when you're not playing.

Additional Reading

Levine, B.D., Stray-Gunderson, J. (1992). A practical approach to altitude training. *Int. J. Sports Med.* 13: 209-212.

Rusko, H.K. (1996). New Aspects of Altitude Training. *Am. J. Sports Med.* 24:S48-S52.

Wilber, R.L. (2001). Current trends in altitude training. *Sports Med* 31:249-265.

Chapter Seventeen

The Traveling Athlete and Jet Lag

Carl Petersen

Almost every athlete and traveler has a story about jet lag, how it affects them, or what they do to combat it. The jet set lifestyle of the high performance or elite tennis player and coach is not always as glamorous as it sounds. Each week a new country, the pampered lifestyle of five star hotels, social events, and parties is not the norm for most players. Long flights in economy class, missed connections, no airport pickup, and the jet lag that goes with it is more likely than not. By following the guidelines set out below, you will be able to recover quickly, train, and perform better without suffering too much jet lag.

TRAVEL CONCERNS

Remember:

- Get immunizations based on a physicians recommendation for the area you are traveling to.

- Take a traveling first aid kit.

- Purchase health insurance and carry medical records or documents outlining any allergies or special medical conditions in case of emergency.

- Have access to medical and physiotherapy personnel.

- Pack your medicine—make

sure you have any regular medication you need, including asthma inhalers or angina sprays in your hand luggage.

- Pre-book an aisle or exit row seat for more leg room and to be able to get up often. Avoid the middle seats.
- Order special meals if needed. They always get served first.
- Carry water and snacks with you, especially when traveling on airlines that do not provide them (ask ahead of time).

JET LAG IS DEFINED AS THE CUMULATIVE PHYSIOLOGICAL AND PSYCHOLOGICAL EFFECTS OF RAPID AIR TRAVEL ACROSS MULTIPLE TIME ZONES.

Jet lag is scientifically referred to as disruption in the body's natural (circadian) rhythms or biological clocks. Circadian rhythms run in 24–26 hour cycles and are oscillations in the body's physiological systems (temperature, heart rate, strength, etc.). These rhythms are synchronized by diet, meal timing, sunrise and sunset, rest and activity, as well as social contact.

WHAT CAUSES JET LAG?

The Aircraft

Jet lag is caused by a series of events. First, there is the aircraft. The pressure changes associated with flying and the cabin environment of a commercial jetliner are not optimal for the human body. Even worse are newer airplanes, while more efficient, they often re-circulate cabin air which is already harboring pollutants that are not healthy for the body. Long flights cause dehydration because the high altitude and low humidity (1-10%) pulls the moisture out of the passengers, quickly dehydrating the body at a rate of 300 ml (10 ounces) an hour. Consumption of alcohol and caffeine laced beverages can contribute to this dehydration problem.

Time Zones

Your body's clock is managed by a small sector of the brain that controls the timing of biological functions like sleeping and eating and sets the peak times for your mind and body. The body's clock is designed for a regular cycle of daylight and darkness. This biological cycle becomes out of sync by changing time zones and is completely confused when it experiences daylight and darkness at the "wrong" times in a new time zone. The more time zones you cross, the greater the disruption to your body's clock. It may take the body's clock a week to adjust to travel across five time zones. (Eastern Canada or the USA to Western Europe. Experts say that traveling eastward when the day is shortened is more stressful on the body as compared to westward travel when the day is lengthened. However experience dictates that this is an individual stressor depending on whether or not you are a late night person (owl) or an early morning person (lark).

THE POTENTIAL EFFECTS OF JET LAG

Physical

- Changes in blood pressure and heart rate.
- Lethargy, fatigue, and general malaise.
- Insomnia.
- Headache.
- Indigestion.
- Drowsiness.
- Losses in reaction time and coordination.

Psychological

- General disorientation.
- Mood swings.
- Feelings of general irritability.
- Poor decision making.

WHAT CAN YOU DO ABOUT JET LAG?

Unfortunately, there is no cure for jet lag, but understanding how the human body functions with jet lag is the first step in helping you cope with it. Some companies are touting miracle cures for jet lag, like acupuncture, aromatherapy, and special diets. While these may help relax and soothe the body, they do not offer a cure. Although some people adjust better than others, jet lag and dehydration are both serious problems for traveling athletes. The following are some tips for frequent flyers, pros, athletes, and coaches who cross continents more frequently than many people cross their city.

TIPS TO COMBAT JET LAG AND DEHYDRATION WHILE TRAVELING

- If you have had a recent injury, surgery, or illness, including coronary artery disease or blood clotting disorder, you should check with your physician before flying.
- Before and during your flight consume a diet high in complex carbohydrates (fruit, vegetables, pastas, breads). This maximizes glycogen (muscle fuel) storage and the water stored with it helps prevent dehydration.
- Avoid fatty food to allow easier and more rapid digestion.
- Eat one half of what they feed you or take your own snack.
- Consume plenty of cool fluids (bottled water, juices, other clear soft drinks). Start with 2–4 cups before take off and add at least 1 cup per hour of flight.
- The more fluids you drink, the more you have to get and go to the toilet (exercise).
- If you drink alcohol or caffeine beverages (coffee, cola), take 2 glasses of water for each beverage consumed. Better still, avoid these altogether since they can promote dehydration.
- Avoid crossing your legs as this may impair return circulation from the lower extremities.
- Wear loose clothes when you fly. The low air pressure on the commercial jets makes our bodies swell up.
- Ensure a better sleep with earplugs, eye shades, and a neck pillow.
- Set your watch to the new destination time and try to eat and sleep accordingly.
- Coat the inside of your nostrils with edible oil or antibacterial cream to help block the spread of airborne germs (flu, TB).
- Try soothing nasal sprays or creams (not decongestants) and use eye drops to eliminate germs in the corners of the eyes, especially if you wear contact lenses.
- Cloudy ears can be cleared by yawning, sucking sweets, chewing gum, or pinching your nose and blowing out.

- Styrofoam cups filled with hot, moist towels placed against the ears on takeoff and landing may decrease the discomfort felt from pressure changes.

TIPS FOR EXERCISING ON BOARD

- Exercise as much as possible on board to minimize potential of blood pooling in the lower extremities and causing a deep vein thrombosis (DVT).

- Contract and relax every muscle in your body while seated.

- Do dynamic exercises like foot pumps or leg swings to promote circulation and prevent pooling of the blood. These exercises will reduce the swollen-ankle syndrome and other symptoms of jet lag.

- Stretch regularly but focus on your calves and hamstrings. Hold your stretches for 30 seconds and repeat 2–3 times.

- Avoid putting bulky items under your seat so you can fully stretch your legs out.

- Wearing thongs or sandals not only keep your feet cooler but force you to scrunch your toes to keep them on when walking.

- If reading or working on a laptop, ensure you take frequent breaks to decrease the stress on joints and muscles of the upper back, neck, and arms.

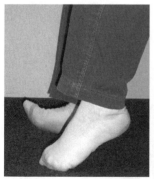
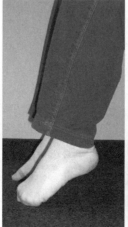

Ankle pumps and twirls.
Pump both of your ankles up and down and twirl them from side to side. Another good trick is to write the alphabet with you toes every hour.

Heel raises and toe lifts. Lean forward and put your elbows on your knees. Now do 10 repetitions of heel raises and toe lifts.

  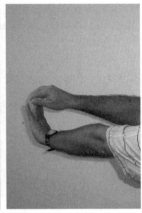

Hamstring stretch. Bend forward from the hips to stretch the hamstrings or put your foot on a low chair and hold for 15–20 seconds and repeat 2–3 times.

Neck stretch. Do a variety of stretches in all directions for your neck. Also do some chin tucks where you try and give yourself a double chin (easier for some of us). Hold each one for 6 seconds and repeat 6 times in each direction.

Finger stretch. Interlace your fingers and stretch them out in front of you so palms face forward. Hold 6 times for 6 seconds, feeling the stretch in the shoulders as well.

Shoulder shrugs, squeezes and rolls. Do 10 repeats of shoulder shrugs, shoulder depressions, shoulder blade squeeze, and shoulder rolls forward and backward.

Knees to chest (knee lifts). Pull knees to chest one at a time or both together and hold for 15–20 seconds and repeat 2–3 times.

- Mental exercises can be very helpful for the many stresses of air travel, including fear of flying.

TIPS TO PREVENT MOTION SICKNESS

- Avoid or minimize reading.
- Do not eat too much.
- Keep away from alcohol or aspirin because both affect the inner ear, making you feel worse.
- Looking up at a 45 degree angle and staring at a fixed object can also minimize this common discomfort.

POST-FLIGHT WORKOUT (JET LAG PROTOCOL)

- Try a warm-up and stretch of about 10–15 minutes.
- Follow this with a light 15–20 minute run or 20–25 minute cycle.
- Do 5 x 20 meter running sprints or 5 x 30 second cycle sprints or pool run sprints about 4 hours before bed. This releases muscle protein in the blood and helps trigger the sleep mechanism.
- If a sauna or whirlpool is available, use it (See Chapter 31 for guidelines.)

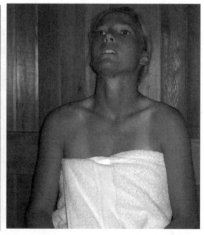

Cycle

Sauna. *Be sure to drink plenty of fluids to make up for those lost in the sauna.*

Fit to Play™ Post-Flight Travel Tips

If You Arrive in the Morning

- Try to sleep on board.
- Set your watch to new destination immediately upon boarding and adjust your eating and sleeping to new time zone.
- Ensure you are well hydrated.
- Eat a good breakfast, have some coffee or tea and get a little exercise.
- Upon arrival get out in the daylight and avoid dark places.
- If you must sleep, it should be no longer than 1–2 hours.
- Do your jet lag exercise protocol.
- Take a warm bath or shower well before bed.
- Stay awake at least until 8 or 9 PM.

If You Arrive in Daytime

- Avoid sleeping too much on the plane, short naps will not leave you as sleep lagged.
- Set your watch to new destination immediately upon boarding and adjust your eating and sleeping to new time zone.
- Ensure you stay well hydrated.
- Upon arrival get out in the daylight and avoid dark places.
- If you must sleep, it should be no longer than 1–2 hours.
- Do your jet lag exercise protocol.
- Take a warm bath or shower well before bed.
- Stay awake at least until 8 or 9 PM.

If You Arrive at Night

- Avoid sleeping on the plane if it arrives at night.
- Ensure you stay well hydrated.
- Do your jet lag protocol, have a light snack, and go to bed.
- Eat fast carbohydrates with dinner (potatoes, corn, sugar). This also helps trigger the sleep cycle.
- Take a warm bath or shower well before bed.
- Utilizing relaxation techniques or listening to music can help promote a good night's sleep as well.

- Stay awake at least until 8 or 9 PM.
- Sleep 8–10 hours only. Sleeping late will postpone adaptation and make you feel more tired by adding sleep lag to jet lag.
- Get up next morning on local time, eat a good breakfast, have some coffee or tea, and get a little exercise.

SHORT TRIP TIPS

- If traveling for only 1–2 days for charity or sponsor events, it may be best to keep your body clock on home time so you don't have to try and switch back upon return.

KEEP TRAVEL INTERESTING. DO YOUR WORK, THEN GET OUT AND ENJOY THE SIGHTS. UNLESS YOU WANT TO BE LIKE JONAH IN THE BELLY OF THE WHALE—TRAVELED LOTS AND SAW LITTLE.

COACHES/PARENTS PROGRAM TO COMBAT JET LAG (NOT FOR ATHLETES)

- Get to the frequent flyer lounge early.
- Help yourself to the free drinks, but drink two waters for each drink.
- Try and get an upgrade to "J" Class.
- Eat the salad and appetizer only.
- Drink several glasses of wine or champagne of choice.
- Fall asleep within the hour.
- Wake up several hours later and start drinking water.
- Pick at the breakfast-fruit and juices.
- Follow the post-flight travel tips.

Prevention is the key to avoiding the maladies of frequent travel. Precautions taken early on and observed throughout your travel will not only decrease the severity of jet lag and dehydration but also will ensure you arrive happy, healthy, and ready to play and train.

Additional Reading

Aerospace Medical Association: www.asma.org.. ·

Air Canada Health Tips: www.aircanada.com/en/travelinfo/onboard/healthtips.html.

Canadian Physiotherapy Association: www.physiotherapy.ca.

Petersen, C.W. (2004). *Fit to Ski: Practical Tips to Optimize Dryland Training & Ski Performance.* Vancouver, Canada: CPC Physiotherapist Corp/Fit to Play Int. Inc.

Petersen, C. "Tennis medicine" "frequent flyer blues." *International Tennis Federation Coaches Review.* Issue #7, October, 1995. London, England. .

Chapter Eighteen

Footwear for Playing and Training

Phil Moore

PLAYING SHOES

With the complexity of movement patterns including forward, backward, lateral, and rotation, as well as the acceleration and deceleration speed changes, your tennis shoes are a critical part of your equipment. They can influence your performance in a number of areas and aid in injury prevention. Visit a reputable sports store and speak with a knowledgeable and experienced staff member.

Wear and Tear

- High performance players tend to toe drag, so the composition of the midsole as well as the wear guarantee will significantly influence your pocketbook.
- Goodyear Indy 500 max rubber or polyurethane remain the most durable compounds. Six-month wear guarantees are common as well.

Grip

- Hard court soles will vary in their grip, so you will have to try them on and take them courtside and do a few starts and stops. Purchase the best fitting model.
- Some grip too well, and you run the risk of catching a sole thereby inverting or rolling your ankle (particularly on rubber based surfaces).
- Avoid the Tretorn canvas porous rubber that was originally designed for clay courts.
- Herringbone patterns do well on clay as well as hard courts.
- Ultimately, there is no need to give up durability to enhance traction.

Breathability

- Most shoes have leather uppers which, in theory, will breathe, being of natural fiber. But remember they are all lined with nylon or foam to keep them from stretching with all the lateral stress.

- This lining often makes them hot unless there is sufficient ventilation by way of the nylon tongue and punched holes in the upper. Some will line the upper with a Coolmax-type lining or footbed to manage the moisture.

- There are very few mesh-uppered tennis shoes because it is considered a less supportive material than leather. But when it's done properly, you get great breathability without compromising the lateral support.

Lateral Support

- Without a doubt, the most important feature of the tennis shoe is the ability of the shoe to keep your foot over the sole plate.

- As you change direction from side to side at high speed, your shoe grips and stops, but your foot continues to slide in the shoe towards the sideline.

- Unless the shoe has sufficient lateral support, your foot will spill over the side and you will roll your ankle (inversion sprain). If the sole plate is made very wide it will aid in keeping your foot stable.

- The cost, however, of a wide base is that the shoe may feel and move more like a flipper than a shoe.

Lateral support. *This is the most important feature of a tennis shoe.*

- Manufacturers are always trying to find ways to keep the shoe sleek, yet give you support for lateral movement. The best way to do this is to wrap the midsole or outersole up the side of your foot, sitting you in a sort of foot frame or cup-sole. That way, as your foot tries to slide off the side of the shoe it comes up against a lateral bumper or shell. This framework stops your foot and keeps it from rolling over.

- Quick recovery of your foot to the neutral position means better balance and faster feet.

- High tops seem a natural choice for this problem but are basically non-existent in tennis! Why? Fashion!

- The basketball shoe option is one, but that means added weight and/or poor durability. So, for the "chronic sprainee," air casts and ankle supports combined with a good laterally supportive shoe remains the best choice. Rarely, if ever, opt for the super-light model.

LIGHTWEIGHT OFTEN MEANS MORE EXPENSIVE AND LESS DURABLE!

Cushioning

- The shock absorption is important but less critical than many of the above mentioned considerations.

- For the high rigid arched cavus foot, it is always important. But due to this foot type's tendency to inversion sprains, the cushioning should come by way of shock absorbing insoles/orthotics rather than soft, thick midsoles.

- In fact, thick bottomed "high heeled" tennis shoes/cross-trainers put the foot on a tall platform and planter flex the forefoot, leaving the foot and ankle vulnerable to sprains.

- Make sure the shoe is relatively flat and has good technical cushioning in the midsole such as air absorb, gel, hexalite, etc.

- Add shock-absorbing footbeds such as sorbothane and other similar polymers in place of the insole in the shoe.

- Cushioning is important to all of us, but in tennis it should not be at the cost of good lateral support and durability.

Finally, all of these considerations must be kept in perspective as fit is the most important feature of any shoe for any sport. What has worked for you in the past is likely best. Given that models are discontinued so often, the new version of an old shoe would be your next best choice. Keep in mind that your needs are different from your partner's, so choose wisely based on your feet and your game.

TRAINING SHOES

Being successful on the court requires more than just hitting deep crosscourt backhands day in and day out. It involves a sound balance of on-court and off-court training. Staying fit is critical.

The demands of on-court play as far as footwear is concerned are managed well with a solid, good fitting tennis shoe as outlined earlier. But those shoes are not appropriate for the high impact demands of road running and sprint training. Where tennis involves a certain amount of high impact, it is dominated by lateral motion as well as quick stops and starts. Running, on the other hand, is more straight ahead and far more repetitive with over 2,000 heel strikes per mile. The body is airborne for a split second, creating an impact of 2 to 4 times your body weight with each step.

Running Gait

The running gait pattern involves four motions:

- Heel strike.
- Midstance pronation.
- Supination and toe off.
- Swing phase.

In looking at these four stages, we get a better understanding of why a training shoe is needed and why the proper training shoe is critical to injury prevention.

Heel strike. At heel strike the foot lands at about a 40 degree angle and impact is 2–4 times body weight and even higher going downhill. The calf muscle and Achilles tendon is elongated so some heel height to the shoe as well as heel shock absorption are important. You get this kind of shock attenuation with a running shoe, not with a tennis shoe.

Midstance pronation. Midstance pronation is the critical phase because it is here that your foot naturally attenuates or absorbs impact. If your foot is very rigid with a high arch, then you will likely have trouble absorbing shock and will likely require a shoe with maximum cushioning and flexibility (i.e., those things your foot does not give you naturally). Conversely, if your foot is flexible and flattens when you put your weight on it, then your foot will likely roll inwards, squinting your knees towards each other. Thus presupposing you to

258

almost every lower limb injury imaginable. This rolling in or "excessive pronation" remains the root evil of most running related injuries, including patella femoral pain, shin splints, and planter fasciitis, just to name a few. The "pronated" foot needs to be supported with a firm soled shoe that is straight lasted and harder on the inside aspect of the shoe. This "motion control" shoe, combined with an arch support or custom orthotic, helps limit the excessive motion of the foot at midstance. Only then can this individual repeat the running, high impact heel-toe gait pattern over and over again.

Supination and toe off. Supination and toe off involve taking a loose bag of bones (i.e., the foot at midstance when it is absorbing shock) and making it rigid enough to propel the body forward. To do this, the foot must roll to the outside as it gets rigid and then push off the middle part of the ball of the foot.

Swing phase. After toe off the leg enters the swing phase. While swinging it relaxes, blood vessels get nutrients to the muscles, the leg recovers.

Running Gait Mechanics and Shoe Choice

By understanding this gait cycle you will hopefully appreciate the

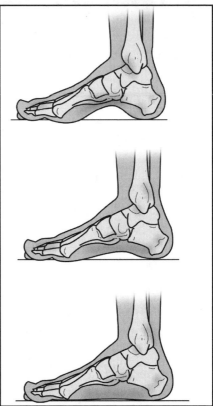

High, normal, flat arch

need for a very different training shoe from your relatively flat, firm, laterally supportive tennis model. Your mechanics must dictate your choice of shoe.

Shoe choice

- If you are less fortunate and have very rigid feet (supinator), then a "neutral cushioned" shoe with lots of shock absorbing bells and whistles may be best.

- If you are blessed with sound biomechanics and "normal alignment," you can likely wear any running or training shoe that fits.

- If you have flexible feet or alignment problems that leave the foot in an excessively pronated position, then a "motion control" shoe with more firmness on the inside or medial aspect of the foot may prove more useful.

Keep in mind that every major manufacturer has a number of shoes in these categories, so find out what mechanical model you resemble and choose the shoe that's right for your gait and that fits your foot.

FIT TO PLAY™ SHOE TIPS

- Treat your shoes like a piece of equipment, not a fashion statement.

- When choosing shoes, consider:
  - ‣ Do they provide good foot stability?
  - ‣ Do they attenuate or decrease impact forces?
  - ‣ What is your foot type and any irregularities your feet have?
  - ‣ What surface are you playing on? Do your shoes provide appropriate friction or traction as needed?
  - ‣ Do your shoes dissipate heat? Are they comfortable?

Additional Reading

Moore, P., Taunton, J. (1991). Medially based athletic footwear—design and selection. *New Zealand Journal of Sports Med.* 22-25.

Pluim, B. & Safran, M. (2004). *From Breakpoint to Advantage.* Vista, California: Racquet Tech Publishing, pages 33-37.

WTA Tour (2004). Physically speaking foot fitness. *Physically Speaking.* August.

Chapter Nineteen

Traveling Medicine and Fitness Kits

Carl Petersen and Dr. Bill West

Since you cannot avoid injuries completely, it is best to have the right items handy for relief. To treat minor injuries such as sore muscles, abrasions, and blisters at home or at the courts, it is prudent to keep your playing bag and home medicine chest stocked with some essential first aid remedies. However, be sure you do not self-treat when you really need medical attention. If you fall and twist a knee or an ankle, go ahead and ice it yourself, but then get to the doctor. Any pain or swelling that doesn't fade in a few days should send you to see your medical professionals.

Here is a list of some products for you to stock in your bag and on your shelves, depending on your potential problems:

Sun protection

- Always use sunscreen. If you miss a spot with your sun screen, try an après-sun cream with aloe. Wear a hat when training under sun and possibly sunglasses.

Over-the-counter medications

- Pain reliever. Speak to a physician about what is best for you. Try Advil™ for relieving muscle soreness. If you have a tender stomach, try acetaminophen (Tylenol plain)—it also can relieve pain and generally is tolerated well.
- Antacids. Take along your favorite.
- Pepto Bismol. Often touted as aspirin for the stomach, Pepto Bismol or a similar generic product can help decrease some of the stomach symptoms you may have from eating unfamiliar foods.

- Gravol for nausea.

- Immodium for diarrhea.

- Cough syrup or lozenges.

- Antihistamine. Ask your physician for suggestions.

- Antifungal. You also might keep anti-fungal sprays or creams in your medicine chest since sweaty sneakers and locker room floors can make you susceptible to outbreaks of athlete's foot.

- Antibacterial. Scrapes and cuts should first be cleaned with warm soapy water. Then, apply an antibacterial cream or spray and a clean bandage that's large enough to cover the area. Change the dressing once or twice a day, or whenever it gets wet.

- Hydrocortisone. Insect bites and rashes may occur when training outdoor.

Medication cautions

- Always read the instructions carefully.

- Check the expiry date.

- Pain killers relieve symptoms, they are not a cure.

- Don't take unfamiliar medication.

- Talk to a qualified professional if you have any concerns.

- Drug testing/dope testing does occur. Obtain a list of banned substances from your sport governing body and avoid them (see Chapter 13).

Adhesive tape

White medical tape can be used to wrap a joint before playing. Put pre-wrap under the tape to keep it from tearing the skin or if you have a lot of hair.

Foot and blister care

Calluses and blisters are common if playing sports with sudden changes in direction such as soccer and tennis. Doughnut-shaped pads can provide some relief. Try using flexible fabric Band-Aids for blister prevention, but one step better is moleskin or Second Skin™ which you stick directly on the hot spot before play. Spenco™ makes a nice small Blister Kit with Second Skin™. Sterile needles should be used if you need to drain a blister before it pops.

Talcum powder

Absorbent talc, such as baby powder, is good for soaking up sweat and cutting down on friction in your shoes. Wear two pairs of socks and put some in between if you get blisters often.

Tensor bandage

Great for strapping on ice packs or to provide compression for swelling or minor muscle strains. Never go to sleep with a tensor bandage on as it can cut off your circulation. Take a 4-inch and 6-inch tensor with you.

Sandwich bags

Zipper bags are convenient for making ice packs. Once you've made an ice pack, wrap it in place using an elastic bandage. This way you get compression and ice.

Gel ice pack

Take one or two with you on the road and have them put in the freezer of the hotel.

Cycle shorts

They will prevent uncomfortable chafing from training on a stationary or road bike. Great for holding ice packs in place on the low back, groin, and thigh area. They also can be worn over a tensor or tape job of the upper thigh to hold it on.

Compression shorts

Anyone who has suffered from a groin, hamstring, adductor, hip flexor, or lower abdominal strain may consider carrying compression shorts with them. Compression shorts can help aid in keeping the hip and groin area warm as well as providing compressive support to spread the load to other muscles around the thigh. Information on Coreshort® is available at www.coretection.com.

Traveling athlete's fitness kit

To assist yourself in your quest for improved fitness, take along the following exercise gear to use on the road:

• Physio ball, extra plug, and small pump.

• Assorted strengths and lengths of stretch cords and bands.

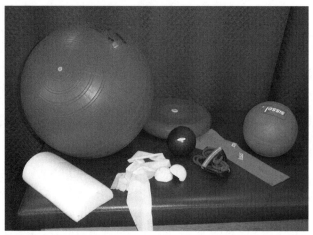

Traveling fitness kit

- Skipping rope.
- Tennis ball (cut in half) or flat cones for agility drills.
- Five-inch myofascial fit ball.
- Four- to eight-pound medicine ball (optional).
- Sissel disc, one-half foam roll, wobble board (optional), or use a rolled towel for balance exercises.

PART FOUR

FOUR

Structured Mental Training

Chapter Twenty

Mental Training

Nina Nittinger

To succeed in tennis and optimize performance, athletes must work on physical conditioning, on-court technical skills, and mental training skills.

YOU WORK HARD TO TRAIN YOUR BODY FOR SUCCESS ON COURT, BUT DO YOU TRAIN YOUR MIND?

Every player and coach knows that psychology has an incredible effect on sports performance. Most elite athletes believe that optimal performance at the top tier of competition is more mental than physical. Today all professional tennis players are fit and very well trained on court, but most athletes do not practice mental training techniques on a regular basis.

We often hear the comment, "I don't need a shrink to play well." Well unfortunately these athletes have missed the point. They employ coaches to work on technique, physiotherapists to work on injuries, and strength and conditioning coaches to work on fitness, but they deny themselves the performance enhancing benefits of mental training. The brain not only controls the movement of the legs, arms, and torso, but also controls the input and output of all information and knowledge about tactics and techniques and must be trained as well.

MANY ATHLETES WOULD LIKE TO WORK ON THEIR MENTAL SKILLS BUT THEY ARE UNSURE HOW TO GO ABOUT IT.

It is important to understand that there are three parts to the body: the physical (everything you do), the mental (everything you think), and the emotional (everything you feel). The three parts are connected like a chain. Every athlete has to train and take care of each part to optimize performance. You need a good balance between the three parts. None of them would work without the other one. If only two parts of the chain are strong or trained, there is too much pressure on the third one, and it may break down. With mental training, every athlete can learn a lot about their own body, body language, feelings, emotions, and how they influence performance.

It is comparable to driving a car without gas. You can have the best car and the best driver in the world, but without fuel the car won't go very far.

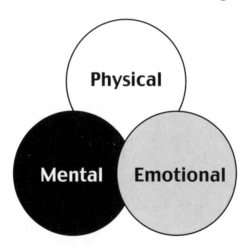

Three parts of the body. *Each part must be trained for optimum performance (adapted after Drasksal & Nittinger, 2002).*

EMOTIONS IN TENNIS

You are an athlete not a machine. You are human and have feelings and emotions. During a match you go through all possible ups and downs. First you are looking forward to the match, then you are nervous. On court the tension starts, you make a few mistakes and get tight and start pushing the ball or being too aggressive. You feel the pressure at important points, the swearing starts, your racquet flies, and the fear of losing arises. But then your opponent starts to miss some balls. The match changes, and you start to fight, see a chance, pump yourself up, and start to play out of your mind.

What is happening here? It is clear that emotions control the behavior and the outcome of your actions.

EMOTIONS INFLUENCE EVERY ACTION AND DECISION IN OUR LIVES INCLUDING EVERY DECISION AND ACTION ON COURT.

To be a successful tennis player you must be in very good physical, mental, and emotional shape. If you know your body and your emotions well, you can control the outcome. It doesn't mean that you always feel great or that you can always compete at your highest level. No one is perfect, as we are only human. But it means that no matter what kind of trouble or situation you are in during a match, you need to control your thinking and emotions to get out of it.

DIRECT YOUR EMOTIONS, DO NOT THINK WITH THEM. BE TRUTHFUL ABOUT YOUR EMOTIONS, AND USE THEM IN YOUR FAVOR, NOT AGAINST YOU.

Positive thinking produces hormones in your body that make you happier. These hormones automatically change your appearance, the way you walk, and the way you perform. On the other hand negative thoughts like fear, anger, and hopelessness set hormones free that will stop you from performing well.

GOAL SETTING

To optimize your performance, you have to know where you want to go and what you want to achieve. It is very important that as an athlete you know what your limits are and what kind of work you have to do. Dreaming unrealistic dreams does not help anyone. Setting realistic short-term and long-term goals is an important step toward improving and optimizing performance.

We suggest athletes start a diary and use one part for goal setting. This way you can control and check your goals after a period of time, modify them, and set new goals for yourself (see Chapter 22 for the Fit to Play™ Training Diary). To set goals, you have to ask yourself certain questions.

Ask yourself these questions

- What am I doing right now?
- What do I want to achieve?
- How much effort am I willing to put in?
- Is my family supporting me?
- How are my practice conditions?
- How can I improve them?
- Do I have the right attitude to be an athlete?

Set your long-term goals, then set your short-term and middle-term goals accordingly.

Long-term goals

- Where do I want to be in one year?
- What are my goals for the next year?
- How can I reach them?
- Who is helping me?
- What are my strengths and how am I going to use them?
- What are my weaknesses and how can I improve them?
- What kind of problems could occur?
- How can I solve them?

Short-term goals

- What are my goals for the next two weeks?
- How can I reach them?
- What are my goals in the next four weeks?
- How can I reach them?
- Who is helping me?
- What are my strengths and how am I going to use them?
- What are my weaknesses and how can I improve them?

- What kind of problems could occur?
- How can I solve them?

Middle-term goals

- What are my goals in the next 3 months?
- How can I reach them?
- Who is helping me?
- What are my strengths and how am I going to use them?
- What are my weaknesses and how can I improve them?
- What kind of problems could occur?
- How can I solve them?

Tips for goal setting

- Set challenging yet realistic goals. They shouldn't be too easy or too hard to attain.
- Write them down (use your training diary, see Chapter 22).
- Reaching your goals will improve your confidence.
- If you don't reach your goals in the planned time, try to find the reason why. Then try again or change the goals to be more realistic.

IF YOU DON'T KNOW WHERE YOU WANT TO GO, YOU MAY END UP SOMEWHERE THAT YOU DON'T LIKE.

SOCIAL ENVIRONMENT

The social environment can be one of the most critical parts in the life of a tennis player. Coordinating schedules between practices, training, tournaments, family, friends, travel, as well as organizing your finances are only a few of the things to think about. Being a competitive tennis player means managing this environment as professionally as possible.

The player must have

- Support from family and friends.
- Well structured and planned training and practice.

- Access to good practice facilities.

- Appropriate nutrition and hydration.

- A well-structured and planned fitness program and recovery plan.

- Well-planned and easily-managed travel.

- Good coordination between time for tennis and working.

- An alternative plan B in case an injury sidelines you.

- Balance among tennis, travel, tournaments, family, friends, and fun.

Ask yourself questions about these topics and add them into your training diary. Try to determine what situation you are in right now and imagine and plan how it should be and what you can change to improve it.

OPTIMIZE YOUR SOCIAL ENVIRONMENT AS IT IS THE WORLD IN WHICH YOU LIVE, TRAIN, AND PLAY, AND YOU WANT IT TO BE AS PERFECT AS POSSIBLE.

MENTAL IMAGERY

Developing your imagery skills is one key to being a more successful athlete. All professional athletes have an excellent capacity for clear, vivid imagery and they use it extensively. Imagery is about creating images with your brain drawn from your experience and inner feelings. To make the image clearer, call up an image or feeling and keep repeating it. Make it a goal to try and use imagery daily so you can become highly proficient and skilled at it.

Try to do your imagery training as perfectly and precise as possible. You have to see, feel, and experience yourself going through the actions as you would like them to happen.

Use imagery to

- See yourself achieving your goals.

- Motivate yourself before and during training or competition.

- Perfect your skills through seeing and feeling them.

- Familiarize yourself with different things like the tournament site, playing in the wind, etc.

- Run through the key elements of your performance—technical, tactical, emotional, etc.
- Refocus during training or competition by imagining what you should focus on.

CONFIDENCE

Having confidence throughout the match is crucial to performing well. When players compete at the same level, it is confidence that determines the outcome of a match. To be confident means to trust yourself and to know that your body, shots, and mental toughness will not let you down under pressure. It is easy to be confident about the strong parts of your game, but it is important to build some confidence around your weaker areas because they may break down first.

Develop a Routine for Pre-Match Preparation

- If you want to build up your confidence, you need a pre-match preparation routine (see Chapter 12 for ideas).
- Your routine should include things that make you feel strong, confident, and well prepared for the match.
- Familiarity improves chances for success.
- Practice and experiment with different warm-up and activation routines before training or hitting sessions and see what works best for you.
- A set pre-shot routine can give you a safe haven during rough points in the match.
- Choose a routine that suits your playing style and personality. Stick to it, practice it, and fine tune it.
- The more prepared you are to go on a court, the higher your confidence level and better your performance.

Check Your Practice Partners and Match Opponents

- Do you have favorite partners?
- Who do you usually hit with?
- Why do they make you feel confident?
- Try to find a good mix between partners you beat, lose to, and who are at the same level.
- If away traveling for tournaments, choose practice partners from different countries for variety. Don't just practice with your home-based partner.

- Winning matches easily will build up your confidence.
- Close matches will train your mental, physical, and tactical skills in critical situations.
- When playing against stronger players, you can be very relaxed because you have nothing to lose. However, you can learn a lot from them. They can show you where your weaknesses are and what you need to work on.

Watch Your Fitness

- The fitter you are, the more physical, mental, and emotional stress you can handle during a match.
- If you are fitter than your opponent, then splitting sets is to your advantage.
- The fitter you are, the faster you recover from hard matches, practice, and training.
- Fitness will help you play better and recover faster at altitude and in the heat.

On-court fitness

- Fitness will help you to prevent injuries and illness.
- Fitness will improve your positive body language, making you more confident.

Always Think Positive

- Positive thinking has a positive influence on your performance.
- Positive thinking will improve your body language.
- Negative thinking will break down your confidence level and give you negative body language.

Off- and on-court fitness

Positive Self-talk

Below are some positive statements that you can use as a player to bring yourself up and improve your attitude. Players need to be aware of the level of player they are competing with. All the positive thinking in the world won't help you if you are ranked 800 and playing a top 50 player.

Exude confidence

Positive statements for tennis players

- I am strong and quick.
- I make things happen.
- I keep my eyes open and head up.
- I am a sharp player.
- I love to win.
- I play with calm, composure, and confidence.
- I am a winner.
- I play smart, tough, and fast.
- Throughout the match, I breathe power and direct my energy.
- My mind is a force I use to make things happen.
- I am responsible for playing to the maximum of my ability and optimizing my performance.
- I see and feel myself playing well, head up, controlling the points.

MENTAL AND PHYSICAL MATCH PREPARATION

Activation and Relaxation

As a tennis player performing in tournaments, you have to find out how best to prepare for a match. Some players are very nervous and excited before they get on the court. As soon as they are on the court, their stress level gets too high, they are too activated, they can't think straight, and they start to miss shots which makes them feel even worse.

Other players are also nervous, but the reaction of their body is different. They can't move or hit well because they are completely blocked.

There are two ways to prepare for a match: activation and relaxation. Players who tend to be very nervous, hectic, and overexcited should learn to relax and calm down before going on court, otherwise performance may be inhibited. Players who tend to be too tight, blocked, or have heavy and slow legs should learn to activate themselves to optimize performance from the beginning of the match.

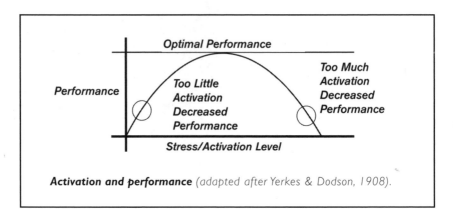

Activation and performance (adapted after Yerkes & Dodson, 1908).

Tips to promote activation

- Run or cycle to get well warmed up.
- Try some skipping or shadow boxing.
- Listen to your activation/motivation CD or music.
- Talk to highly motivated and funny people, let them infect you.
- Keep yourself busy; keep your mind off the match.
- Imagine you are arguing with someone.

IF YOU ARE NOT PROPERLY ACTIVATED OR PREPARED, DON'T BE SURPRISED IF YOU DON'T PERFORM WELL.

Tips to promote relaxation

- Look for a quiet place.
- Listen to slow relaxing music.
- Control your breathing, inhale and count to 4, exhale and count to 5.
- Tighten and relax every muscle for 5 seconds each.
- Daydream about calm, quiet places.

STRESS MANAGEMENT ON COURT

Stress management is about being well prepared for difficult, tight, and stressful situations on court. If you are not well prepared for critical situations, you won't know how to react and panic sets in. Panicking on court or in practice situations will lead to mistakes and poor performance.

Stress does not have to be threatening. Stress can also be the thrill to perform better. Professional athletes have the ability to perform at their best in tight situations. But that's because they have learned this and are prepared to handle stressful situations. To learn how to handle stressful situations, you must first find out what stress means to you.

Stress related questions

- When do I feel pressure?
- How do I perform under pressure?
- When do I feel stressed?
- In what situations do I perform badly?

After answering these questions you should start writing down all the possible stressful situations you can imagine. Then create a plan on how to react in each situation. You can practice this in training sessions and then use it in your matches.

Tips to Manage On-Court Stress

- Always have a plan on how you will react or behave in certain stressful situations. If you are prepared for those situations, they won't influence your game.
- When you are very nervous or tight, choose match goals that are easily achieved, such as not hitting the balls to close to the lines and moving well between strokes. Long rallies and a lot of movement will loosen you up and get you back into the match.

- Control your eyes, your breathing, and your thoughts (see below).

- Create and use your on-court rituals and pre-shot routines; remember, habit is like an armor.

- Be cheerful and courteous and have fun on court.

THE ONLY TRUE STRESSOR IS ENVIRONMENTAL. THERE IS NO STRESS UNLESS YOU THINK THERE IS.

CONCENTRATION

The match is not over until you are shaking hands, packing your racquets, and heading to the shower. Sometimes a few crucial points can decide winning or losing. Keeping up your concentration for the whole match is very difficult. You will always want to have a refocusing strategy in mind if you need it. If you can keep your level of concentration up longer than your opponent, chances are high that you'll leave the court a winner. Keep cue cards in your racquet bag to help you refocus on the four most important elements of concentration:

Keep control of your

- Eyes.
- Thoughts.
- Body language.
- Breathing.

Control Your Eyes

- Find a spot on court you can always look at or go to when you feel distracted or lose your concentration. Switch on your concentration when you look at or go to this spot.

- You will see a lot of pros actually touching a certain spot like the doubles alley or going to their towel before playing the next point.

Stay focused

Towel to refocus   *On court spot to refocus*

- Avoid looking directly at spectators, friends, or other matches.
- Do not glance around—look at your strings or your on-court spot.

Control Your Thoughts

- When you lose your concentration, a million unimportant thoughts will go through your head—try to focus on the next point.
- Talk to yourself: "Stop, this doesn't belong here!"
- Positive self-talk is very important: "I can do it!", "Come on!", "Let's go!"
- Coach yourself: "Next time I'll pass him/her down the line," or "Keep it deep to his/her backhand."
- Always remember: your body reacts to everything you are thinking—the more positive you think, the better you will feel and the better you will perform.

REMEMBER—NO WHINING!
NO COMPLAINING! NO EXCUSES!

Control Your Body Language

- Even if you don't feel well, you have to pretend you feel better than ever.

- Pretending on the outside will automatically change you inside. Your body and muscles react to actions and emotions.

- Show your opponent that you are very positive and that you love the game.

- Don't make your opponent happy by telling him/her that today is a horrible day and your backhand doesn't work.

- Smile once in a while but don't be arrogant.

- Be friendly to other people, even if they are very noisy and disturb you.

Avoid negative body language

- When you are very nervous or tight, hop and jump around—this will loosen up your muscles and show your opponent that you are motivated and energetic.

Control Your Breathing

- When you're out of breath after a long point, take your time and walk around; take small steps to help clear out the lactic acid from the muscles.

- When you're very nervous or out of breath, inhale and exhale slowly (count to 4) a couple of times until your heart rate decreases, then settle in for the next point.

- Always take a deep breath or two before an important point—never rush.

- Always take a deep breath if you miss your first serve.

Example

> ‣ Someone or something distracts me momentarily during my second serve—I double fault because I lose focus—I'm very upset.

▸ I will go to my towel and dry my hands. When I'm calm I'll walk back and focus on the next point. Next time I'm distracted I'll catch the ball, take a deep breath, and serve again.

CREATING ON-COURT RITUALS

Be deliberate and perform the same physical and mental actions for each shot. This helps decrease tension by making preparation for each shot consistent. Your own on-court ritual will make it easier to refocus and keep up your concentration. Try the following rituals and see what works best for you.

Rituals

- Resetting strings.
- Drying with a towel.
- Hopping up and down or side to side.
- Brushing your hair back.
- Banging your racquet on your shoe.
- Straightening shirt sleeve.
- Wiping the sweat off.
- Pulling or tugging on your cap.

Reset strings

Tug at your cap

EVERY PLAYER MAKES MISTAKES. BAD PLAYERS REPEAT THEM BECAUSE THEY IGNORE THEIR MISTAKES OR BLAME THEM ON SOMETHING ELSE. GOOD PLAYERS LEARN FROM THEIR MISTAKES AND TAKE THE CHANCE TO IMPROVE FOR THE NEXT TIME.

MENTAL COACHING FOR MATCHES

A key point to becoming a successful tennis player is thinking the right things before, during, and after a match. Many coaches, players, and parents tend to speak and think way too much and complicate things before upcoming matches. The result is that the player gets overloaded and confused with so much information and then can't hit a ball in the court. A player who is already nervous cannot handle much information and shouldn't be confronted with people who are overexcited. All information before a match should be short and to the point. It's better not to talk at all about the match than to talk too much about it.

Depending on the character of the player, it is important to build up an individual routine on how to best prepare for a match. The coach or self-coached player should talk or think about the player's strengths and only a few important tactical plans, including a plan B if the primary plan does not work out. Also, thinking about the opponent should focus on weaknesses, not strengths, in order to build confidence.

GOOD COMMUNICATION BETWEEN PLAYER AND COACH IS THE FOUNDATION FOR A SUCCESSFUL TEAM. THERE IS NO COACH IN THE WORLD WHO CAN READ THE MIND OF A PLAYER.

During a match coaches cannot influence the outcome, and they are not responsible for winning or losing. The only thing a coach can do is to behave correctly and support the player by being as outwardly positive as possible. Usually, players have eye contact with their coaches. The player should let the coach know what behavior he or she expects. For some players, a nod after a bad ball is a big positive help. Some players hate it when the coach talks to somebody else or is on the phone or text messaging.

Speaking together about a match after it finished is always difficult. As soon as the player exits the court, people either congratulate him on his fantastic play or comment on and analyze all his mistakes and bad shots. The last thing a disappointed and emotional player needs after a loss is criticism.

IT IS VERY IMPORTANT TO DEVELOP A MATCH ANALYSIS ROU-
TINE, FOR NO MATTER THE RESULT OF THE MATCH, MATCHES
ARE THE MOST IMPORTANT LEARNING SITUATIONS.

Tips for Coaching before a Match

- Set goals for the match.
- Have a short but intense talk.
- Focus on a few very important things.
- Short analysis of the opponent's strengths and weaknesses.
- Highlight the player's own strengths and how to use them against the weaknesses of an opponent.
- Put together a tactical plan.

Tips for Coaching during a Match

- Exhibit positive body language while watching.
- Encourage players with, nodding, pumping a fist, or verbal cheers such as, "Come on!"
- Don't show negative emotions such as shaking your head.
- Always keep eye contact.
- Don't interfere.
- Stay cool.
- Don't talk to other people.
- Don't leave the court.
- No telephone calls and minimize text messaging during the match.

Tips for Coaching an Underdog

- Take away a player's fears.
- Build the player's self-confidence while focusing on his strengths.
- Highlight specific weaknesses of the opponent.
- Don't focus on winning but on achievable goals.
- Explain that being an underdog is a big mental advantage.
- The underdog can only win, there's nothing to lose.
- The favorite has a lot to lose and not as much to win.

Tips for Coaching the Clear Favorite

- Build up the self-confidence of the player, but avoid arrogance.
- Focus on strengths.
- Highlight the weaknesses of the opponent.
- Set interesting goals.
- The player has to take the match seriously even though he is the clear favorite.

Tips for Coaching during a Delay

- Depending on length of the delay, the player should be left alone for a while to cool down and relax.
- Depending on the score, the player needs easy, short, and objective tips how to turn the match around when losing or keeping it going when winning.
- Set goals for restarting the match.
- Talk about the players strengths.
- Pump the player up emotionally.
- Keep the player warm and begin a warm-up early enough to get back on court.

Tips for Coaching after a Match

- A player should communicate what he or she expects from the coach after a win or loss.
- Always get together quickly after the match to shake hands or hug.
- Don't talk about the match immediately after. Let the emotions of both player and coach settle down first.
- The player should do his or her post-match recovery protocol, shower, and take care of hydration and nutrition.
- Match analysis should be done when both player and coach have clear heads and can speak about the match objectively.
- Parents or friends should not interfere during the coaches match analysis.

MENTAL TRAINING TIPS AND STRATEGIES (SUMMARY)

Success in tennis means managing many different psychological factors. High-performance players must work on strokes, technical skills, and physical training, but they must also develop mental skills and strategies that help optimize on-court performance. Dedicated tennis players at all levels spend a large amount of time and effort to develop on-court skills, tactics, and strategies. Unfortunately considerably less time is spent on the mental side of the game.

By learning, practicing, and refining the simple high performance mental training strategies outlined below, one can regain or maintain the emotional competence necessary for on-court success.

Control your emotions

- Emotional control and competence both off and on court help create a path to consistent results.
- Always show positive emotions to your opponents.

Set your goals

- Knowing where you want to go, what you want to achieve, and the first steps to get them are key.
- Set realistic goals that are not to hard or to easy to achieve.

Use imagery and visualization skills

- Use visualization in training to improve your technique.
- During practice, before your match starts, and at changeovers close your eyes and visually remind yourself of times when you played extremely well.
- Utilize these images of past performances as a short film clip to stay focused, boost your confidence, and improve performance.
- Use imagery of nice things when you feel very stressed or under pressure.
- Visualize your goals and how you are going to reach them.

Exude confidence both off and on court

- Be acutely aware of your behavior during warm-up, while playing, and while socializing.
- Being and acting confident will have a significant effect on how your opponents view you and how you view yourself.
- Stand tall—practice good posture, move deliberately, and speak quietly and surely.

- Be confident in your positive off- and on-court behaviors and consciously repeat them.

Practice relaxation control

- Keep your relaxation-tension level under control.
- Before getting ready to return serve, do some quick side-to-side jumps to activate the nervous system.
- Take a couple of controlled breaths from deep in your belly. Exhale slowly and think, "athletic stance, switch on the core, and drop shoulders."

Practice self-coaching and positive self-talk strategies

- Work with your coach to develop your own positive statements for self-talk.
- Create cue cards to help you stay positive and refocus.

Ensure proper activation levels to optimize performance

- Be able to bump it up a notch if needed or drop down a level, if feeling overexcited or overactivated.

Practice concentration control to avoid distractions including

- Eye control.
- Thought control.
- Body language control.
- Breathing control.

Use on court rituals to create consistency

- Rituals will make you feel more comfortable when you are under stress and pressure.
- By following your own on-court rituals you can set the pace of play and keep some familiarity and routine to your competitive environment.

Believe in yourself and think positive

- If you don't believe in yourself, why should somebody else?
- Believing in yourself means knowing what you can do and what you can't do.

- Always think and speak positive about yourself. You always want to push your self-esteem up and never down.
- Show your opponent that you believe in yourself.

Using the above tips and strategies either by themselves or in combination allows you to build your repertoire of mental training strategies. Practicing these skills will ensure you are able to access them on demand and contribute to high performance training and play.

References

Draksal, M., Nittinger, N. (2002) .*Mentales Tennis Training*. Ein praktische Arbeitsbuch fur Spieler und Trainer, Linden.

Yerkes, R.M. & Dodson, J.D. (1908). The relationship of strength of stimululi to rapidity of habit formation. *Journal of Comprehensive Neurology and Psychology* 18: 459-482.

Additional Reading and General References

Andrews, J.R., Harrelson G.I. (1991). *Physical Rehabilitation of the Injured Athlete*. Philadelphia: WB Saunders Company.

Draksal, M. (2002). *Mentales Aufbautraining nach Sportverletzungen*. Linden.

Gilbert, B. & Jamison, S. (1993). *Winning Ugly, Mental Warfare in Tennis—Lessons from a Master*. A Fireside Book.

Linz, L. (2004) *Erfolgreiches Teamcoaching. Ein sportpsychologisches Handbuch für Trainer*. Mayer & Mayer Verlag

Loehr, J. (1991) Persönliche Bestform durch Mentaltraining für Sport, Beruf und Ausbildung. BLV Verlagsgesellschaft

Loehr, J. E. (1997). *Stress For Success*. Random House.

Loehr, J. E.(1995). *The New Toughness Training For Sports; Mental, Emotional*, and *Physical Conditioning of the World's Premier Sport Psychologist*. A Plume Penguin Book.

Loehr, J. (1998) Die neue mentale Stärke. Sportliche Bestleistung durch mentale, emotionale und physische Konditionierung. BLV Verlagsgesellschaft

Orlick, T. (1986). *Coaches Training Manual to Psyching for Sport*. Champaign, IL: Leisure Press.

Orlick, T. (1986). *Psyching for Sport: Mental Training for Athletes*. Champaign, IL: Leisure Press.

Orlick, T. (1990). *In Pursuit of Excellence*. Champaign, IL: Leisure Press.

Prentice, W.E. (1990). *Rehabilitation Techniques in Sports Medicines*. St Louis: Times Mirror/Mosby College Publishing.

Weinberg, R. (1988). *The Mental Advantage, Developing your Psychological Skills in Tennis*. Leisure Press.

Chapter Twenty-One

Mind Games— Psychological Skills, Spills, and Thrills

Josef Brabenec Sr. and Dr. David Cox

THE ANXIOUS MIND (Josef Brabenec Sr.)

Sport psychologists have all kinds of advice on how to keep cool and composed in tense and mentally trying match situations—take time between points to relax, look at the racquet after a point is finished, take deep breaths and focus on the next point (it's the only one a player can win).

This advice is all correct. All top players practice such tactics. Why, then, when the score is 4-3, 5-4, 6-5 or serving to confirm a break, the ability to keep cool and collected very often evaporates to a degree. The only explanation is the score.

Even the best player who enters the "danger zone" of a possible win experiences added pressure distorting momentary concentration and coordination that sometimes results in unexpected and untimely errors. Players who are leading are much more susceptible to this type of let-down than players who are trailing.

The most pressure-bearing points in a match are discussed below in the order of their importance on a player's mental wellness and on the final result of a match.

Break Points

These are the opportunity to win opponent's service (0-40, 15-40, 30-40 and receiver's advantage). To win a match, a player must be able to convert at least 35–40% of these points.

Game Points

These are the opportunity to win service (40-0, 40-15, 40-30 and server's advantage). In a relatively even match, the server must be able to win 75–90% of his own serves to win the match. However, there is no guarantee that if a player wins all his serves he will win the match, as Edberg experienced in the 1991 Wimbledon semifinals when he lost to Stich 6-4, 6-7, 6-7, 6-7.

Playing according to a score is an art. Any action a player initiates on the court during a match relates to the score. The mental view of the score influences the game. Any action a player initiates on court during a match relates "psychologically" to the score. "To convert or not to convert" translated by tennis Hamlets is "to win or not to win." Conversions or no conversions demonstrate the player's mental stability or frustration in a match. Imagine a player trailing 2-5 and having two break points in each of his opponent's last two service games and then losing his own serve after leading 40-15.

In the final of the 1989 French Open, Edberg was leading Chang 2-1 in sets, played brilliantly in the fourth set, creating 10 break points, but converted only one. Chang had two break points and converted both, winning the fourth set and the match. In the 1980 Masters, McEnroe lost to Becker 4-6, 4-6 after having nine break points and converting none, while Becker converted one break point in each set and won. Repeated non-conversions of break points, and eventually game points, is the single most common cause of players' frustration, anger, and mental let-down leading to defeat in a match.

How should you treat those golden opportunities when they occur? When receiving, it is imperative to put the ball in play. When serving, a first service with reduced power is the best tactic. If a player has two to three successive opportunities in a game, he should try to force the issue on the first break or game point. The second or third such point should be played more conservatively, because the trailing player is well aware that he cannot afford an error.

To create match situations offering many more break points while training, the players can play sets with games starting at 0-30. This will give the receivers many more opportunities to break and will teach the servers to come from behind when serving. Both situations are crucial in close matches.

Positive Conversions of Set and Match Points

These give a player needed confidence or utmost frustration. These situations are usually dependent on how successful a player was in conversions of break and game points. Missing opportunities at set point or match point have more serious consequences for a player's mental stability. On any first set or match point a player should stick to what he does best in a particular match. If a player has a third or fourth set (match) point, a surprising shot or unexpected move is in order.

The Third and Fourth Point in a Game

These points are "mentally" more valuable than others. In tennis scoring, all points are even, counting for -15. But within a game, some points are more even than other points. Good players always know the score and play the next point accordingly. Excluding break and game points, the third point in a game gives a player a lead of 40-0 or 30-15. When trailing 0-30, the third point brings a player within striking distance to even the score. The fourth point may give a player a game or commanding lead of 40-15 (60–70% assurance of winning a game), or even the score in a game to 30-30. If a player trails 0-40, the fourth point is mentally the easiest to play. Smart strategy calls for a high risk shot (going for it), which, if successful, may inspire the player's confidence and sometimes may turn the game around.

Winning more points, and eventually more games, does not guarantee a match victory. However, it is statistically shown that in over 95% of matches, the player who wins more points is the winner of the match. But, winning more points and eventually more games does not always guarantee a match victory. In the final of the 1985 US Open, Martina Navratilova lost to Hana Mandlikova 6-7, 6-1, 6-7, winning more points and more games, but losing the match because of two well-played points by her opponent in each tie breaker. Winning more points in a match is not so important as *winning key points* in a match. Here is a graphic hypothetical example of this fact: Player A plays against player B, who starts serving. Both players hold their serves until 4-4. Player B holds very easily (all love games). Player A holds with some difficulties, always from a deuce game. At 4-4, player A breaks and holds his own service to win 6-4. The winner is Player A, winning four points less than Player B.

Winning the First Point in a Game

In the final stages of a set, *winning the first point* in a game seems to be crucial for the confidence of a player attempting to close out the set.

Tiebreak Points

These points have four times higher mental value than a regular point in a game. A player must win four points to win a game. One point in a tiebreak represents one game. The most important points in a tiebreak seem to be the first and the seventh point. Losing the first point often sets back the server 0-3, creating a pressure-packed "must win" situation for his next two serving points. The seventh point may bring the score to 6-1 or 5-2, giving a player a good chance to serve out the set or keeping the score at 4-3 or 3-4 on serve.

The Last Two Points in Multi-deuce Games

Games with 4, 6, or 8 deuces create additional pressure on both players. Such games are very often a turning point in a match. Winning the last two points in such a game could be the key to winning a set or a match.

If a player receives "a gift" in the form of double fault or easy unforced error, it is important not to reciprocate with the next point. If the recipient of a gift wins the next point, this will increase the magnitude of a preceding unforced error in his opponent's mind.

SMART PLAYERS WILL ALWAYS TRY TO USE THEIR MOST RELIABLE SHOTS ON IMPORTANT POINTS.

The Two Most Important Games

As some points are more important than other points, so are some games more important than others.

The two most important games in a best of three sets match are the *first two games of the second set*. If a player wins a set 6-1 or 7-6, and then wins the first two games of the second set, he not only confirms his domination, but very often breaks the fighting spirit of his opponent. In contrast, if this player loses the first two games of the second set, his short mental let down is an inspiration for the fighting spirit of the opponent, who suddenly feels he is back in the match.

DO NOT GET COMPLACENT AFTER WINNING A SET, BUT WHEN YOU LOSE A SET, DO WHATEVER IT TAKES TO WIN THE FIRST TWO GAMES OF THE SECOND SET.

Seventh Game of a Set

Bill Tilden's theory of the *seventh game* in a set still deserves a lot of credit. It gives a player either a 6-1 set or a commanding lead of 5-2 and a chance to serve for the set. In the case of an even score of 3-3, it gives one player an important lead, with increased pressure on the server to hold, because otherwise his opponent will serve for the set. When a player trails 2-4, the seventh game may bring him back within a game (3-4). If a player wins 6-0, the seventh game gives him the first game of the second set, establishing his continuing dominance in the match. Even though it is only a "myth," if you or your opponent believes in it, it will have a big influence on your game. Our hats are off to Bill Tilden for starting such a myth and having so many people believe in it.

Winning a service game after breaking an opponent's service has great mental importance. Very few people realize that service break is achieved only after a player wins his own serve after breaking his opponent's serve. The player's best effort is needed after winning the opponent's serve, not relaxation.

The games most difficult to win, and mentally most demanding, are those in which a player serves for a set or a match. The smell of victory somehow triggers the "fear of winning," which is very common at all levels of play. In contrast, the trailing player in such a situation often risks more to make it really difficult for the server, feeling that he has nothing more to lose. The first two points in such games are crucial. The server should make sure he gets his first serves in, even at the price of reduced power. The trade-off is increased mental pressure on the receiver.

There are the misleading leads of 3-0, 4-1, and 5-2. They appear to be three game leads, but in most cases they represent only one service break. Experienced players do not relax with such leads, but also do not panic when trailing by those scores.

Holding and breaking serves as described above apply predominantly to men's tennis. Only a few women, such as the Williams sisters, Davenport, Capriatti, and occasionally 4-5 others, can rely on holding serve in their matches. Usually in women's tennis, it seems to be much more important to "hold the return" (i.e., to win the opponent's serve more than to hold your own serve). There are several reasons for this:

• The percentage of double faults committed in women's matches is generally higher than in men's matches.

- Many women have slower, weaker, and shorter second serves, which are asking for punishment.
- Women's serves break down in crucial match situations much more than men's serves.

Therefore, the return of service is the key stroke in women's tennis on a club level and the lower levels of the professional circuit. My advice for junior girls and coaches: spend lots of time developing a forcing, threatening return of service which will make life difficult for the server. It is very important to realize that the receiver knows where the serve will land before it is hit. To be good, it must land shorter than the service line, which is in midcourt. Therefore, it should be treated like a midcourt shot, with all possible disrespect.

THE WORRIED MIND (Josef Brabenec Sr.)

Would you believe that when you book a court at the club for one hour, you actually play a maximum of 12–15 minutes? This is about 10 percent longer than it would be in a tournament match because you don't follow the same rules regarding breaks between points or games. The real time of a tennis match consists of 80–85 percent intermissions and breaks. During this time, players are on the court but are not actually playing. Real playing time equals 15–20 percent of the time the players are on the court.

Table 23.2 Actual Playing Time during a Match.	
Duration of the match: 2 hours	120 minutes
Rules stipulate that after each odd game players change ends and take a 90-second break: 15 x 90 seconds equals	22.5 minutes
Another rule gives a player the right to take up to a 20 second break following each point: 210 breaks x 20 seconds equals	70 minutes
Time elapsing between missed first serve and second serve in play is approximately 6 seconds. If it happened 80 times in a match that would equal	7.5 minutes
Total time when the ball is not in play equals	100 minutes
Total real playing time equals	20 minutes

This can be illustrated (Table 23.2) by documenting a hypothetical match with scores of 6-4, 4-6, 6-4, thirty games lasting 2 hours. Suppose each game consists of 8 points, the total is 240 points.

Most important are the breaks between the points. Players of any caliber should relax for 8–12 seconds and then refocus for 4–6 seconds on how to win the next point because the next point is *the only point that a player can win at that moment*. It is the mental preparation for the upcoming point that makes good players excellent ones.

Advice for club players: do not rush between points (do not stall either). Take your time to refocus for the next point. Think and play one point at a time.

THE THINKING MIND (Josef Brabenec Sr.)

Tennis is a decision-making sport. The ability to make correct decisions and execute them efficiently separates novices from advanced players. Tennis challenges a player's intellect as well as his neuro-muscular coordination.

A match can consist of 150–300 points. Each point represents an individual concentration unit consisting of several strokes. During each stroke, either in training or in a match, the player performs the following mental exercise:

- When the player has completed his stroke, he starts OBSERVING his opponent.
- The player then EVALUATES his opponent's response (stroke) in relation to his own and the opponent's position on the court.
- Finally, the player makes a DECISION for his next response and he EXECUTES.

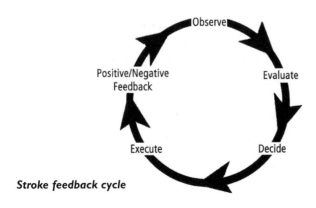

Stroke feedback cycle

The player will immediately feel total satisfaction, partial satisfaction, or frustration, and will start again to observe his opponent in order to get prepared for the next shot. The more satisfaction the player feels, the higher his confidence will be and, consequently, the better his performance. This is an example of a full circle concentration unit repeating itself with each stroke while the ball is in play. This applies to all matches and to all practices.

Decisions involved in every single stroke a player performs deal with the variables of power, speed, depth, placement, spin, court position, and offense or defense. Each stroke challenges the player's decision-making ability. This is the attraction of tennis, and it is the challenge you face as a player every time you step on the court.

Decisions and executions get more difficult as a player's technical and tactical skills advance. A beginner is predominantly concerned with *how* to hit the ball. An intermediate player combines *how* to hit a stroke with *where* to place the ball. A tournament player's knowledge of *how* to hit is usually automatic; the decision of *where* to hit is 80% accurate. The problem they face is *when* to hit a particular shot.

You can see why you can be your worst opponent, but if it's any consolation, each of your opponents faces the same problem.

Decision-making ability is one of the vital elements in tennis and separates excellent players from all the others. Depth perception and good judgement are essential for early decision-making (EDM) ability. The earlier you can judge depth, spin, and speed of the coming ball, the earlier you can prepare for its return. A player's decision to move forward and attack the ball must be made a long time before the oncoming ball passes the imaginary line of the net.

The diagram below shows graphically the flight of the ball from Player B to Player A. If you as Player A are able to make the decision anywhere between points EDM1-EDM2, you will be able to challenge the coming ball, gain commanding position on the court, and return it early (an early contact, or EC, point). This will result in:

- Good forward weight transfer (pace) behind your stroke.
- Cutting short your opponent's time for recovery or proper position. This is particularly vital for approach shots and passing shots.

On the other hand, if Player A is able to make the decision *only* after the ball has passed over the net—anywhere between the points LD1-LD2—this will result in late stroke preparation, late contact (LC) and considerable loss of time. Consequently, such a player will not be able to gain the commanding position on the court during any rally and will be chased by the opponent from corner to corner.

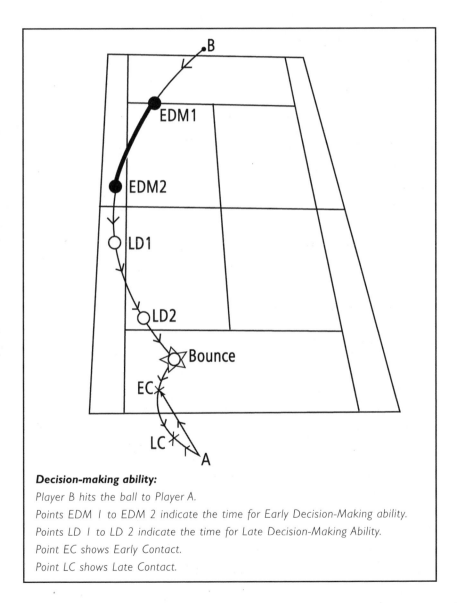

Decision-making ability:

Player B hits the ball to Player A.

Points EDM 1 to EDM 2 indicate the time for Early Decision-Making ability.

Points LD 1 to LD 2 indicate the time for Late Decision-Making Ability.

Point EC shows Early Contact.

Point LC shows Late Contact.

The Responsible and Accountable Mind (Josef Brabenec Sr.)

As a 17-year-old in Czechoslovakia, I (Brabenec) read a book by Czech ex-Davis Cup player Karel Ardelt. The quote attracted my attention: "It is the infinite number of choices and solutions with which each stroke challenges the ingenuity and discipline of our minds that brings us back on the court day after day."

Many years later I realized how true this statement is. Not only each match, but also each practice session is an intellectual contest. It constantly challenges our decision-making ability. The result, we hope, is the best possible stroke representing our response and solution to the ever-changing situation on the court.

Most players try to analyze their opponents to find a weakness in their game, which could later be exploited in a match. All assumptions made about their opponents have one weakness—they are completely beyond your control during a match.

The fact is, it is you that you must worry about, not your opponent.

It is almost impossible to master your opponent in a match or improve your game if you lack determination, will to work, self-discipline, and positive sense of final achievement. Tennis creates an automatic intellectual contest within you. Every single stroke is different. Every single situation calls for a different response. As a player, you must make 300–600 split second decisions during a match or a training session, and you must take full responsibility for them. Errors are an indispensable part of a tennis match. Good players accept their errors with dignity and a certain generosity. They fully understand that it is human- and tennis-like to err. So walk away from mistakes with your head up, and quickly switch your attention to the next point. This requires enormous inner strength, as tennis is totally unforgiving in this respect.

On the court you can only control *yourself*. If you lose control over the only element of the match you can control, you are asking for trouble. Tennis training and matches systematically and mercilessly challenge your inner strength. No matter how well or how badly you perform on a given day, you always have that distinct feeling you can and will do better tomorrow. This eternal bait brings us back on the courts day after day.

Tennis presents to the player an internal intellectual contest. If you can handle it successfully, you can master your opponent more easily. As Jim Loehr, the American sport psychologist, said, "If you always give your best effort, stay positive about yourself, accept full responsibility for what you did, YOU ARE DOING THE BEST YOU CAN AND YOU CAN BE ONLY THE BEST YOU ARE." The ultimate challenge in tennis is to win the contest with yourself.

TWO MINDS: THE PSYCHOLOGY OF DOUBLES (Dr. David Cox)

Although we tend to think of tennis as an individual sport, in reality it is a team sport for the many club players who play primarily doubles. From a psychological perspective, this is interesting because the psychological differences between individual and team sports are significant. Yet, it appears that most tennis players do not give this difference the attention it deserves. If we think historically about the elite levels of the game, there have been few situations where individuals have excelled in both singles and doubles.

In the modern professional game there are "doubles specialists" who make their living focusing entirely on doubles. Part of this specialization recognizes that doubles is a unique game within the sport that requires a special technical, physical, and psychological skill set. When one thinks about doubles players, this often occurs in the context of pairs (e.g., Hewitt and McMillan, McEnroe and Fleming, Navratilova and Shriver, Woodbridge and Woodforde) rather than individuals. It has been reported that when the Australian Mark Woodforde was asked who is the best doubles team in tennis, he indicated it was "McEnroe plus anyone." In the women's game this might translate to "Navratilova plus anyone."

Clearly, the *technical skills* required to play doubles involve the elements of the game that are highlighted in doubles play such as serve, service return, and volleying. The *psychological elements* relate to the concept of team dynamics and the possibility of creating a synergistic effect in which the sum is greater than the parts. Crucial to this goal is the concept of cohesion, which describes the possibility that a group, in this case two tennis players, will work together and overcome obstacles to achieve identified goals. Several issues will be important in this process. One is communication on the court, which is both verbal and nonverbal. Between points good teams typically discuss the next point, focusing on tactical decisions and the process of playing the game rather than the outcome. For example, it is not very useful to tell your partner, "Get the first serve in," as one would assume he will want to do this. It is more useful to focus on tactical decisions that relate to executing skills well. The crucial mindset is to focus on the process and let the outcome take care of itself.

The nonverbal components of communication will be obvious in good teams. These are displayed in positive body language and the use of potent nonverbal cues such as touch. It is interesting that good doubles teams often have some form of physical contact between each point regardless of whether it was a point won or lost. Role definition or clarity is important as it is crucial that each member of the team understands the different roles for which he is responsible. Alternatively, many teams do not perform well because of role conflict. The good doubles teams often represent a curious blend of skills. For example, one player will have a big serve and be capable of making the big shot while the other will play a more conservative game with dependable service returns and deft touch around the net. What is most important here is that both players are aware of, and comfortable with, their roles. In good teams individuals will enjoy their partner's successes and will work to make their teammate look good. This might be defined as the assist in basketball or the set-up in tennis.

Finally it is important for teams to have goals. These may take three forms.

Types of goals

- Outcome goals.
- Performance goals.
- Process goals.

Outcome goals relate to winning and losing and are defined entirely by the score, which, in tennis, guarantees there will be a winner and a loser. Consequently, in a tournament, there will ultimately be one winner and many losers. From a psychological perspective, outcome goals will be less useful than performance and process goals.

Performance goals are concerned with how a team "plays the game" and can be defined in technical, physical, and psychological terms. For example, a team might focus on increasing its first serve percentage or making sure that it communicates between every point.

Process goals are concerned more on how one prepares to play the game. For example, a team might focus on its nutrition, equipment, or being well rested before a match. What is most important about performance and process goals, in comparison to outcome goals, is that they are under the athletes control and are independent of winning or losing (i.e., we can experience success with these goals while losing the match in outcome terms).

The dynamics within a doubles team is an ongoing process and the good teams are constantly searching for ways to get better. When one observes a good doubles team play, it is obvious that the cohesion it generates has much more to do with psychological issues than with technical or physical concerns.

Fit to Play™ Tips for Better Doubles (Josef Brabenec Sr. & Nina Nittinger)

- Communicate with your partner between points.
- Talk about tactics before the match and what to do if the tactic doesn't work out.
- Talk before every point about what you plan to do.
- Have a strategy for every point. For example: "I serve down the T and you cross," or "I serve wide, you fake and stay."
- Surprise your opponents with different strategies, use strategies you have practiced before, and don't try new things in an important match.
- Use physical contact like a knuckle touch, hand slap (high five) or hand on a shoulder between points to reconnect.
- Be aware of how your non-verbal cues such as head shaking, sighing, rolling your eyes, etc., might affect your partner.

- Attempt to capitalize on the strengths of each partner and utilize them to your advantage.

Chapter Twenty-Two

Weekly Training Diary

Carl Petersen and Nina Nittinger

K eeping track of your on-court physical training and tournament schedule and how they are affecting you technically, physically, and mentally will help you to:

- Analyze the effects of your training.
- Monitor your progress.
- Develop ways to improve.
- Keep a record of fitness training and on-court practice.
- Stay motivated.
- Set challenging yet realistic goals.
- Avoid overstress and potential injury.

The training diary is set up to allow you to record as much information as you think helpful on each page.

How To Use the Diary

- Make one copy for each week.
- Fill in weekly date.
- Circle day of the week.
- Fill in AM (morning) heart rate daily
- Circle how you feel
    - ▸ Attitude to train and play. How do you feel?

> ‣ Physically. How do you feel?

> ‣ Mentally. How do you feel?

> ‣ Sleep/Rest. How good was it?

> ‣ Nutrition/Hydration. How good was it?

> ‣ Recovery routine. How good was it?

- Fill in what you did for physical training, mental training, and on-court training.

- Fill in any comments, personal notes, coaches comments, and relevant environmental conditions (time of play, surface, altitude, temperature, and wind condition, etc.).

FIT TO PLAY™ TRAINING DIARY (photocopy for use)

Diary Week of:_____   (+ felt above average; = felt average; - felt below average)

Day 1	M T W Th F S Sun	am HR =	(Feelings) (circle one)		
Training:		Attitude	+	=	-
		Physical	+	=	-
		Mental	+	=	-
Comments:		Sleep/Rest	+	=	-
		Nutrit/Hydr	+	=	-
		Recovery	+	=	-
Day 2	M T W Th F S Sun	am HR =			
Training:		Attitude	+	=	-
		Physical	+	=	-
		Mental	+	=	-
Comments:		Sleep/Rest	+	=	-
		Nutrit/Hydr	+	=	-
		Recovery	+	=	-
Day 3	M T W Th F S Sun	am HR =			
Training:		Attitude	+	=	-
		Physical	+	=	-
		Mental	+	=	-
Comments:		Sleep/Rest	+	=	-
		Nutrit/Hydr	+	=	-
		Recovery	+	=	-
Day 4	M T W Th F S Sun	am HR =			
Training:		Attitude	+	=	-
		Physical	+	=	-
		Mental	+	=	-
Comments:		Sleep/Rest	+	=	-
		Nutrit/Hydr	+	=	-
		Recovery	+	=	-
Day 5	M T W Th F S Sun	am HR =			
Training:		Attitude	+	=	-
		Physical	+	=	-
		Mental	+	=	-
Comments:		Sleep/Rest	+	=	-
		Nutrit/Hydr	+	=	-
		Recovery	+	=	-
Day 6	M T W Th F S Sun	am HR =			
Training:		Attitude	+	=	-
		Physical	+	=	-
		Mental	+	=	-
Comments:		Sleep/Rest	+	=	-
		Nutrit/Hydr	+	=	-
		Recovery	+	=	-
Day 7	M T W Th F S Sun	am HR =			
Training:		Attitude	+	=	-
		Physical	+	=	-
		Mental	+	=	-
Comments:		Sleep/Rest	+	=	-
		Nutrit/Hydr	+	=	-
		Recovery	+	=	-

Chapter Twenty-Three

The Psychology of Injury Rehabilitation

Dr. David Cox, Carl Petersen, and Nina Nittinger

A Sport Psychologist's Perspective (Dr. David Cox)

An injury can be a highly emotional and very disruptive experience for an athlete. Although the ability to remain free of injury can be very important in determining athletic success, injuries are extremely common at all levels of sport. In some cases injuries can be so severe that the individual will not be able to return to the level of performance at which he/she previously participated, or, in worst case scenarios, return to sport in any form may be greatly compromised.

For the purposes of this discussion it will be assumed that we are dealing with individuals who will eventually be returning to participation in their chosen sport. Traditionally, we have focused our attention on the physical aspects of rehabilitation from injury, the implication being that physical readiness was all that was considered necessary to return to play. We know now that this is clearly not always a reasonable assumption. For some athletes the mere knowledge that they are physically ready to return to competition appears to allow for a confident return to play; however, for many it is clear that, while they may be deemed physically capable of returning to action, they are not ready psychologically.

It has been suggested that apprehension following athletic injury has actually increased due to improvements in surgical techniques that have reduced the time required for physical rehabilitation and therefore the time available for psychological adjustment.

New attitudes toward psychological recovery

- It is apparent that athletes have become much more sensitive to the needs of their bodies.

- Increasingly, we recognize the importance of helping athletes cope with the psychological implications of an injury, even at a point when the physical issues may no longer be of concern.

- We encourage athletes to deal positively with their psychological concerns as compared to making them feel that such concerns are irrelevant and reflect weakness.

An athlete's reaction to an injury will vary according to factors such as the nature and severity of the injury, the significance of sport for the individual, and the support system available. Clearly, a wide range of emotions may be experienced in response to a sports injury, including fear, anger, depression, guilt, and anxiety.

Different models have been proposed to help us better understand the psychological processes involved in the reaction to a sports injury including a stages of reaction model which proposes that injured athletes will pass through stages of adjustment in a set order in much the same manner as has been used to explain the process of death and dying. Kubler-Ross describes five stages that she believes an individual goes through when faced with death—denial and isolation, anger, bargaining, depression, and acceptance. It is generally recommended that although such a model can be useful in anticipating emotional reactions to injury, a more flexible approach that recognizes individual response patterns is necessary.

The more cognitive approach focuses on personal appraisal of the event and places more emphasis on a model of stress and coping. Emotional and behavioral responses to an injury will be influenced by an individual's appraisal of the event and the particular coping strategies he/she has available, some of which are viewed as a positive response to the situation while others would be considered negative.

Prerequisites for dealing with injury

It is important that injured athletes:

- Develop good relationships with supportive and empathic caregivers.
- Are well educated as to the nature of the injury and the expected course of recovery.

- Are taught psychological skills such as goal-setting, relaxation, positive self-talk, visualization, and imagery to assist in the recovery process.

- Are prepared for possible setbacks or variability during recovery.

- Have social support networks available to provide both emotional and informational support to the injured individual. These are important in determining the coping resources used.

In this context, it is clear that most athletes cope well with injury, although we need to be aware that, for some, recovery may be difficult, and they will require psychological intervention to assist in this process.

THE PHYSIOTHERAPIST'S, ATHLETE'S AND COACH'S PERSPECTIVES

(Carl Petersen and Nina Nittinger)

Having had the opportunity to work with thousands of athletes from a variety of sports, ranging in skill level from weekend warriors to Olympic Gold medalists, we have made some observations about the psychology of injury rehabilitation.

Injuries are part of an athlete's life. Daily training and competing under extreme conditions dramatically increase the risk of getting injured. Besides the physical pain, injuries can cause traumatic feelings such as depression and fear or result in a severe loss of self-confidence. The more important the sport is in the athlete's life, the more stressful the negative impact can be, especially for young athletes who tend to identify themselves through their success.

The physical recovery from injury can mostly be done with medical help in a certain period of time. But the mental recovery from injuries is a critical part that has to be taken care of very carefully and planned well. Mental training can reduce stressors during and after the injury. It can build up the confidence level during the injury and when returning to training and competing. Players who have a lot of self-confidence may be more able to keep a positive outlook and not become frustrated with the rehabilitation process. Players with good concentration and imagery skills may be able to focus on the rehabilitation, training, and recovery needed to overcome injury.

Factors affecting rehabilitation (Adapted after Brukner & Khan, 2002)

- Type of injury (acute or chronic).
- What caused it?
- Athlete's pain tolerance.

- Support—player/player, player/coach, player/family, player/physiotherapist.
- Player's coping skills—psychological attributes.
- External pressures:
  - ▸ Fear of losing support from federation.
  - ▸ Fear of losing support from sponsors.
  - ▸ Fear of losing ranking.

Potential ankle roll

IF YOU CHOOSE TO PLAY, YOU MAY AT SOMETIME PAY THE PRICE WITH AN INJURY.

Life Stressors Causing Injuries

Injuries are not always caused by physical factors only. The psychological stressors in an athlete's life, such as traveling, pressure, loneliness, etc., can have a severe effect on the body. Life stressors are psychological risk factors, and they can weaken the ability to handle stress in those people training and competing at a high level.

Stressful conditions can increase an athlete's anxiety, which can contribute to abnormal muscle tension, altering the relaxation-contraction coordination and control.

If an athlete is over-aroused, the relaxation ability may be impaired and cause changes in technique and promote abnormal patterns of movement. The result or outcome for the athlete is poor performance, sustained muscle pain, and even more stress.

Each athlete should try to figure out what kind of life stressors confront and effect him/her. After finding those stressors, the goal is to find a way to eliminate or handle them the best way possible.

Strategies for dealing with life stressors

- Respect yourself as a whole well-rounded person, not only as an athlete.
- Find and confront your life stressors.
- Prioritize your activities.
- Refocus your personal goals.
- Set priorities for both your private and sporting life.
- Eat well and ensure you get enough rest and sleep.
- Use recovery techniques on a daily basis to promote healing.
- Consider using mental training, including visualization, as part of your daily routine.

Injuries Causing Life Stressors

An athlete who suffers from injury has a drastic change to his/her life which takes him/her out of his/her and daily routine. Separation from practice and competition can lead to feelings of despair and depression. The isolation and anxiety of re-engaging in the sport after a long rehabilitation can cause extreme psychological responses.

An athlete's coaches, friends, and parents have to be aware that these feelings exist and that they have to be addressed. It is very important that the athlete gets support and help from his/her social environment to handle the difficult situation.

The first step after starting the healing process with doctors, physiotherapists, strength and conditioning specialists, etc., is to set goals for the psychological recovery. When you are injured, you don't want to waste your time, but you want to get the best out of the situation.

Making the best of the situation

- Follow the advice of your doctors, physiotherapists, and other care-givers.
- Accept your situation.
- Do not let your injury negatively influence your private life.
- Communicate with your parents, friends, teammates, and coaches.
- Set goals for your time out (stay busy).
- Use and plan your spare time carefully (study, read, learn something new).
- Consider mental training, including visualization, as part of your daily routine.
- Get help in structuring your daily activities and planning your weekly training cycles.

Recovery Guidelines after Injuries

Etiology of Injuries

First, you have to find out what caused your injury. Excuses and explanations such as "just bad luck" won't help you. Take full responsibility for what happened, accept it, and then start working on your new goals.

Possible contributors to injury

- Equipment, training material, and training venues (are they appropriate).
- Training schedule (daily, weekly, monthly, yearly).
- Warm-up routine (for both on-court and off-court activities).
- Lack of recovery routine.
- Flexibility of muscles, tendons, and hypo- or hyper-mobility of joints.
- Muscle strength and imbalances.
- Malalignment and postural concerns.
- Life stressors.
- Hidden fears.
- Lack of balance between training activities and rest and relaxation.
- Lack of emotional, mental, and physical balance in daily life.

IT IS IMPORTANT FOR THE ATHLETES TO UNDERSTAND THAT AN OVERUSE TYPE INJURY IS A MESSAGE FROM THE BODY AND NOT JUST "BAD LUCK."

Medical Rehabilitation

Contact your doctors and physiotherapists for their assessment of your situation, what you have to do for rehabilitation, and how long it will take. Don't think about rushing your rehabilitation time. If the doctor tells you not to train for six weeks, you shouldn't try to train after four weeks. Listen and follow the advice of the experts. They want to help you, so accept the help. If you don't follow the guidelines, you might delay your recovery and make things worse. Speak to your therapists to help structure activities and training appropriate for you.

Psychological Rehabilitation

To get the best mental effect out of your rehabilitation time, you need a good team. Your team will be your physiotherapist, other therapists, coach, family, and friends. Everybody on this team should work on the same goal—your recovery. Be thankful to everybody and listen to their advice. Don't think you can handle everything alone—you can't. Negative emotions will go through your mind sooner or later; don't let them distract you.

To do list for psychological rehabilitation

- Put your team together.
- Communicate with your team.
- Accept and appreciate their help.
- Include mental training as part of your daily routine.
- Stay motivated and positive.
- Set new goals for every day, week, and month.
- Use relaxation techniques regularly.
- Visualize your healing process.
- Visualize your comeback.
- Use high performance recovery tips and strategies (see Chapter 31) to rest your mind and spirit from your sport.
- Use the time out to develop weak areas in your training and to improve mental abilities and skills.

Back on Court after an Injury

Getting back on court after a long absence can be problematic for players. They often start too fast, too hard, too soon and expect too much of themselves. Coaches and players must slow down and plan the comeback very carefully. Players should be mentally, physically, and emotionally prepared to get back on court. There is no reason to rush things, risk re-injury, or to get frustrated after bad practices. It is important to be very patient and to take the time needed to recover.

Tips for returning to the court

- Get clearance from and follow the instructions of your physician and physiotherapist. They should, with your permission, communicate with your coach.
- Don't start too early, too soon, or go too hard, too long, or too fast.
- Give yourself time to get used to practicing and playing again.
- Build up a daily training routine for both mental and physical training.
- Put a schedule and plan together for how much and how long you train in the beginning and stick to it. Review and revise regularly based on how you feel.
- Don't expect too much from yourself.
- Use visualization for technique on and off the court.
- Start visualizing your first competitions and how you will succeed.
- Stay positive and motivated.
- Use relaxation and recovery techniques regularly.

Remember, the athlete's rehabilitation and subsequent off- and on-court training require careful planning with all members of the TEAM.

References

Bruckner, P., Khan, K. (2002). *Principles of Injury Prevention in Clinical Sports Medicine.* Roseville: McGraw Hill Australia Pty Ltd.

Kinch, M. (2002). Principles of rehabilitation in Brukner & Khan. *Principles of Injury Prevention in Clinical Sports Medicine.* Roseville: McGraw Hill Australia Pty Ltd. 183.

General References and Additional Reading

Draksal, M. (2002). Mentales Aufbautraining nach Sportverletzungen. Ein praktischer Ratgeber für Leistungssportler, (Mental)-Trainer und Physiotherapeuten. Linden. Verlag Michael Draksal.

Kinch, M. (2002). Principles of rehabilitation in Brukner & Khan. *Principles of Injury Prevention in Clinical Sports Medicine.* Roseville: McGraw Hill Australia Pty Ltd. 160-185.

Kleinert, J. (2003). Erfolgreich aus der sportlichen Krise. Mentales Bewältigen von Formtiefs, Erfolgsdruck, Teamkonflikten und Verletzungen. BLV Verlagsgesellschaft.

PART FIVE

Structured Physical/Medical Assessments

Chapter Twenty-Four

Self-Assessment and Functional Testing

Randy Celebrini and Carl Petersen

THE ATHLETE SELF-SCREENING EXAM™ (Randy Celebrini)

T he Athlete Self-Screening Examination™ has been developed to make athletes and those treating or training them aware of any musculoskeletal problems that may affect the athlete's ability to meet the specific demands of the sport. First, it is important to recognize that the purpose of the self-screening exam is not to establish a specific diagnosis to a problem or orthopedic complaint. The primary goal is to identify the presence of muscle and joint problems that may or may not preclude you (the athlete) from taking part in training or competition for the short term. Secondly, it is used to identify the presence of biomechanical or functional limitations that may predispose you to the development of noncontact and overuse injuries as well as limit your potential to optimize athletic performance.

If any problems are identified, you should speak to your coach, physiotherapist, or strength and conditioning coach to develop a rehab program. If these problems are not improved after performing *functional corrective exercises* (FCE), a more detailed *comprehensive orthopedic examination* (COE) by a physiotherapist or physician working with you would be recommended. The goal is to make you (the athlete) and the sports medicine and science personnel working with you aware of the predisposing factors to dysfunction and potential injury.

The Athlete Self-Screening Exam™ is comprised of the following tests:

- **Test 1**: Lower extremity squat (heels planted).
- **Test 2**: Upper extremity elevation.
- **Test 3**: Lower extremity dynamic stability (balance).
- **Test 4**: Trunk (core) mobility (lumbo-pelvic-hip extension).
- **Test 5A**: Trunk (core) stability (lumbo-pelvic-hip flexion).
- **Test 5B**: Trunk (core) stability (lumbo-pelvic-hip extension).
- **Test 6**: Hip/Pelvis mobility A, B, and C.

Note: These tests are a pass or a fail in order to identify the presence of dysfunction. For each test you should note the presence and location of any discomfort whether pass or fail. These subjective comments will be noted and may help to focus the detailed functional corrective exercises or COE (Comprehensive Orthopedic Exam) done by your physical therapist or physician.

Test 1—Lower Extremity Squat (heels planted)

> **Purpose:** To identify the presence of dysfunction in the mobility and stability of the lower extremity.

> **Action:**
> - Stand with feet shoulder width apart and heels planted.
> - Keep eyes facing straight forward and shoulders square.
> - Perform a complete lower extremity squat.
> - Knees aligned over feet with feet facing straight forward.

> **Pass Criteria:** You are able to complete the motion and maintain a full squat without the presence of pain, unusual stiffness, or tension.
> - Ability to maintain a position of thighs parallel to the ground.

Lower extremity squat (heels planted)

- Maintain your balance for 10 seconds.
- Keep knees aligned over feet and facing forward.

Fail: You are not able to complete the motion and maintain a full squat without the presence of pain or unusual stiffness or tension.

Test 2—Upper Extremity Elevation

Purpose: To identify the presence of dysfunction in the mobility and stability of the upper extremity.

Action:

- Stand with feet shoulder width apart and heels planted.
- Keep eyes facing straight forward and shoulders square.
- Place the hands together in front of the body with elbows extended.
- Perform the motion of upper extremity elevation.

Pass Criteria: You are able to complete the motion of a full upper extremity elevation without the presence of pain, unusual stiffness, or tension.

- Maintain a position of arms overhead in relation to the trunk at an angle of 180 degrees.
- Maintain for 10 seconds.
- With chin tucked in with trunk in neutral.

Fail: You are not able to complete the motion of a full upper extremity elevation without the presence of pain, unusual stiffness, or tension.

Upper extremity elevation

Test 3—Lower Extremity Dynamic Stability (balance)

Purpose: To identify the presence of dysfunction in the dynamic stability of the lower extremity.

Lower extremity dynamic stability (balance)

Action:

- Stand with feet shoulder width apart and heels planted.

- Keep eyes facing straight forward and shoulders square. Bring one thigh up to 90 degrees hip flexion along with 90 degrees knee flexion and ankle dorsiflexion (toe pulled up).

- Allow yourself to set then close eyes.

Pass criteria: You are able to complete the motion and maintain the position without the presence of pain, unusual stiffness, or tension.

- Ability to maintain a position of hip/knee flexion at 90 degrees and ankle dorsiflexion to neutral.

- Maintain position for 10 seconds.

- Chin tucked in with trunk in neutral.

Fail: You are not able to complete the motion and maintain the position without the presence of pain, unusual stiffness, or tension.

Test 4—Trunk (Core) Mobility (lumbo-pelvic-hip extension)

Purpose: To identify the presence of dysfunction in the mobility and stability of the lumbar spine, pelvis, and hips.

Action:

- Stand with feet shoulder width apart and heels planted.

- With eyes facing straight forward and shoulders square, place the hands on opposite shoulders and arms facing outwards 45 degrees to the body.

- Keeping knees extended, lean straight back until arms are parallel to the ground.

Pass criteria: You are able to complete the functional motion of backward bending without the presence of pain, unusual stiffness, or tension.

- Ability to maintain a position of trunk extended (arms at angle parallel to the ground).
- Maintain position for 10 seconds.
- Chin tucked in with knees fully extended.

Fail: You are not able to complete the functional motion of backward bending without the presence of pain, unusual stiffness, or tension.

Trunk (core) mobility. *Lumbo-pelvic-hip extension.*

Test 5A—Trunk (Core) Stability (lumbo-pelvic-hip flexion)

Purpose: To identify the presence of dysfunction in the dynamic stability of the lumbar spine and pelvis.

Action:

- Lie flat on your back with knees bent to 90 degrees and heels flat.
- Place hands on opposite shoulders and keeping chin in line with trunk lift the shoulder blades off the floor and dorsiflex the ankles.

- The lower back should be firmly placed against the floor (without arching) and hamstring muscles remain relaxed.

Pass criteria: You are able to maintain the position without the presence of pain, unusual stiffness, or tension.

Trunk (core) stability. *Lumbo-pelvic-hip flexion.*

- Ability to maintain position of the lower back firmly fixed on the floor (no arching).

- Maintain position for 10 seconds.

- Chin tucked in with shoulder blades off and ankles dorsiflexed (toes pulled up).

Fail: You are not able to maintain the position without the presence of pain, unusual stiffness, or tension.

Test 5B—Trunk (Core) Stability (lumbo-pelvic-hip extension)

Purpose: To identify the presence of dysfunction in the dynamic stability of the lumbar spine and pelvis.

Action:

- Lie flat on your stomach with knees extended and feet pulled up (dorsiflexed).

- Place elbows on the floor directly below the shoulders and forearms facing straight forward.

- Keeping chin in line with trunk lift the pelvis off the floor and assume a position parallel to the ground (without arching or sagging).

Trunk (core) stability. *Lumbo-pelvic-hip extension.*

Pass criteria: You are able to maintain the position without the presence of pain, unusual stiffness, or tension.

- Ability to maintain position of the trunk neutral (without arching or sagging).

- Maintain position for 10 seconds.

- Chin tucked in shoulders and elbows at 90 degrees and ankles dorsiflexed (toe pulled up).

Fail: You are not able to maintain the position without the presence of pain, unusual stiffness, or tension.

Test 6—Test Hip/Pelvis Mobility A, B, and C

Purpose: Identify the presence of dysfunction in the mobility of the hip and pelvis.

Test 6A

Action:

- Lie flat on your back with knees bent to 90 degrees and heels flat.

- Place hands on knee of the same side and keeping the head on the ground and chin in line with trunk bring knee to the chest and dorsiflex the ankles.

- The lower back should be firmly placed against the floor (without arching). Ability to complete the motion with thigh contacting the chest and lower back firmly fixed on the floor (no arching).

- Maintain position for 10 seconds with chin tucked in, neck and shoulder blades in contact with the floor, and ankles dorsiflexed.

Hip/Pelvis mobility A

Pass criteria: Athlete is able to complete the motion without the presence of pain, unusual stiffness, or tension.

Fail: You are not able to complete the motion without the presence of pain, unusual stiffness, or tension.

Test 6B

This alternate biases the test towards mobility of the hamstring muscles which can become tight with activity and dysfunction.

Action:

- Lie flat on your back with knees bent to 90 degrees and heels flat.
- Extend hip and knee on one side and dorsiflex (toe pulled up) the ankle.
- Slowly raise the foot straight up to a 90 degree position at the hip.

- The lower back should be firmly placed against the floor (without arching).

Pass Criteria: Athlete is able to complete the motion without the presence of pain, unusual stiffness, or tension.

- Ability to complete the motion with lower extremity at 90 degrees and lower back firmly fixed on the floor (no arching).

- Maintain position for 10 seconds.

- Chin tucked in with neck and shoulder blades in contact with the floor and ankles dorsiflexed (toe pulled up).

Hip/Pelvis mobility B

Fail: You are not able to complete the motion without the presence of pain, unusual stiffness, or tension.

Test 6C

This alternate biases the test towards mobility of the hip flexors which can become tight with activity and dysfunction.

Action:

- Lie flat on your back with knees bent to 90 degrees and heels flat.

- Extend hip and knee on one side and on the other side dorsiflex the ankle (toe pulled up) with the knee pulled to chest.

- Slowly straighten the knee to contact flat against the floor bringing the hip into extension and foot pulled up (ankle dorsiflexion).

- The lower back should be firmly placed against the floor (without arching).

Pass criteria: Athlete is able to complete the motion without the presence of pain, unusual stiffness, or tension.

- Ability to complete the motion with lower extremity (hip knee and ankle all in contact with the floor) and lower back firmly fixed on the floor (no arching).

- Maintain Position for 10 seconds.

- Chin tucked in with neck and shoulder blades in contact with the floor and ankles dorsiflexed(toe pulled up)

Fail: You are not able to complete the motion without the presence of pain, unusual stiffness, or tension.

Hip/Pelvis mobility C

Fit to Play™ Additional Functional Strength Tests (Carl Petersen)

- **Test A:** Lower extremity dynamic stability (single leg repeated squat).
- **Test B:** Lower extremity dynamic stability (repeated lunge).
- **Test C:** Lower extremity dynamic stability (flat hop).
- **Test D:** Lower extremity dynamic stability (step hop).

Test A—Lower Extremity Dynamic Stability (single leg repeated squat)

Purpose: To identify the presence of dysfunction in the dynamic stability and balance of the lower extremity.

Action:

- Stand on one leg on flat ground or a step, keep heel flat.
- Raise opposite leg up so knee is at 90 degrees.
- Raise arms out in front to horizontal.
- Keep eyes facing straight forward and shoulders square and do a single leg squat (to 60 degrees) up and down three consecutive times, then repeat opposite leg.

Pass criteria: You are able to complete the motion without the presence of pain, unusual stiffness, or tension.

Single leg squat

- Ability to keep knees tracking over toes.
- Front foot stays flat on ground.
- Hip does not thrust forward.
- Low back does not hyperextend.

Fail: You are not able to complete the motion the position without the presence of pain, unusual stiffness, or tension.

Test B—Lower Extremity Dynamic Stability (repeated lunge)

Purpose: To identify the presence of dysfunction in the dynamic stability of the lower extremity.

Action:

- Stand with feet shoulder width apart and heels planted.

- Keep eyes facing straight forward and shoulders square. Lunge forward onto one leg and back three consecutive times, then repeat opposite leg.

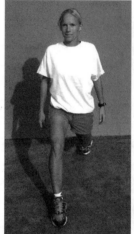

Pass criteria: You are able to complete the motion without the presence of pain, unusual stiffness, or tension.

Lunge. *Correct and incorrect (knee does not track over toes).*

- Ability to keep knees tracking over toes.
- Front foot stays flat on ground.
- Hip does not thrust forward.
- Low back does not hyperextend.

Fail: You are not able to complete the motion the position without the presence of pain, unusual stiffness, or tension.

Test C & D—Lower Extremity Dynamic Stability (flat hop & step hop)

Purpose: To identify the presence of dysfunction in the dynamic stability of the lower extremity. NOTE: Do not do this test if your knees are already sore or you suspect instability.

Flat hop

Action:

- Stand on a flat ground or a low step with feet shoulder width apart and heels planted.

- Keep eyes facing straight forward and shoulders square. Bring one thigh up to 90 degrees hip flexion along with 90 degrees knee flexion and ankle dorsiflexion.

- Place the hands together in front of the body at shoulder height with elbows extended.

Step hop

- Hop off the low step or hop forward if on flat ground and attempt to stick the landing.

Pass criteria: You are able to complete the motion and control the landing position without the presence of pain, unusual stiffness, or tension.

- Ability to stick the landing on one foot without hopping forward, backward, or to the side.
- Knee stays tracking over foot with no undue valgus (knee in) movement.
- Ability to maintain a position of hip/knee flexion at 90 degrees and ankle dorsiflexion to neutral on non-hopping leg.
- Chin tucked in with trunk in neutral.

Fail: You are not able to complete the motion and control the landing position without the presence of pain, unusual stiffness, or tension.

Many sport-specific field and laboratory tests have been developed over the years for tennis and other sports. For a tennis-specific set of fitness tests, see Chapter 2 in the USTA book *Complete Conditioning for Tennis* and Chapter 2 in the ITF book, *Strength and Conditioning for Tennis.*

Additional Reading

Cook, G. (2003). *Athletic Body in Balance*. Champaign, IL: Human Kinetics.

Daniels, L., Worthingham, C. (1980). *Muscle Testing (4th edition)*. Philadelphia: W.B. Saunders.

Kendall, F. & McCreary. E. (1993). *Muscle Testing and Function.* Williams & Wilkins, PA.

MacDougall, J.D., Wenger, H.A., Green, H.J. (1992). *Physiological Testing of the High Performance Athlete*. Champaign, IL: Human Kinetics.

Magee, D.J. (2002). *Orthopedic Physical Assessment*. Philadelphia, PA: W.B. Saunders Company.

Roetert, P. & Ellenbecker, T.S. (1998). *USTA Complete Conditioning for Tennis*. Champaign, IL: Human Kinetics.

Sahrmann, S. (2002). *Diagnosis and Treatment of Movement Impairment Syndromes*. St. Louis: Mosby.

Quinn, A. & Reid, M. (2003). Screening and Testing. In: M. Reid, A. Quinn, and M. Crespo (Eds). *Strength and Conditioning for Tennis 17-45*. London: ITF.

Walsh, M. & Nolan, M. *Clinical Assessment and Treatment Techniques for the Lower Extremity*. Vancouver, Canada: Kilkee Publishing.

PART SIX

SIX

Structured
Recovery & Injury
Prevention

Chapter Twenty-Five

Common Back Problems and the Malaligned Player

Carl Petersen, Martha Sirdevan,
Dr. Wolf Schamberger, Dr. Robert Morrell

As an athlete who plays tennis, you are susceptible to back injury. Very few competitive players make it through an entire season without experiencing some form of back pain. A healthy back must be associated with good flexibility and strong upper and lower core strength. As well, there should be a good balance between the upper and lower core stabilizing (axial) muscles, which include the transversus abdominus and multifidus, and the moving (phasic) muscles, which include the quadriceps, hamstrings, hip adductors, latissimus dorsi, and other muscles. The axial muscles are prone to weakening, and the phasic muscles are prone to shortening, which can alter the balance between the low back, hips, and pelvis and cause problems. The chief function of the back is to support the body and to house and protect the spinal cord, but it must also work as a stabilizing power platform as the extremities move.

The lower back (lumbar spine) is composed of five vertebrae, each separated by shock-absorbing discs and surrounded by associated nerves, muscles, and ligaments. The spine is moved on the pelvis by groups of muscles. The front (anterior) has the abdominals, the back (posterior) has the back extensors, and the sides have the lateral flexors and rotators.

Tennis players subject the lower back to greater mechanical stresses than other parts of the back, which increases the potential for injury. The rotation or torsion required to hit a backhand, extend into a serve, overhead, or reach for a low volley all stress the spine and muscles supporting it. The force of gravity makes the on-court pounding tough on the body, and any weaknesses or flexibility imbalances put more stress on the back. The supporting muscles around the spine are always hard at work dynamically to protect against these significant gravitational and rotational forces.

The causes of back pain are complex and varied. Medical advice should be sought if pain persists more than a few days, and x-rays or other special tests may be done under the supervision of your physician to rule out other potential problems. Back pain in tennis players is usually due to sprains and strains, facet joint syndrome, and pelvic and hip malalignment syndromes (discussed in next section). The severity can range from a nagging, nuisance-type ache to an incapacitating pain that prevents training and playing.

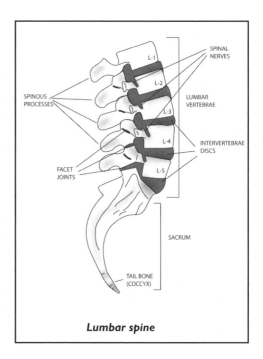

Lumbar spine

LUMBAR LIGAMENT SPRAINS AND MUSCLE STRAINS

Pelvic and lumbar ligament sprains and muscle strains secondary to malalignment make up the majority of all back problems. They originate from microscopic tears of the muscles and ligaments that occur when the body's ability to adapt is overwhelmed by the forces applied. These are common injuries associated with a specific event such as inappropriate lifting, overuse, or a fall.

As well, the quick-twisting and rotational action of the upper body on the pelvis and hips may cause injury when the fatigued muscles fail to keep the joints of the spine within their normal range of motion. The ligaments are stretched and sprained or the muscles are strained. The severity of these injuries depends on the number of fibers affected.

Sprains and strains are often described as first, second, and third degree depending on severity. First degree indicates stress to some of the fibers, second degree indicates some fibers torn and stretched, and third degree denotes a complete rupture of the fibers. These injuries are characterized by localized pain which has a specific mechanism of injury and no neurological involvement; however, pain can also be referred to a distant site in the extremities.

Quick twisting and rotation

You can also get pain or instability from muscles that are fatigued and under chronic increased tension and fail to do their supportive job.

Treatment consists of rest, local physiotherapy modalities, and ice to decrease inflammation, swelling, and associated pain and muscle spasm. Anti-inflammatories and analgesics may be appropriate under a physician's prescription. The initial rest period is followed by a rehab and strength program, which includes return to normal range of motion, flexibility, and strength.

FACET JOINT SYNDROME

Facet joint syndrome is the culprit in an estimated 10 to 15 percent of back injuries. This syndrome occurs when the facet joints connecting the vertebrae become strained and inflamed after undergoing extreme forces. The forces can either be in the form of an extension injury during the service motion or compression and torsion injury from quick stops and starts with the forces of gravity and rotation acting on the body. This injury is characterized by localized pain with only moderate radiation. The surrounding muscles are generally in spasm. There may be loss of movement as well as pain in the facet joint that is injured. It is differentiated from a disc protrusion in that there is no pain or associated numbness or tingling in a nerve root distribution radiating down the leg.

Treatment consists of physiotherapy modalities to decrease muscle spasm and pain as well as manual therapy techniques to mobilize the facet joints.

MALALIGNMENT SYNDROME

Malalignment is the most common injury associated with back pain in both recreational and professional tennis players. The alignment of the lower back, pelvis, and extremities must be symmetrical to avoid abnormal stresses resulting in pain and

Jamming or compressive forces

myofascial tension symptoms. Malalignment syndromes are frequently seen in athletes that either jump from one leg to the other, engage in rotational activities, or sit for prolonged periods of time at work or traveling. It is also common in athletes with poor three-dimensional lower core strength or increased tightening of the phasic muscles like the hamstrings and hip flexors. This can result in the imbalance and jamming of the sacroiliac joint producing low back pain. This common cause of injury is explored in detail later in this chapter.

ACUTE DISC SYNDROME

This syndrome is characterized as acute severe lower back pain with radiation to one extremity. The pain usually radiates to the foot. The exact radiation will

ANYONE EXPERIENCING PAIN OR NUMBNESS AND TINGLING DOWN THE LEGS OR WEAKNESS IN LEG MUSCLES SHOULD BE EVALUATED BY A PHYSICIAN OR PHYSICAL THERAPIST TO RULE OUT A DISC PROBLEM.

help determine which disc is involved. Neurological examination shows associated reflex changes and weakness of the muscles supplied by that nerve root.

Treatment involves stabilization to ensure spinal cord continuity and anti-inflammatories and analgesic medication per a physician's prescription. Only when appropriate, the athlete should return home for treatment and consultation. Rehabilitation includes corrective realignment where required and a progressive stretching and strengthening program that leads to a return to training and tennis program.

Tennis athletes can help reduce their potential for back injury by taking preventative measures.

Tips to Minimize Back Problems

- When traveling for long periods in a car or plane, use a back support or place a rolled-up towel behind your lower back.

- Lifting heavy suitcases is all part of travel. Avoid undue and or asymmetrical stress by keeping your back erect, bending your knees to lift with your legs, and keeping lower abdominals switched on throughout the movement.

- Use correct form and perform appropriate pre-season strength training exercises, especially for the three-dimensional upper and lower core musculature.

- Achieve adequate flexibility in the hamstrings, gluteals, and hip flexors.

- Don't try and touch your toes first thing in the morning when the discs are hydrophylic (filled up with water) because bending forward puts more stress on them, potentially leading to increased chance of disc protrusion or other problem.

- Focus on three-dimensional core strength in a variety of functional activities that put you in the hip extended position. (See exercises to hold neutral in Chapter 26 as well those in Chapter 6.)

- Switch on your core (contract your lower abdominals at a low level like a dimmer switch) throughout the day.

- Do a comprehensive dynamic warm-up before any activity (Chapter 2).

Obviously, there is no simple solution to either the cause of back pain or to its treatment and prevention. But a little knowledge goes a long way in preventing problems. If you have any concerns about your back, you should consult with your primary caregiver.

THE MALALIGNED PLAYER SYNDROME

A sport like tennis is asymmetrical in nature and can torque the body's muscle and fascial systems, leading to an imbalance in length and strength of muscles and tendons. Tennis requires asymmetrical strength and flexibility of the dominant hand, arm, and upper torso for proper execution of strokes. While upper body development is asymmetric, resulting in overdevelopment of one side of the upper body, symmetrical strength and flexibility of the legs and lower torso are necessary for optimum court mobility.

The flexed posture of competitive sport further adds to this imbalance. Simple symmetrical stretches for the low back and hips will help keep you aligned. However, if you're experiencing low back, sacroiliac joint, or hip pain, or tightness or discomfort down the leg or into the torso, talk to your therapist to see if your pelvis is malaligned. He or she can give you some simple hold-relax exercises followed by some key stretches to remedy it.

Flexed posture

WHAT DOES MALALIGNMENT MEAN?

Do you ever feel like your body is crooked or twisted? Do you ever feel like one foot seems to be scuffing the ground more than the other foot? If this is accompanied by pain or stiffness in the lower back, groin, or into the buttocks, this could be a symptom of a malaligned pelvis. Although there are many areas of abnormal biomechanics, a common one, malalignment of the pelvis, spine, and extremities, is sometimes overlooked. This malalignment syndrome remains one of the frontiers in medicine, unrecognized as a cause of over 50% of back and limb pain (Schamberger, 2002). The associated biomechanical changes—especially the shift in weight-bearing and the asymmetries of muscle tension, strength, and joint range of motion—affect soft tissues, joints, and organ systems throughout the body. Abnormal pelvic motion during training can put undue strain on a variety of structures that lead to overuse problems.

The pelvic ring of bones is a symmetrical structure which has about 36 muscles attached to each side as well as numerous ligaments. The pelvis consists of two large hip bones, the innominates, which are attached together in the front at the symphysis pubis. The back and bottom of each innominate has a bony protuberance that is called the ischial tuberosity (sitz bones). At the back, between the two innominates, is the sacrum. The sacrum is an extension of your spine. The connection

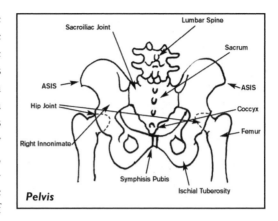

Pelvis

between the innominates (pelvic bones) to the sacrum forms the right and left sacroiliac joints.

The legs are attached to the pelvis at the hip, and the torso sits on top of the pelvis. The pelvic ring is therefore an area of extreme torsion and stress. In the healthy body, the pelvis is able to withstand repeated gravitational and torsional strains. If the repeated strains are largely asymmetrical due to the nature of the sport or the nature of a playing field, the pelvic ring can become malaligned. Unequal muscle pull on each side of the pelvis can result in the ring becoming distorted. Distortion of the pelvic ring as a result of torsion of the pelvic bones or sacrum and loss of movement in one of the sacroiliac joints results in some of these muscles and ligaments being put under tension while others are put in a relaxed position.

It is difficult to prove that muscle strength imbalances are the primary cause of injury or decreased performance. We can, however, view muscle imbalances as one of the many potential risk factors increasing the chance of injury or decreased performance (Chandler, 2001).

"ATHLETES WHO ARE OUT OF ALIGNMENT MAY HAVE DIFFICULTY PROGRESSING IN THEIR SPORT AND, AS A RESULT, SOMETIMES HAVE TO ABANDON THEIR EFFORTS ALL TOGETHER. MALALIGNMENT ALSO PUTS ATHLETES AT INCREASED RISK OF INJURY, AND ONCE INJURED, THEY ARE LIKELY TO TAKE LONGER TO RECOVER, OR MAY EVEN FAIL TO DO SO AT ALL."
— DR. WOLF SCHAMBERGER

The body has a strong propensity to adapt to gravitational and rotational forces. However, if the pelvic ring is distorted for a period of time, the body's ability to adapt is overwhelmed, and pain and stiffness usually result. Pain and stiffness can be felt in the area of the sacroiliac joints, the buttocks, the surrounding musculature of the hip, or in back symptoms, or they can refer to the groin and down the leg.

Who Is Commonly Affected?

Athletes of all different levels and sports are vulnerable to this injury. Here are some common risk factors:

- Playing asymmetrical sports that require a lunging and rotation action such as tennis and other racquet sports, golf, and baseball.
- Repeatedly landing from a jump with one leg first as in a tennis serve, volleyball, or skiing.
- Running on a sloped surface, such as the side of the road.
- Playing a field sport on a field with a slope.
- Driving for long distances.

A common mechanism causing malalignment involves bending forward while twisting the trunk either the right or the left side as in picking up a ball or weights that creates a combined action of forward flexion with side-bending and rotation. As well, hitting repeated shots or reaching forward lunging for a shot can create the same scenario. The onset of pain is usually immediate, often felt on trying to get back to the upright position. It can however come on more gradually over the next few hours or even days, as inflammation in the supporting ligaments occurs (Don Tigny, 1993).

How To Tell If You Are Malaligned?

The most common presentation of malalignment syndrome is rotational malalignment. Other conditions like upslip, pelvic inflare and outflare, and other presentations can also occur but should be dealt with by an appropriately trained therapist who has had special training to recognize, diagnose, and treat the malalignment syndromes.

There are a number of simple alignment checks that will help you decide if you are rotationally malaligned. While these are effective tools to help you find the root of the problem, they are not meant to be looked at in isolation. A health professional such as a physiotherapist can help you to put all the signs and symptoms together to come up with a clinical picture.

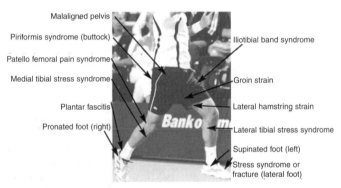

Malalignment injuries. *If you have experienced any of the overuse injuries listed, then you should definitely consider a closer look at pelvic biomechanics.*

One Leg Stance (balance)

Stand on one leg with the knee slightly bent. Watch yourself in the mirror to compare. You need to look more closely at your pelvic biomechanics if:

- Balance is harder on one side.
- One side seems weaker.
- One side seems tighter or stiffer.
- One side is more painful.
- One side is less coordinated.

If you had no problem with the above self-check, try to stress yourself further with a one leg squat as described below.

One Leg Squat

Perform a one leg squat, first with one leg and then the other. Go down to about a 30–60 degrees bend in the knee. Watch yourself in the mirror to compare. You need to look more closely at your pelvic biomechanics if:

- Balance is harder on one side.
- One side seems weaker.
- One side seems tighter or stiffer.
- One side is more painful.
- One side is less coordinated.

One leg squat

Leg Length Check

- Lie on your back with your knees bent up and lift your bottom up off the floor and return it to the starting position. This neutralizes your pelvis.

- Straighten out both legs. Get a friend to check to see if both of your legs are the same length. Some people can tell on themselves by the feel of their ankle bones hitting together.

- It is best to have someone else take a bird's eye view from the top and look to see if your ankle bones line up.

- If you have the most common presentation (right pelvis forward, left pelvis backward), the right leg will most often look longer than the left.

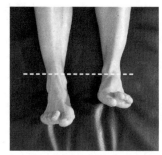

Leg length check. Right longer.

Hip Bone (ASIS) Check—Supine Lying

- Lie in supine (on your back) with your legs out straight, use the next test to confirm or disprove a rotation or malalignment.

- Put one finger on each of the bony protuberances at the front of your hips. These are the anterior superior iliac spines (ASIS). Make sure to land-

ASIS check. Right lower.

mark on the same point of each ASIS (e.g., on the top or just below).

- Again, get a friend to look at you from above and decide if the ASIS's are level or if one appears to be higher than the other.

- Most commonly, with the right innominate rotated forward and the left rotated backward, the right ASIS will appear lower than the left.

PSIS Check

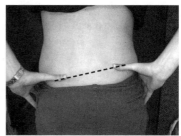

- Lie on your stomach.

- Get a friend to landmark the posterior superior iliac spines (PSIS). These are the bony protuberances at the back of your hip bones. They are most commonly just above the dimples.

- Landmark on the same part of each PSIS and get a friend to see if these points are level or not.

PSIS check. *Right higher.*

- Most commonly, with the right innominate rotated forward and the left rotated backward, the right PSIS will appear higher than the left.

Sitting Check (illiac crest)

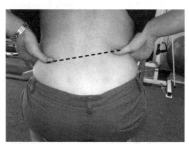

- Sit on a stool or a chair with both feet not touching the ground.

- Find your waist and slide down to the iliac crest of your hip bones.

- Get a friend to look or check in the mirror and determine if the iliac crests are level.

- This test can appear level, and it may still mean that you have a rotated pelvis. If they are not level, note which side appears higher.

Sitting check (illiac crest). *Right higher.*

- If one side is higher and it is accompanied by unusual pain and stiffness, you could have an innominate which is upslipped and you should see a qualified therapist.

Potential Signs of Malalignment

Any of the factors accompanied with pain or stiffness in the low back and hips should key you to recognize that something is wrong:

- Change from sitting to lying test.
- One leg short.
- If the above mentioned bony landmarks don't match.

How to Fix it

A qualified health professional would use these and other tests to help put together the clinical picture and determine whether you have pelvic malalignment and what type of presentation. This section will discuss the most common direction and presentation of a malaligned pelvis (anteriorly rotated right innominate/posteriorly rotated left innominate) and provide simple exercises which will help you to correct yourself. Rotational malalignment is by far the most common presentation, occurring in isolation in 80–85% of those with pelvic malalignment (Schamberger, 2002).

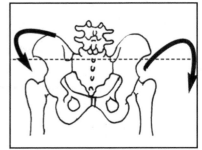

The most common presentation

Most common presentations

- Leg length test: Right leg looks longer than the left.
- Supine lying ASIS check: Right ASIS appears to be lower than the left.
- PSIS check: Right PSIS appears to be higher than the left.
- Sitting check: No asymmetry between the two crests of the innominates or the right is slightly higher.

This condition occurs when the pelvis is unable to balance out the different directions of pulls that are generated through the pelvis with movement. The pelvis becomes malaligned as the different muscles which attach to it provide asymmetrical pulls. If your findings correlate with the findings listed above, you can go on to perform an exercise to help to self-correct. The self-correction technique uses your own muscles isometrically to pull the pelvis back towards a neutral position. NOTE: The opposite presentation can occur. A left forward, right backward rotation, which occurs less frequently (approximately 10–15%), would require the opposite corrective maneuver. If you are unsure, speak to a qualified therapist.

This is a specific exercise that uses an isometric muscle energy technique called the "6 x 6" because you do it 6 times and hold each time for 6 seconds.

- To self-correct, lie on your back with both knees bent.
- Lift the right leg up and hook your hands behind your right knee.
- Using only 30% of your power, push the right leg away from your chest and into your hands. Your hands should be resisting the pull. This is an isometric (without movement) contraction of your hamstring and hip extensors (e.g., gluteus maximus and piriformis muscles).
- Hold for 6 seconds.

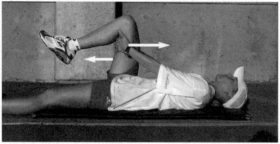

6 x 6 right leg

- Return the right leg to the ground and now lift up the left leg.
- Place your hands on the front of the left thigh and pull your left thigh toward your chest and against your hands.
- This is an isometric contraction of the left hip flexors.
- Hold the contraction for 6 seconds (30% power only).
- Repeat the 6 x 6 contraction with the right and left leg as above 6 times.

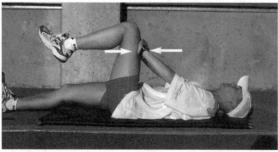

6 x 6 left leg

The pelvis, lower back, and hips work together to provide stability and power to a multitude of movements and any number of problems can occur. The presentation described in this section is the most common one that we see at City Sports & Physiotherapy Clinic and on the professional tour.

FOR THIS PRESENTATION OF (RIGHT FORWARD/LEFT BACKWARD) MALALIGNMENT PROBLEM, YOU WILL ALWAYS PUSH THE RIGHT LEG AWAY AND PULL THE LEFT LEG TOWARDS YOU. FOLLOW THIS WITH STRETCHES, INCLUDING THE SPINAL ROLL, HAMSTRING, HIP FLEXOR, AND A GLUTEAL/PRETZEL STRETCH (SEE BELOW).

Spinal roll

Quad stretch

Pretzel stretch

Hamstring stretch

Hip flexor stretch

344

Remember, if your findings do not correlate with the findings outlined above, do not panic. You may have a combination of the presentations described or you may be rotated in the opposite direction as the one described or you may have another condition of the pelvis that has not been described here, such as upslip or pelvic inflare or outflare.

Other presentations or combinations can occur and are common if:

- The pelvis has been rotated for a long period of time or acutely rotated from a fall or twist.
- The muscles have become adaptively shortened.
- There is reactive muscle spasm affecting the hips and pelvis.
- There is pain and associated muscle inhibition present.

In these circumstances, the 6 x 6 corrective exercises may not be as effective, and you should consult with an appropriately trained therapist who has had special training to recognize, diagnose, and treat the malalignment syndromes.

The more athletes and patients can do for themselves, the better their chances of recovery. We look at the qualified therapist as doing the "fine-tuning," whereas the athletes and patients need to get involved in their day-to-day treatment to help to maintain alignment between treatment sessions. It is important that they learn to recognize any recurrence of malalignment; the sooner they do, the sooner they can get on with self-correction maneuvers and/or seek help. A spouse or friend can be taught how to help with the assessment of malalignment and help with some of the techniques that may correct it or at least achieve a partial correction and decrease the pain and spasm until the athlete can see a physiotherapist.

Once you have effectively self-treated your malaligned pelvis, other stretches and core strengthening exercises should be added to your daily routine (see Chapter 26, Core Training To Hold Neutral, and Chapter 6, Upper and Lower Core Training in 3-D).

It is important to address the common causes of the rotated pelvis and not just the symptoms (pain) and muscle tension.

COMMON CAUSES OF MALALIGNMENT SYNDROME

Flexibility Limitations

- As mentioned above, often the pelvis becomes malaligned as a result of tight muscles pulling asymmetrically.
- It is important to keep all the muscles that attach to the pelvis supple and long.
- Include stretches for your gluteals, quadriceps, hip flexors, hamstrings, and adductors in your daily stretching routine.

Core Strength Limitations

- The pelvis can become rotated when your core muscles are weak.
- Bending over to pick something up or improper lifting techniques can accentuate this.
- After any period of injury and dysfunction, it is important to re-address the core muscles.
- Begin by isolating your transversus abdominus and progress from there. This is covered in detail in Chapter 26 "Core Training to Hold Neutral."

Poor Posture and Lifting Techniques

- In normal alignment the back's natural curves keep the spine and pelvis strong.
- Putting your back into a position like forward bending, twisting and rotation, or deep side bending makes it harder for the spine to stay protected.
- Poor posture fatigues the muscles causing spasm and, over time, pain.
- When lifting loads, use two hands, bend your knees, keep your back straight and head up.
- When doing repetitive work that involves rotation, turn your body by moving your feet.
- If doing repetitive tasks, change postural positions as often as possible to distribute the load to different body areas.

Our intention with this section is to create an awareness of the malalignment syndrome and problems it can create for athletes. Tennis players are more at risk of developing malalignment because of the rotational and torsional nature of their sport as well as the flexed competitive posture of tennis. Athletes can learn to recognize the subtle changes that may occur at the time of a recurrence such as a change in walking, changes in ease of movement, or abnormal tension. Earlier recognition of your malalignment allows for earlier treatment, earlier correction, and often an avoidance of the discomfort and other problems that will come to bother the athlete the longer malalignment persists.

WORDS OF CAUTION

A malaligned pelvis may be a source of lower back and buttock pain. There are many other possible sources of problems in this region and doing the self-correction exercises in the presence of a different injury may make that injury worse. It is therefore wise to seek professional advice if you are not sure what is causing the pain. Also, it is possible to over-correct yourself with these exercises. It is important to continue to self-test during treatment, and if you are succeeding to hold neutral, you should cease the self-correction exercises.

More information on the malalignment syndrome can be obtained below:

Video/DVD: Schamberger, W; Boyd, J.. *The Malalignment Syndrome—Treating a Common Cause of Back, Leg and Pelvic Pain.*

DVD: Boyd, J., Schamberger, W. (2003). *Alignment—The Missing Piece of the Puzzle.*

Book: Schamberger, W.. *The Malalignment Syndrome: Implications for Medicine and Sport;* Churchill Livingston, Edinburgh, 2002

Websites:

www.malalignmentsyndrome.com

www.boydhealthworks.com

References

Chandler, T.J., (2001). Muscle strength imbalances in tennis. In: M. Crespo, B. Pluim & M. Reid (Eds). *Tennis Medicine for Tennis Coaches.* London: ITF.

Don Tigny, R. (1993). Mechanics and treatment of the sacroiliac joint. *The Journal of Manual & Manipulative Therapy* 1(1) (1993): 3-12.

Schamberger, W. (2002). *The Malalignment Syndrome–Implications for Medicine and Sport.* London: Churchill Livingstone.

Chapter Twenty-Six

Core Training
To Hold Neutral

Carl Petersen and Martha Sirdevan

In order to hold your pelvis, lumbar spine, and hips in a neutral position, a strong core (trunk) is fundamental. The muscles of the trunk act as stabilizers for the three-dimensional upper core (scapula, thoracic spine, and shoulder) and lower core (torso, pelvis, and hips) (Petersen, 2004). Whether starting from the center or not, the trunk muscles help transfer energy from the legs through the central core (trunk) to the upper body and arms. This is especially important in rotational or asymmetric sports like tennis. Human movement outside a single plane is a complex blend of muscles and joints working in three dimensions to shorten, lengthen, stabilize, and provide optimum function. Tennis training requires acceleration, deceleration (Petersen, 2005) power, coordination, and agility in all three planes of movement .

The lumbo-pelvic core (trunk) muscles form the stable power platform from which the body's extremities move. This "inner unit" (Richardson et al., 1999) consists of four main muscles— the transversus abdominus (TA, i.e., lower abdominals), multifidus (deep, small muscle of the back), the pelvic floor muscles, and the diaphragm (under the ribs). Collectively these muscles work together to form a corset-like cylinder of support for the back and pelvis (Lee, 1999).

Three planes of movement

349

While the core muscles work to stabilize the trunk, the larger and longer muscles of the body (gluteals, quadriceps, hamstrings, etc.) can then work optimally. These larger muscles provide the links between the upper and lower extremities, while the core provides the strong, stable platform from which to work. They also help to protect the back and pelvis against injury. Proper function and recruitment of each of these muscles is essential for stability. Inadequate function of any of these muscles compromises the entire core.

Importance of
Transversus Abdominus

The transversus abdominus (TA) is the innermost abdominal muscle that connects to the spine at the back and wraps around the trunk to meet its counterpart in the front. It has a large attachment to the lower six ribs and the top of the entire pelvis. When the transversus abdominus contracts, it causes a slight narrowing of the waist and drawing in of the lower abdomen something like a tight corset. It functions to stiffen the spine and stabilize the pelvis prior to movements of the arms and legs. Thus, in persons who use proper stabilization strategies, the transversus abdominus is frequently active at a low level throughout the day. This is the goal with all of the exercises in this chapter as well as Chapter 6.

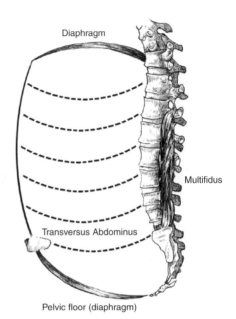

Diaphragm

Multifidus

Transversus Abdominus

Pelvic floor (diaphragm)

Core cylinder *(adapted from Lee, 1999)*

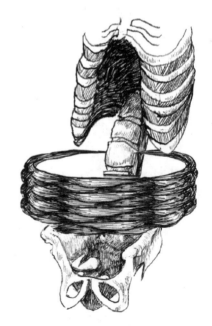

Transversus abdominus
(adapted from Celebrini, 2001)

The idea of core stability is many things to many people (Comerford, 2004). Depending on the country, county, gym, or health and fitness professionals and coaches you talk to, they will have different ideas about "core stability," how to train it, and how to cue it. For the purposes of this book, I will use the cue "switch on your core" or the cue used by Vancouver physical therapist Alex McKechnie of "fire the core and sustain" (McKechnie & Celebrini, 2002). Thinking of "switching on your core" or "fire the core and sustain" will help connect the upper and lower core musculature through the central core "inner unit." You switch your core on at a low level—like turning up the dimmer switch on a light. Other descriptions for cueing or isolating the core muscles that are used include "pelvic tilt," which has been replaced by "pelvic tension," and "suck your belly button to your spine." As well, strength coach Ian King from Australia speaks of keeping the "tummy thin" (King, 2003). Use whatever cue you need, but use it regularly and "switch on your core" or "fire the core and sustain" before all movements including exercise.

SWITCH ON YOUR CORE, OR "FIRE THE CORE AND SUSTAIN"

Before each exercise think of the following things:

- Contract the pelvic floor muscles.
- Contract the transversus abdominus (lower abdominals) at a low level.
- Remember to breathe.
- Keep knees soft (slightly bent) if standing.

To effectively switch on your core and connect the upper and lower core, you must follow these principles:

- Ensure that the initial contraction is isolated (no other muscles substituting).
- The contraction should begin slowly with control (like turning on a dimmer switch).
- Low effort to produce light tension is all that is required.
- Breathe normally.

BASE WORK—FOUR-ON-THE-FLOOR, AND MORE
(adapted after Richardson et al., 1999)

1. Switch on Your Core with Leg Slide

- Once you have mastered isolating the TA with a normal breathing pattern, progress to sliding out one leg at a time.

- Keep the TA switched on or under tension during the entire exercise. Slowly straighten one leg while sliding it along the surface of the floor and then returning to the start position to a count of 10.

- Repeat with the other leg, making sure to keep TA on the entire time and to continue to breathe.

- Repeat 10 times on each leg.

Leg slide

- This exercise can be made more challenging by lifting the foot off the floor as you slide it out and back.

2. Switch on Your Core with Leg Fall Out

- Again, find your TA while lying on your back, knees bent up.

- Now let one leg fall out to the side and back up to a count of 10.

- Repeat 10 times on each leg.

Leg fallout

- Don't let the opposite hip come up off the floor.

3. Switch on Your Core with Leg March

- Again, find your TA while lying on your back, knees bent up.

- Now march your feet up and down several inches for a count of 10 seconds.

- Don't raise knees too high (not over 90 degrees).

- Repeat 10 times.

Leg march

4. Switch on Your Core with Alternating Limb Movement (Dying Bug)

Dying bug

- Find your TA while lying on your back, knees bent.

- Now bring opposite arm and knee to 90 degrees (head and shoulder blades can come slightly off floor) and lower to a count of 10.

- Alternate sides doing 10 repetitions on each.

These "4-on-the-floor" exercises are ideal base work when correcting malalignments. Whenever you have been malaligned or have had lower back or hip and groin pain, you should return to these base work exercises.

BASE WORK PROGRESSIONS

Next are some progressions of base work exercises.

Pony Back to Neutral

Pony back

- Start in a kneeling position with shoulders over hands and hips over knees.

- Let your back arch down like an old pony.

- Now switch on your core, including lower abdominals, and suck your belly button up towards your spine and pull back to neutral position.

- Hold for 10 seconds and repeat 10 times.

Prone Bridging and Twists

- Start prone (lying face down); keep foot dorsiflexed; arms at side and back straight.

- Switch on the core and elevate body with only floor contact points of forearms, hands, and feet.

- Do not hyperextend low back or rotate the pelvis forward (anteriorly).

- As control and endurance improve, try doing a quarter-rotation to the left and right.

  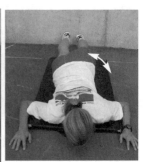

Prone bridging   **Prone bridging with twists**

Supine Bridging (stomach up)

- Lie face up on a mat with your feet on the floor and knees bent to 90 degrees.
- Keep the head and arms relaxed and switch on your core at a low level (like a dimmer switch).
- Lift your hips and low back (from tail bone to rib cage) until trunk is level. Keep your weight on your heels.

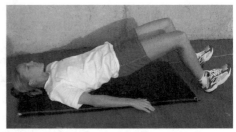

- Keep your spine neutral.
- Hold for 4 seconds and do 2–3 sets of 10–15 repetitions.
- Strengthens core and hips.

Supine bridge (stomach up)

Supine Bridging (with stretch cord abduction)

- Start as above.
- Switch on your core and push knees apart against stretch cord and lift your hips as above.

- Hold for 4 seconds and do 2–3 sets of 10–15 repetitions.
- Strengthens core and hips.

Supine bridge (abduction with stretch cord)

Supine Bridging (with ball squeeze)

- Start as above.
- Switch on your core at a low level and squeeze the ball lightly with knees and lift.
- Hold for 4 seconds and do 2–3 sets of 10–15 repetitions.
- Strengthens core and hips.

Supine bridge (adduction with ball)

Supine Bridge with Quarter Rotation

- Start as above, switch on your core at a low level.
- Lift your hips and low back (from tail bone to rib cage) until trunk is level with thighs.
- Breathe out slowly and rotate your pelvis to the right or left.

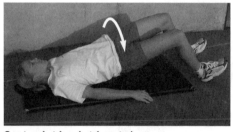

Supine bridge (with twist)

- Hold for 4 seconds. Breathe in and out to return to neutral.
- Movement is smooth and the knees remain still.
- Do 2–3 sets of 4 repetitions to each side.
- Strengthens core and hips.

Now that you are able to properly fire the core and sustain in lying, kneeling, and bridging, it is time to connect the core to the extremities (arms and legs) with functional weight-bearing exercises (described in Chapter 6, Core Training in 3D). These exercises have been chosen because they are functional in nature and reflect the current research on how our muscles and fascial tissue link together to form sling systems connecting the core (Lee, 2004) to the extremities. .

Training Note

• These exercises are not exhaustive and you may add others based on your experience or the advice of a healthcare or fitness professional.

"I BELIEVE THAT CORE MUSCLE EXERCISES ARE THE MOST FUN-
DAMENTAL PART OF MY TRAINING. THE CORE MUSCLES ARE
EXTREMELY IMPORTANT TO KEEP MY BACK HEALTHY. IF MY MUS-
CLES STAY STRONG AND STABLE, I DON'T SUFFER FROM BACK
PAIN. EXERCISING MY CORE MUSCLES HELPS ME TO BE REFLEX-
IVE AND MAINTAIN THE CONTROL, WHICH ALLOWS ME TO
EXCEL IS MY SPORT."

JEAN PHILLIPE (JP) ROY—OLYMPIC SKIER

References

Celebrini, R. (2001). Illustration from lecture on The Athlete Self Screening Exam™. Vancouver, Canada (Spring)

Comerford, M. (2004). Performance stability. Presented at STMS Joint Congress, London, England.

King, I. (2003). *The Book of Muscle* 162-163. Rodale Inc. St. Maartens Press.

Lee, D. (1999). Postpartum Health for Moms. www.dianelee.ca/postpartum/

Lee, D. (2004). Principles of the integrated model of function and its application to the lumbopelvic-hip region. In: *The Pelvic Girdle (3rd Edition)*. Churchill Livingstone.

McKechnie, A., Celebrini, R. (2002). Hard core strength: A practical application of core training for rehabilitation of the elite athlete. Course Notes. Vancouver, BC April.

Petersen, C. (2005). Fit to play: practical tips for faster recovery (part 2). *Medicine & Science in Tennis*. 10(2): August 2005.

Petersen, C., Sirdevan, M., McKechnie, A. & Celebrini, R. (2004). Core connections 3-dimensional dynamic core training (balls & stretch bands). In: C. W. Petersen. *Fit to Ski: Practical tips to Optimize Dryland Training and Ski Performance*. Vancouver: Fit to Play/CPC Physio. Corp. 267-281.

Richardson, C.A., Jull, G.A., Hodges, P.W., Hides, J. (1999). *Therapeutic Exercise for Spinal Segmental Stabilisation in Low Back Pain*. Churchill-Livingstone.

Additional Reading

Kendall, F. et al. (1993). *Muscles—Testing and Function (4th edition)*. Baltimore, MD: Williams and Wilkins.

Lee, D. (1999). *The Pelvic Girdle*. Churchill Livingstone.

Richardson, C.A., Jull, G.A. (1995). Muscle control-pain control. What exercise would you prescribe? *Manual Therapy* 1995, 1:2-10.

Chapter Twenty-Seven

Outsmarting Your Injuries

Carl Petersen

O ver the years many effective treatments and tips on the management of sports injuries have been identified. As individuals respond differently to the physical, psychological, and emotional parameters of treatment, it is best to combine different treatment forms (shotgun effect) in an attempt to maximize effectiveness. Athletes, coaches, parents, and sport medicine and science personnel need to be aware of the variety of treatments available and understand when and how they may be used.

Two basic types of injuries can occur in training for sports—those due to trauma and those from overuse. Trauma is easy to identify. It's either from a fall or being hit by someone or something. Obviously, injuries related to falls and collisions such as fractures, contusions, and lacerations (cuts) demand immediate medical attention and will not be our focus.

Overuse injuries develop as an accumulation of repetitive stress rather than the result of a single event. It can result from numerous micro-traumas to the tissues when doing too much, too hard, too fast, too soon and can occur anywhere in the musculoskeletal system, including tendon, muscle, ligament, nerve, and bone. For example, during running, the foot strikes the ground between 800–1,200 times per mile with a force of 2–3 times body weight. The repetitive nature of this type of stress can be the starting point for any number of overuse injuries. Rarely is an injury an isolated event. Exercise causes a certain amount of damage to the tissues which respond when given adequate rest by getting stronger. If the tissues receive too much stress too soon, they cannot adapt and break down. When the body's ability to adapt is overwhelmed, overuse injuries can be the result. The first symptom of overuse is usually pain, which can be followed by swelling and inflammation.

Injuries are often preventable, and with early intervention and proper exercise progressions, their incidence and severity may be decreased. Recognizing the signs and symptoms of injuries and learning what to do about them can help reduce your recovery time. What follow are some common sense guidelines to help you understand the injuries and know their potential causes, as well as some tips on treatment and prevention.

INJURY PREVENTION

As physical therapists, we regularly assess players with a comprehensive orthopedic exam and the Fit to Play™–Additional Functional Tests (see Chapter 24). As well, we encourage the athletes to use the The Athlete Self-Screening Exam™ (see Chapter 24) to self-monitor their physical well being. Identifying potential causes or precursors to injury is a vital part of injury pre-habilitation and improved management and rehabilitation of injuries in tennis.

Potential factors contributing to injury

- Poor biomechanics (e.g., pronation—flat feet).
- Inadequate flexibility (e.g., tight hip flexors or hamstring).
- Inadequate strength in the upper and lower core.
- Poor balance and 3-dimensional core control.
- Poor equipment (e.g., worn out shoes).
- Previous injuries (always a strong indicator for future problems).
- Training errors (e.g., too much, too hard, too fast, too soon).
- Increased volume, density, and intensity of off- and on-court training.
- Lack of proper yearly periodization and daily, weekly, and monthly planning.
- Judgment errors (e.g., practicing 300 serves in one session).
- Lack of recovery time in competitive season.
- High performance recovery tips and strategies not built into daily, weekly, and monthly plans.

OLD INJURIES ARE PERHAPS THE BIGGEST RISK FACTOR TO GETTING INJURED AGAIN.

Without a doubt, one of the most important aspects of injury treatment is promptness. Do something about it right away. If identified early, many injuries respond well to self-treatment. Understanding is the key to prevention and allows safe, pain-free activity. However, no chapter in a book can replace a proper diagnosis or treatment plan, and all persistent injuries should be evaluated by a competent health care professional.

DON'T PLAY OR PRACTICE WHEN INJURED OR ILL.

TIPS FOR INJURY TREATMENT AND PREVENTION

Injury Treatment—The "PRINCE" Principle

Initial treatment. The first 24 hours following an acute soft tissue injury are the most important. Injured tissue usually means injured blood vessels. When blood accumulates and causes swelling and compression around adjoining tissues, the lack of blood flow can cause further damage. This swelling and pressure increase can inhibit the healing of the tissue and cause pain and muscle spasm and decreased use. Therefore, every effort should be made to reduce the amount of bleeding at the site of the injury. Following the treatment guidelines represented by the PRINCE acronym will help ensure that you treat your injury properly.

Protection. Protect the site from further injury or aggravation. This may range from wearing high-top or more stable shoes to protective taping and bracing to orthotic devices to correct foot alignment.

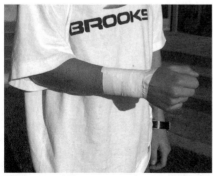

Protection. *Wrist tape and ankle brace.*

Rest (complete or modified). Depending on the severity of the injury, you may need to have complete or modified rest. If possible cease activity immediately following injury. Moving the injured part may result in increased bleeding and swelling. In more serious injuries, the injured part may need to be rested completely with the use of crutches for the lower extremity or a sling or splint for the upper extremity. If activity causes pain and swelling, don't do it. Changing to a non-weight-bearing activity such as cycling, elliptical training, swimming, or water running can help reduce discomfort and keep you active.

Modified rest. *Elliptical trainer and water running.*

Ice. Applying ice or cold packs minimizes pain and causes a local vasoconstriction, thus reducing bleeding and swelling by reducing blood flow to the injured area. Pain is decreased due to the numbing effect of the cold. The cold reduces the metabolic rate of tissue and lowers its demands for oxygen and nutrients. It may also help decrease inflammation and muscle spasm.

Ice. *Ice or cold water from a hose to cool the calf.*

Use a gel pack, bag of frozen peas, crushed ice, or ice in a bucket of water to apply cold to the area for 10–15 minutes, depending on the size of the area and the depth of the tissue to be targeted. Repeat every one to three hours. Do not apply ice directly to the skin because doing so can cause frostbite. If ice is not available, use cold water. Ice should not be applied if there is impairment to the local circulation as in Reynauds disease or peripheral arteriosclerosis or if the person suffers from a cold allergy.

NSAID. Non-steroidal anti-inflammatory medication taken under a physician's supervision can be effective in decreasing inflammation and pain and thus speed the healing process. Other over the counter remedies such as ibuprofen can also be helpful (speak to your physician).

Compression. External compression with a firm bandage helps to decrease the amount of bleeding and swelling into the injured area. Using a tensor bandage, begin wrapping below the injured area and work upwards, unwinding the bandage evenly without too much tension and overlapping the layers by half. Using compression during and after the application of ice will improve its effectiveness.

 Do NOT APPLY ICE OR COMPRESSION IF YOU HAVE CIRCULATORY PROBLEMS OR TROUBLE DISTINGUISHING HOT FROM COLD.

Compression

Elevation. Elevating or raising the injured area reduces blood flow to the area and encourages venous blood flow. Raising the upper extremity above the heart and lower extremity above the pelvis helps prevent swelling and aids in draining the swelling into large blood vessels.

Elevation

Treatments to Avoid

Treatments that should be avoided in the initial injury phase (first 24 hours) are:

- Heat, including hot packs and whirlpool.
- Heat rub or liniment.
- Hard or vigorous massage.

A physical therapist or sports physician can teach you precautions, advise you on return to participation, and help adjust training techniques and exercise progressions based on your age and fitness level. Being smart about your training means learning the rules of thumb for recognizing nonadaptive responses to training.

Treatment Rules of Thumb

- If it hurts during an activity or for more than one hour after the activity and does not go away with rest and ice, you need to cut the activity by 50 percent.
- Pain, swelling, or redness that occurs immediately after playing or training and lasts more than one day needs evaluation by a professional.
- Any pain that interferes with your ability to play needs to be evaluated by a professional.

Physiotherapy modalities such as ultrasound, interferential current, laser, TENS, muscle stimulation, and magnetic field may help decrease pain and muscle spasm. Talk to your physiotherapist about the benefits and timing of these modalities and others.

TRAIN SMART AND PAIN FREE!

Injury Prevention Guidelines

- Do a medical and physiotherapy screening two times per year, whether injured or healthy.
- Seek prompt help for any and all injuries, either acute or overuse.

- Don't try to play through an injury.
  - Always identify the structures involved and the extent or severity of the injury. See your physician or your sports physiotherapist.
  - Trying to play through an injury that is small only leads to micro-trauma or macro-trauma to the tissue, causing further damage.
  - Instead of playing, try some cross-training activities that won't aggravate the injury.
  - Most injuries respond well if treated properly.
  - Don't trivialize the injury by saying, "it is not a real injury" or that it is, "something that I can play through."
- Ensure equipment and clothing are up to standard.
- Ensure proper technique in training on and off court.
- Ensure an appropriate periodized and well-planned physical training program that includes five phases:

  Pre-Competition
  - Phase A: Training for training.
  - Phase B: Building the base.
  - Phase C: Getting sport specific.

  In-Competition
  - Phase D: Tournament competition and maintenance.

  Post-Competition
  - Phase E: Rest and recovery.
- Always perform a structured dynamic warm-up and cool-down.
- Always monitor overstress.
- Always use high performance recovery tips and strategies (see Chapter 31).
- Respect a DRUG FREE SPORT POLICY (see page 224).

References

WTA, Sport Sciences and Medicine Department, Sony Ericsson WTA Tour. Personal communication.

Additional Reading

Brukner, P., Khan, K. (2002). *Principles of Injury Prevention in Clinical Sports Medicine*. Roseville: McGraw Hill Australia Pty Ltd. 103-4.

Crespo, M., B.M. Pluim, and M. Reid (Eds) (2001). *Tennis Medicine for Tennis Coaches*. London: ITF.

Cross, R. & Lindsey, C. (2005). *Technical Tennis: Racquets, Strings, Balls, Courts, Spin, and Bounce*. Vista, CA: Racquet Tech Publishing.

Maquirran, J. (Ed) (2002). Medecina deportiva aplicada al tennis. Buenos Aires: Gr fica Integral.

Pluim, B. & Safran, M. (2004). *From Breakpoint to Advantage*. Vista, CA: Racquet Tech Publishing.

Wenger, H.A., McFayden, P.F., and McFaydon, R.A. (1996). Physiological principles of conditioning. In: Zachazewski et al. (Eds). *Athletic Injury and Rehabilitation* 189-205. Philadelphia: WB Saunders.

Chapter Twenty-Eight

Overtraining and Recovery Guidelines

Carl Petersen and Nina Nittinger

RECOGNIZING AND PREVENTING OVERSTRESS (OVERTRAINING)

Staleness, burnout, overtraining, overstress, overreaching, and monotony are all terms bantered around when talking about overtraining. This can be confusing for the athlete. For our purposes, we have adopted the Sport Medicine Council of British Columbia's (see references) definition of overstress to clarify things.

Overstress is a condition in which an athlete suffers from a number of signs and symptoms such as:

- Overuse injuries.
- Chronic fatigue.
- Mood disturbances.
- Blood chemistry changes.

This is said to occur when physical and/or emotional stresses exceed the individual athlete's coping capacity. However, physical stress is the primary factor, while other sources of stress are additive.

THE FATIGUE-OVERTRAINING CONTINUUM

In a training context, the achievement of a certain level of fatigue appears to be necessary to the development of physical abilities. Even at significant levels, fatigue is usually a temporary condition which disappears within a few hours if the athlete has access to adequate rest, nutrition, hydration, and emotional support. However, if the training load is excessive and/or if it is administered before recovery has occurred, the state of fatigue can persist and even worsen. The same may be true if the training load imposed on the body significantly exceeds its present capacity (i.e., if the loading is not progressive), or if the conditions following exercise are not conducive to recovery. Over time, this can lead to a relatively chronic state of fatigue and to a situation where the athlete's performances begin to stagnate or decline. Under such conditions, the reaction of many athletes is to increase the volume and/or the intensity of their training, thus establishing a vicious circle that only serves to aggravate the problem. Ultimately, the result may be a condition of overtraining (Marion, 1995).

Your body responds to the stresses of training and practice in a manner known as the general adaptation syndrome. In 1956 Canadian biologist Hans Selye first described this three-stage response to stress as including:

- Alarm.
- Resistance.
- Exhaustion (Selye, 1974).

The first phase is experienced when your body comes under new or more intense stress stimulus (e.g., training longer or harder, running farther, starting strength programs, etc.). This shock or alarm phase may last several days or several weeks depending on the stress and include the following symptoms:

- Excessive soreness.
- Stiffness.
- A temporary drop in your ability to perform.

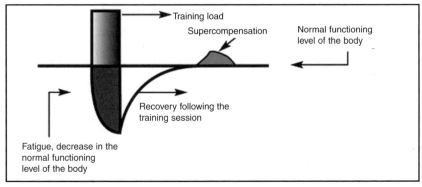

Fatigue Training Load (with permission NCCP Level 4/5 Task # 6 Pre-Readings, copyright Coaching Association of Canada)

The second phase is the resistance phase whereby your body adapts to the new loads or increased stress stimuli and gets stronger, allowing you to return to normal functioning. Your body can withstand and adapt to this type of stress for an extended period of time by making various physiological adaptations in the neurological, biochemical, structural, and mechanical systems that help to improve performance. This is often called super-compensation. Your body tolerates greater training loads, and you can increase them by manipulating training variables like frequency, duration, and intensity of activity.

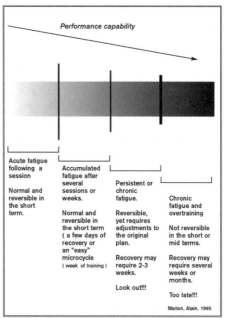

Performance Capability (with permission of Coaching Association of Canada, 1995)

	Generally Agreed Upon Overtraining Signs and Symptoms	

Physical Symptoms	**Psychological Symptoms**
Increased feeling of fatigue	Decreased motivation to train
Decrease in performance	Decreased motivation to compete
Increased muscle tension	Disturbed sleep or ability to relax
Increased muscle tenderness	Increased irritability
Increased susceptibility to Illness or injury	Decline in feelings of self-worth
Decreased appetite and weight	Uncontrollable emotions
Increased resting heart rate	Increased anxiety or insecurity
Increased blood pressure	Oversensitive about criticism
	Listlessness or melancholy

Some of the above signs and symptoms can be experienced following heavy and intense workouts, even though a classic overtrained state has not been reached. One of the best indicators of overstress or over training is how well you are coping as an athlete. You may strive to develop your own set of signs and symptoms that are relevant to you and your sport. A decrease in your general sense of well-being, pain in your muscles upon rising, and poor quality of sleep appear to be linked with excessive fatigue and could be signs that precede overtraining.

STRESSORS

On- and off-court training are just two of the many sources of stress you have to deal with as a tennis player. Being aware of potential stressors and taking steps to minimize their impact on you can help prevent overstress.

Tournaments are stressors

Training and Practice Stressors

- Too much training or practice done too hard, too fast, too soon.
- Lack of recovery time.
- Too many tournaments.
- Training or playing while injured or ill.
- Returning from injury or illness too quickly risks:
  - Compensations from weak and damaged tissues that are unable to fully weight bear.
  - Potential increased damage to already vulnerable injured tissue.
  - Prolonged recovery time.

Lifestyle stressor: "Nice" organized room.

Travel and Lifestyle Stressors

- Unfamiliar or poor quality of food.
- Poor accommodations or living conditions.
- Inadequate acclimatization to cold, humidity, or altitude.
- Irregular routine.
- Lack of sleep.
- Jet lag and travel concerns.

Environmental Stressors

- Constant competitive environment.
- Inadequate acclimatization to cold, humidity, or altitude.
- Lack of support from family and friends.
- Lack of adequate finances.
- Employment or scholastic concerns.
- Personal relationships.

Health Stressors

- Illness or injury.
- Allergies or other health concerns.
- Poor nutrition and/or hydration.
- Large fluctuations in body weight and composition.

Tips to Prevent Overstress or Overtraining

- Individualize physical training and on-court training.
- Involve yourself in your program design.
- Ensure adequate variety in your training. Sometimes, a change is as good as a rest.
- Be flexible in your training routine based on fatigue, attitude to training, and other stressors.
- Maintain good communication with your coach concerning levels of fatigue and stress.
- Ensure proper planning and periodization of training.
- Ensure gradual increase in training loads and progressions.
- Ensure proper sequencing of your training.

- Scheduling and utilizing recovery time and techniques.
- Ensure adequate rest between training sessions and within training sessions.
- Ensure sufficient sleep.
- Ensure proper nutrition and hydration—some athletes may be chronically dehydrated or glycogen depleted during periods of intense training.
- Provide regular scheduled days off from training. It is essential that an adequate recovery period follow several days of intense training.

The response to overstress and overtraining appears to be highly individual, and the signs and symptoms can vary greatly from player to player. The factors contributing to the increase or decrease of overstress are complex and multifaceted. There is no perfect technique to monitor and evaluate fatigue levels; however, keeping a training diary and monitoring it weekly and monthly may help. The main factor responsible for overstress and overtraining is the lack of recovery within the training program. You should enlist the help of your coach and other sports medicine and science personnel to help you make adjustments to your training and practice plans. This will minimize the potential for overstress or overtraining and optimize performance.

REST AND RECOVERY ARE TWO OF THE MOST IMPORTANT COMPONENTS OF YOUR TRAINING AND PRACTICE PROGRAM.

PHYSICAL AND PSYCHOLOGICAL RECOVERY

You can enhance your recovery rate between training or competition sessions by taking action to recover physically, psychologically, and emotionally. See Chapter 31 for more ideas.

Relaxation

Learning to recover and relax is a great advantage for optimizing high performance. When you are competitive, being calm and relaxed in tight situations are two of your best mental weapons. As long as you are in a relaxed state of mind, nobody and nothing can stress you. When you feel stress coming on, you recognize it and have a technique or strategy in mind to respond to it.

The goals of relaxation techniques are to:

- Slow down breathing.
- Slow down heart rate.
- Decrease muscle tension.
- Relax muscles.
- Help control your thoughts.
- Turn negative feelings and emotions into positive ones.
- Produce positive hormones.
- Block out interruptions.
- Increase body awareness.

Relaxation

The exercises listed below will assist in relaxing the mind as well as the body and decrease stress-related fight or flight chemicals. They will also assist in acute and chronic stress management. This list is not exhaustive and other methods and techniques can be used based on your experience.

PMR (progressive muscle relaxation). During PMR you tighten specific muscles for 5 seconds and relax for 20 seconds. By doing this you can learn to identify what tension feels like, and after releasing you will feel the sensation of relaxation.

Autogenic relaxation. This is a self-induced relaxation technique during which your attention is focused upon sensations you're attempting to produce in specific muscles. The two common sensations are softness and warmth.

Controlled breathing. Many relaxation techniques incorporate some component of breathing. Breathing drills incorporate a range of exercises that assist you to focus your attention on breathing and induce a state of relaxation.

Imagery relaxation (visualization). During imagery relaxation you vividly imagine a scene where you feel secure, comfortable, and relaxed (beach, garden, etc.). The scene is imagined with all of the senses.

Music. Choose your own selection of music; use a personal stereo as opposed to the radio. Have variety and include music to soothe.

Videos. Bring a selection of your own favorite videos or CDs; use them to forget about your sport for several hours.

Color therapy. Choose several articles of clothing that make you feel great.

Laughter and fun. Use active socialization such as jokes, card games, and story telling to promote emotional recovery.

Stress control "choices." The only truly stressful situation is environmental. Other situations are not inherently stressful. You can decide if you'll be stressed.

Thought control. Get away from the tennis environment. Break the routine: rather than rushing from point to point to sit in the hotel, take your time, see a museum or a church or a new restaurant. Have coffee by a lake or pack a picnic lunch.

To get better results in relaxation we suggest trying a combination of techniques, and see what works for you. For example, go to a lake or the beach and lie or sit somewhere comfortable. Have a picnic and watch the beautiful scenery around you. Try to feel positive but relaxed. Start off with some controlled breathing. After that you can focus your attention upon sensations you want to produce in specific muscles. To finish you can lie down and tighten and relax every muscle in your body.

Relaxing beach walk

Training and Competition Fatigue (Angela Calder)

Fatigue Type	Characteristics and Recovery		
Metabolic Fatigue (energy Stores)	**Main causes** • Training lasting one hour or more, or • From several shorter sessions a day, and • It can be cumulative when training or performing over a number of days.	**Symptoms** • Athlete fatigues sooner than is normal for that athlete. • Athlete struggles to complete a session or event.	**Recovery Strategies** • Rehydrate and refuel before, during, and after training. • Use contrast temperature showers, pool, spa and cold plunge, or active recovery activities. • Meal within 1–2 hours of training and monitor hydration
Neurological (nervous system) Peripheral Nervous System (muscles)	**Main causes** • After short, high intensity sessions (e.g., weight training, plyometrics, complex skill execution, etc.) • After long but low intensity sessions, especially involving repetitive movements (e.g., steady state swimming, running, cycling, paddling, rowing, etc.).	**Symptoms** • Reduced localized force production (e.g., slow feet, reduced acceleration, poor technique, etc.)	**Recovery Strategies** • Rehydrate and refuel (including small amounts of protein as well as carbohydrates) before, during, and after training. • Within 5-15 minutes after training, use a spa or shower with jets focused on the large and fatigued muscle groups. • After training or later in the day, massage large muscle groups using jostling/shaking techniques.
Neurological (nervous system) Central Nervous System (brain)	**Main causes** • Low blood glucose levels • High pressured training session—especially involving rapid decision making and reactions. • Poor motivation (e.g., monotony of training, emotional factors, injury, etc.)	**Symptoms** • Lack of drive. • Lack of motivation.	**Recovery Strategies** • Steady and regular intake of carbohydrates during training and after training to maintain normal blood glucose levels. • After training—unwind (e.g., listening to music, visualization, etc.)
Psychological (emotional, cultural, and social)	**Main causes** • Lack of team or squad cohesion, personality conflicts, etc. • Competition pressures, event venue and residential conditions, parents, coach, media, national sporting body, etc. • Other lifestyle stresses—home, school exams, personal relationships, etc.	**Symptoms** • Athlete loses self-confidence or self-esteem. • Athlete's body language, increased signs of anxiety, negative attitudes, etc. • Poor sleep patterns.	**Recovery Strategies** • Focus on process rather than outcome indicators. • Debrief by identifying 1–3 things that worked well in training and 1–3 that need more work. • Take mind off training with an escapist or funny movie, TV, book, or socialize with family and friends. • 10–15 minutes before bed, switch off from the day by using relaxation techniques.
Environment and Travel Fatigue	**Main causes** • Disruption of normal routines, especially the biological clock. • Disrupted sleeping, waking, and meal times. • Sedentary and limited body positions on long journeys (i.e., 30 minutes or longer). • Adapting to different climatic conditions to those normally experienced.	**Symptoms** • Athletes take longer to warm-up. • Unforced errors in the first 15 minutes are well above normal rates. • Athletes fatigue sooner than normal.	**Recovery Strategies** • Preparation planning will minimize fatigue. • Stay hydrated and refueled. • Stay cool in the heat—use a pool, shade, iced towels, etc. • Minimize visual fatigue by wearing sunglasses outside and limiting time on computers and play stations.

References

Marion, A. (1995). Overtraining and sports performance. *SPORTS, Coaches Report.* Coaching Association of Canada.

Coaching Association of Canada. NCCP Level 4/5 Task #6 Pre-Readings.

Selye, H. (1974). *Stress Without Distress.* Philadelphia: JB. Lipincott.

Sport Medicine Council of British Columbia (1994). *Science and Medicine Resource Manual for Coaches.*

Additional Reading & General References

www.ask.net.au. Free coach and athlete resources and information on recovery and regeneration.

www.ais.org.au/nutrition. Free information on sport specific post-game nutrition and impartial evidence-based information on nutritional supplements.

Calder, A. (1996). Recovery–Revive, Survive and Prosper. In: R. DeCastella (ed.), *Smart Sport.* Canberra, Australia: RWM publishing.

Calder, A. (2003). Recovery. In: M. Reid, A. Quinn, & M. Crespo (Eds), *Strength and Conditioning for Tennis.* London: ITF.

Calder, A. (2003). Recovery strategies for sports performance. *Olympic Coach,* Summer, 18(3): 8-11. Colorado Springs, CO: US Olympic Committee.

Hogg, J.M. (2002). Debriefing: A means to increasing recovery and subsequent competition. In: M.Kellmann (ed.), *Enhancing Recovery: Preventing Underperformance in Athletes.* Champaign, IL: Human Kinetics.

Hawley, C.J. & Schoene, R.B. (2003). Overtraining syndrome–A guide to diagnosis, treatment, and prevention. *The Physician and Sportsmedicine* 31(6) June.

Hooper, S.L., MacKinnon, L.T, Howard, A., Gordon, R.D. & Bachmann, A.W. (1995). Markers for monitoring overtraining and recovery. *Medicine and Science in Sports and Exercise* 27:106-112.

Kellmann, M. (2002). *Enhancing Recovery: Preventing Underperformance in Athletes.* Champaign, IL: Human Kinetics.

Loehr, J. (1992). *The New Toughness Training for Sports.* Dutton, USA.

Marion, A. (1995). Overtraining and sport performance. *SPORTS, Coaches Report.* Coaching Association of Canada.

Matuszewski, W. Rehabilitative regeneration in sports. In: *Science Periodical on Research and Technology in Sport.* (SPORTS) January 1985.

Petersen, C. (1988). A physiotherapist's role in facilitating regeneration and recovery in elite athletes. *Canadian Sport Physiotherapy Journal* 13:3.

Viitasalo, J.T., K. Niemela, R. Kaappola, T. Korjus, M. Levola, H.V. Mononen, H.K.Rusko, and T.E.S.Takala (1995). Warm underwater water-jet massage improves recovery from intense physical exercise. *European Journal of Applied Physiology* 71: 431-428.

Wilmore, J.H. & Costill, D.L. (1988). Training for Sport and Activity (third edition). Dubuque, IA: Wm C. Brown Publishers.

Chapter Twenty-Nine

Sleep Smarts
for Recovery

Carl Petersen

What does sleep have to do with tennis training? Tennis is a mental game, and if you are not well rested, you cannot think as well. Most touring pros will tell you that when they do not get enough sleep, their memory is bad and they're sluggish and can't concentrate on practice. In terms of recovery, sleep is as important as what you eat or drink. Evidence suggests that lack of sleep may interfere with glucose metabolism, which muscles depend upon for recovery and the brain needs to function.

Lack of sleep can also contribute to injuries. Your muscles need the rest and recovery time during sleep to rebuild the tissue stressed during a workout. Lack of sleep can overwhelm your body's ability to adapt, increasing the poten-

FOR ATHLETES THAT ARE PLAYING AND TRAINING HARD, SLEEP IS A RECOVERY TOOL. IT IS A NECESSITY NOT A LUXURY.

tial for injury. Lack of sleep can also make you prone to illness because the added stress depletes the immune system. It is estimated that those who get less than six hours sleep have 50 percent less immunity protection than those who get eight hours sleep.

Lack of sleep is a problem for most people, athletes included. Experts suggest that we need a minimum of eight hours a night, though nine are ideal; however, most people get closer to seven hours. One's sleep needs must be met per 24 hour period. Both quality and quantity of sleep needs to be in synchrony with one's circadian (daily) rhythm (Yan-Go, 2006). The rule of the day and night used to be "early to bed, early to rise," but that was before the invention of the light bulb. The last time most people really had a good sleep was when they were still in grade school. Beyond that age, there's always a reason to go to bed later— homework, sports, work, text messaging, and television. With all the distractions life can throw your way, you must make sleep happen.

The amount of sleep you need is individual. Some people need nine or ten hours while others are energized after six or seven. To find the number of hours sleep that's perfect for you, Dr. Fricsa Yan-Go from UCLA suggests that you try the following experiment next time you are on vacation.

Sleep experiment (Yan-Go, 2006)

- Go to bed at the same time every night and wake up on your own, without an alarm clock (keep track of the time).
- After 4 days you will have paid off your sleep debt and should wake up feeling energized.
- Make a note of how long you slept that night—that's what you should aim for on a nightly basis.

SLEEP SMART TIPS

The following are a few tips to help you sleep smart and aid recovery.

Minimize caffeine in the late afternoon

- Opt for decaffeinated beverages instead.
- Also avoid chocolate and other foods that contain caffeine.
- People can be affected by caffeine up to 12 hours after drinking it.

THINK OF EACH HOUR OF SLEEP BEFORE MIDNIGHT AS WORTH A DOUBLE HOUR AFTER.

Avoid excessive alcohol in the evening

- Although it makes you sleepier initially, as its effects wear off, sleep will be disrupted.

Make your bedroom a sleep refuge

- That means no eating, reading, or watching TV in bed.
- You want your brain to have a strong association with bed and sleep.
- If you do things in bed that you can do elsewhere, you may confuse your brain.
- Other sleep disrupters are pets in the bedroom, light seeping in through the windows, and any type of noise.

Bedding basics

- Stick with natural fibers such as cotton for your bedding. Since we release a large amount of sweat and oils over the course of an evening, avoid synthetics as they are less absorbent.
- Choosing a comforter style bedding can give you that "swaddled baby" cocoon feeling.
- Choose a pillow or pillows that will keep your neck and spine aligned. A neutral spine keeps the passageways for the nerves and blood vessels from becoming restricted.

Minimize thinking and worry

- Don't allow problems to keep you awake at night.
- If you remember something you don't want to forget, keep a voice recorder by your bedside, write it down, or call and leave the message on your voice mail.
- As well, don't allow problems to keep you awake at night. Minimize thinking and worrying in bed—learn to switch off (Calder, 1996).

Smart eating habits

- Try to avoid going to bed with a full stomach or going to bed hungry.
- Smaller meals or a light snack before bedtime can avoid the two extremes.

Monitor both your own and the bedroom's temperature if you are having trouble sleeping

- A room that's too warm can hinder sleep.
- Avoid hot showers and exercise just before bedtime because a higher than normal body temperature makes it difficult to sleep.
- Use a fan or moist towels on your torso to decrease your body temperature if you have trouble sleeping.

Get up

- If you have been lying in bed for 30 minutes and have not fallen asleep, do something else to help relax.
- Listen to light music, stretch, read, etc., until you feel tired. When you lie in bed and stress out about not falling asleep, all you do is keep yourself awake.

Avoid afternoon naps

- If you sleep during the day, you may be short-changing yourself at night.
- The occasional mid-day snooze won't hurt, especially if you are over-tired, but too much napping throws your sleep clock out.

Keep a schedule

- Go to bed and wake up at the same time every day including weekends.
- If you have the odd late night, force yourself to get up at the same time so you don't get sleep lagged.
- Consistency is a key to a good night's sleep.

References

Calder, A. (1996). Chapter 7, Recovery: revive, survive, and prosper. In: R. de Castella, W. Clews (Eds), *Smart Sport*. RWM

Yan-Go, Frisca (2006). Personal communication.

Additional Resources

Websites: www.ask.net.au; www.mayoclinic.com/health/sleep/HQ01387; www.shut-eye.com; www.sleepfoundation.org; www.helpguide.org/life/sleep_tips; www.sleep-net.com.

Chapter Thirty

Soft Tissue Release (Muscle and Fasciae)

Carl Petersen and Martha Sirdevan

The myofascial system has received increased attention in the past few years. This intricate system surrounds all the muscles, nerves, and blood vessels in the body. It is a complex web-like system that separates muscles into compartments. Dysfunction in this system is common. Because this system wraps around each muscle fibril in the body, it can become twisted and snagged in different places. It is like a nylon stocking surrounding your muscle, and with dysfunction, this stocking can become caught or tight in certain places.

Physiotherapists, massage therapists, and other health professionals have been suggesting to patients to use their hands, tennis balls, foam rolls, and other implements to release sore, tight muscle and fascial tissue for years. Myofascial release refers to a group of techniques used to relieve soft tissue from the abnormal grip of tight fascia (Juett, 1988). Myofascial release is not a new concept—Dr. Janet Travell documented many techniques in the 1940s. Recently, in addition to these, small rubber myofascial release balls are being used to stretch and soften tight muscles (Soleway, 2001). These balls work not only to release trigger points in the muscle but also can work to "smooth out" the myofascial system and decrease delayed onset muscle soreness. The incidence of delayed onset muscle soreness differs between the sexes, as females seem to be less susceptible to it (Tarnoplosky, 1990). But practical experience dictates that both men and women benefit from soft tissue release.

The effectiveness of massage or soft tissue techniques as an adjunct to stretching in order to facilitate flexibility have been demonstrated in the past (Witkorson-Moller, 1983). Physiotherapists use manual techniques to help decrease trigger points that are defined by Travell and Simons as an exquisitely tender point in a taut band of muscle (Travell and Simons, 1998). Active, irritable trigger points that result from heavy training may reduce muscle strength and inhibit the normal contraction-relaxation coordination of the muscles. Obviously, this will not be conducive to pain free training. These problems can impair training and competition and can progress to injury if they are not resolved (Brukner and Khan, 2002).

Small ball body rolling is a great way to stretch and release tight muscles. The concept is very simple: Use the ball to "iron out" tight areas. By rolling on the ball along the muscle and at different angles to the muscle, you are trying to "untwist" the myofascial system. The aim of this technique is to induce a prolonged lengthening of tissue as distinct from a stretch, which may or may not lead to a long-term change (Granter, 2002). If an area is especially tight or sensitive, use the ball as a trigger point release tool and stay on the sore spot (Soleway, 2001). The fascia system seems to respond best when gentle pressure is applied and sustained for more than two minutes.

Soft tissue techniques can be done in a relaxing atmosphere when players are in the bath, showering, or watching television (Clews, 1990). This will help stimulate the tension receptors, induce relaxation, create analgesic response, and deactivate trigger points (Brukner and Khan, 2002).

CHOOSE THE RIGHT SIZE BALL

Myofascial release balls come in 3 or 4 sizes. The larger the ball, the easier it is to roll on and the more comfortable it should be. The smallest of the balls (5–inch diameter) is less comfortable to roll on and is typically used once the person is more experienced with rolling.

PRECAUTIONS AND CONTRAINDICATIONS
(adapted after Soleway, 2001)

Ball rolling and other types of muscle and fascial release techniques are not appropriate for everyone. Be careful with certain body areas or medical conditions.

Ball sizes

Caution areas

- Tailbone.
- Floating ribs (11 and 12).
- Lower tip of the breastbone.
- Upper neck and mid-neck.
- Over the hip bone (bursae sac).

Conditions and diseases not appropriate for small ball rolling

- Malignancy.
- Fractures.
- Systemic or localized infections.
- Open wounds or stitches.
- Acute rheumatoid arthritis.
- Osteoporosis.

GETTING STARTED

Use the ball and simply roll along or across muscles that need to be stretched. Keep in mind that a tight muscle is rarely an isolated case. For example, if you have a tight iliotibial band, it is likely that your hamstrings, quadriceps, and gluteal muscles will also be tight, so use the ball along many muscles to get maximal benefit. Rolling around the pelvis is important as it is the attachment site for numerous muscles. The fascia and connective tissue around the lumbar spine and the sacrum are often associated with lower body muscular dysfunction, so make sure to get to the insertion points of the muscles and tendons.

Gluteus and piriformis

Gluteal muscles and piriformis

- Start at the sacrum and roll out toward the hip.
- Stay on spots of increased tenderness and hold until you feel the tension release.

Hamstrings and calf

- Roll along length of hamstrings and calf.
- Support weight with arms.

- If you have wrist or shoulder problems that make it difficult, you can place the ball on a low bench.

Hamstring on the floor or seated   **Calf**

Iliotibial band

- Roll along the length of the ITB, starting in the buttocks and rolling to the knee.
- Hold on spots of increased tenderness.
- Also move perpendicularly across the iliotibial band.
- If you have wrist or shoulder problems that make it difficult, you can place the ball against the wall.
- Avoid the hip bone area as there is a bursae over top of it that can be irritated with direct pressure.

Iliotibial band and buttock. *On the floor or against the wall.*

Quadriceps

- Support weight with arms and roll down along length of muscles.

- Angle body differently to get lateral versus medial quadriceps and adductors.

- If you have wrist or shoulder problems that make it difficult, you can place the ball on a low bench.

Deep hip flexors (iliopsoas and hip rotators)

- Deflate the myoball so it is a little softer (as shown).

- Lie on your stomach with a pillow in front of your hip bones.

- Place the myoball just medial to your anterior hip bone (groin area).

- Lie flat down and relax into the ball to release the tissue.

- You can add to this stretch by having your physio, parents, or training partner apply gentle rhythmical rocking pressure in a longitudinal direction up your lower back para-vertebral muscles at the lumbar 1 and 2 vertebral level (approximately one hand width above the hip bone).

Quadriceps. On the floor and on a bench.

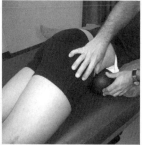

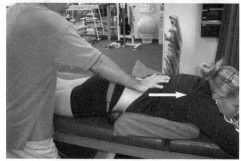

Deep hip flexors. Deflated ball, ball placement, and rocking pressure by a partner.

Training Notes and Precautions for Deep Hip Flexors
This area of the groin contains blood vessels and nerves and is very sensitive. Ensure you soften the ball and stop immediately if you feel pain or any tingling or numbness as you may be putting abnormal pressure on the nerves.

Hip adductors

- Support weight with arms and roll down along length of muscles.
- Use a phone book or block under the ball to allow more pressure to be applied.
- Angle body differently to get to different parts of the adductors.

Hip adductors

Foot

- Step and roll on the ball to massage the muscles of the foot.
- You may find a tennis ball works better.

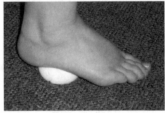

Foot

Lumbar and thoracic spine musculature

- Have the ball just to the outside of your spine and gently roll up and down and perpendicular to the spine.
- Roll up to the bottom of your shoulder blade.

Posterior shoulder and anterior shoulder musculature

- Some people feel it is best to roll against a wall for the muscles of the shoulder.
- Move your arm to different angles to actively stretch the muscles at the same time as rolling.

Lumbar and thoracic spine

Posterior shoulder   *Anterior shoulder*

Forearm and upper arm

- Place the ball against the wall or on a table.
- Stretch out the muscles of the forearm flexors and extensors by sliding your arm back and forth on the ball.

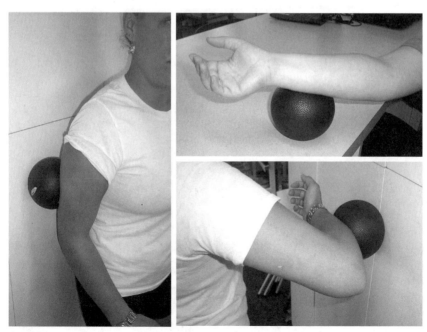

Forearm and upper arm (wall and table)

Cervical spine musculature

- Some people find rolling on the neck muscles too uncomfortable.
- Try a larger ball first for comfort and work the muscles and the vertebrae to soften the area.
- You can also deflate your ball a little to make it more comfortable.

Small ball release work is a fantastic way for coaches and athletes to self-manage tight muscles and stiffened areas, especially when no professional help is available from a physiotherapist, massage therapist, trainer, or other therapist. The balls work well for hard to stretch areas (iliotibial band) and for muscles that are prone to tightening with exercise (hip flexors). Limitations with the ball do exist and should not be substituted for the hands of an experienced therapist.

References

Brukner, P., Khan, K. (2002). Chapter 6, Principles of injury prevention. In: *Clinical Sports Medicine* 103. Roseville, Australia: McGraw Hill Australia Pty Ltd.

Clews, W. (1990). *Sports Massage and Stretching: Self Massage Techniques for all Sporting Activities*. Bantam

Granter, R. (2002). Principles of treatment. In: Brukner & Khan (Eds). *Clinical Sports Medicine (Revised 2nd edition)* 151. Roseville: McGraw Hill Australia Pty Ltd.

Juett, T. (1988). Myofascial release: an introduction for the patient. *Phys. Ther.* 7(41): 7-8.

Soleway, C. (2001). *Body Therapy—Small Ball Release Program*. Longmont, Colorado: Ball Dynamics International. (website-wwww.fitball.com)

Tarnopolsky, L.J., MacDougall, J.D., Atkinson, S.A., Tarnopolsky, M.A., Sutton J.R. (1990). Gender differences in substrates for endurance exercise. *J. Appl. Physiol.* 68(1): 302-8.

Travell, J.G., Simons, D.G. (1998). *Myofascial Pain and Dysfunction—The Trigger Point Manual, Vol. 2. (2nd edition)*. Maryland: Williams & Wilkins.

Witkorsson-Moller, M., Oberg, B., Ekstrand, J., Gillquist, J. (1983). Effects of warming up, massage and stretching on range of motion and muscle strength in the lower extremity. *Am. J. Sports Med.* 11(4): 249-52.

Additional Reading

Lehn, C. & Prentice, W.E. (1994). Massage. In: W.E. Prentice (Ed). *Therapeutic Modalities in Sports Medicine (3rd edition)*. St. Louis, MO: Mosby-Year Book Inc.

Sirdevan, M. (2004). Myofascial release ball therapy. In: C. Petersen, *Fit to Ski: Practical Tips to Optimize Dryland Training and Ski Performance* 165-168. Vancouver, Canada: Fit to Play/CPC Physio. Corp.

Zake, Y. and Golden, S. *The Ultimate Body Rolling Workout*. New York: Broadway Books.

Chapter Thirty-One

High Performance Recovery Tips and Strategies

Carl Petersen

One key to the success of tennis players and other athletes is not just in how hard they train off and on court, but also in how well they recover from training, playing, environment, and travel. With the pressures of work, school, family, and travel it is difficult if not impossible to ensure that proper recovery guidelines are followed after and between training, playing, and competing.

Today's players have to be in great shape and recover well to be competitive on a consistent basis. Most elite athletes are exposed to very demanding training schedule. Under these circumstances, the athletes may be pushed beyond physiological and psychological norms which may result in decreased function (Bompa, 1985).

Too much physical training and too little rest and recovery after hard workouts causes a great deal of stress on muscles, joints, and bones. Further stresses such as worries about money, fear of failure, or conflicts with friends, teachers, or teammates can lead to irreversible damage (Hawley & Schoene, 2003).

Different stressors include training, practice, travel, lifestyle, environmental, and health stressors. Each athlete has a different ability to cope with each stressor: one may cope with training stresses easily but nutritional stress poorly, another the opposite.

Learning survival strategies to prevent injuries is far better than having to learn how to treat them. The effectiveness of any recovery program depends on a good working relationship between the coach, physician, physiotherapist, nutritionist, psychologist, physiologist, and other health professionals (Weinberg, 1988).

The subjective benefits of utilizing recovery techniques have been known by athletes and coaches for years, and the science of recovery is rapidly catching up with art. Recovery is a generic term used specifically with reference to the restoration of physiological systems and regeneration of psychological parameters that have been altered during activity.

Developing an effective post-training and competition routine is very important as it helps players recover physically and psychologically. Recovery sessions must be incorporated into sports-specific training programs. This approach to recovery and regeneration enhances athletic development and contributes to optimal performance.

Players and coaches must constantly strive to find the optimal balance between training and recovery. Some athletes work out or play even when they are sick, and they sometimes do too much, too fast, too hard, and too soon, risking problems associated with over-training or overuse injuries that impair optimal function.

Do not commence heavy training until you have fully recovered from previous training, competition, travel, injury, or illness. Allow adequate time for recovery, and modify training for optimal taper and peak if getting ready for an important tournament. The best treatment for overstress, overtraining, or overreaching is prevention with a well-planned daily, weekly, monthly, and yearly schedule that includes use of a variety of high performance recovery tips and strategies. These are discussed in detail in the rest of the chapter.

Rs of Recovery (adapted after Petersen & Nittinger, 2003)
- Rehydrate
- Refuel
- Realign the body
- Recovery workouts
- Regain and maintain muscle length
- Reset your balance clock
- Reconnect the core
- Release the soft tissue
- Rest (active and passive)

- Relax
- Refresh with variety
- Replay your training or match
- Reinvigorate with recovery menu
- Record and replan

REHYDRATE

Drink plenty of water or clear fluid. Try clear juice or sports drinks diluted with water—the minimum is 0.5–1.0 quarts per hour during training. The goal is to have light colored urine. The harder, higher, and hotter conditions you train or play in, the more you need to drink. Prehydration and immediate rehydration are key. Losing as little as two percent of body weight through sweat can impair an athlete's ability to perform due to low blood volume and less than optimal utilization of nutrients and oxygen. Also, younger players may need to be more vigilant about hydration

Hydration

strategies as dehydration seems to be more detrimental to children than to adults (Bar-Or, 2001). Refer to Chapter 14 on hydration for more information.

REFUEL

Ensure that adequate nutrition (carbohydrate fuel) is consumed post-training. Adequate supplies of glycogen in the muscle and in the liver are needed to support the energy demands of the player and promote recovery for the next training session. Dietary carbohydrate is the primary source for the body to manufacture glucose (Coyle, 1995). Since glycogen stores take 24–48 hours to replenish, they must be replaced daily (Costill, 1992). Each gram of glycogen is stored with approximately three grams of water, so ensure adequate hydration to ensure maximum glycogen synthesis.

There is a window of opportunity within the first 20 minutes after strenuous exercise to replenish muscle fuel stores at a faster rate than if carbohydrate intake is delayed for longer. Small amounts of protein taken with carbohydrates before, during, and after hard training help minimize muscle protein breakdown as a result of heavy workloads. Athletes should consume between 1.2 and 1.5 g/kg body weight of simple carbohydrates as soon as possible after exercise (Costill, 1992). Be sure to check the label on the drinks and sports bars so you know what you are consuming. Refer to Chapter 13 on nutrition for further information.

REALIGN THE BODY

Most training and sports like tennis are asymmetrical in nature and can torque the body's muscle and fascial systems leading to an imbalance in length and strength of muscles and tendons. While upper body development is asymmetrical in tennis, symmetrical strength and flexibility of the legs and lower torso are necessary for optimum court mobility. The flexed posture of competitive sport further adds to this imbalance. Malalignment also puts athletes at increased risk of injury. (Schamberger, 2002). Sport medicine and therapy personnel must recognize malalignment and postural syndromes and ensure that the daily training plans and rehabilitation protocols address these syndromes in a proactive manner. Refer to Chapter 25 on malalignment for further information.

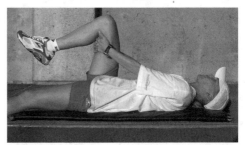

6 X 6 Corrective exercise

Spinal roll

RECOVERY WORKOUTS

The utilization of recovery techniques must become habitual and be performed daily (Bompa, 1985). Studies suggest that light aerobic exercise following anaerobic training (e.g., sprints) might facilitate recovery of force or speed/power by increasing lactic acid removal, thus possibly helping restore normal calcium levels within muscle fibers (Signorile, 1993).

To help flush out the lactic acid and other waste products that build up in the muscle during training and play, try the following cycle routine. Use light resistance and cycle at 85–90 RPM (revolutions per minute) at a heart rate of 100–115 beats per minute for 15–20 minutes. At higher pedaling rates there is a greater recruitment of slow twitch fibers. Since slow twitch fibers are more resistant to fatigue, a higher pedaling rate will prove advantageous and less likely to cause premature fatigue (Hagan, 1992).

Other modalities such as pool running or walking can be used in the absence of a bike. See Chapter 8, Water Recovery Workouts, for more information.

Stationary cycle

Water run

REGAIN AND MAINTAIN MUSCLE LENGTH

Performing static and facilitated stretches optimizes muscle and tendon length post-training. Players should develop, with the aid of a physical trainer or physiotherapist, a stretching routine that is performed consistently (Reque, 2003).

Hold-relax and contract-relax PNF techniques have been shown to be more effective than just static stretching (Enoka, 1994; Lucas, 1984). PNF techniques may be relaxing as players can lie down and perform no work while being stretched passively. This can be an effective means of post-exercise relaxation (Reque, 2003). In a recent study, static stretches prior to exercise did not prevent lower extremity overuse injuries, but additional static stretches after training and before bed resulted in 50 percent fewer injuries occurring (Hartig & Henderson, 1999). The state of tension in other muscle groups should be assessed on a daily basis and new stretches added to ensure that a good length-

Conform stretch hamstring   *Conform quad stretch*

tension balance is maintained in all muscle groups responsible for on-court performance. See Chapter 3, Smart Stretching Guidelines, for more information.

RESET YOUR BALANCE CLOCK

Balance training is a fundamental component of functional mobility and dynamic sports activity and should be part of everyone's daily fitness routine, whether destined for the pro circuit or not. Physical therapists and fitness coaches have long known the benefits of balance and body awareness exercises in rehabilitating injuries and in sport-specific training. Fatigue associated with hard training impairs proprioceptive mechanisms and may directly trigger nociceptors (Bruker & Khan, 2002). This combination of fatigue, impaired

proprioception, and potential inhibition due to pain make it imperative to try and reset the three-dimensional balance clock of the joints before being put in a potential injury situation.

Reset your balance clock with some drills using wobble boards, foam rolls, rolled towels, or the Dynamic (Skier's) Edge. Most gyms will have some balance equipment available. By training on an unstable surface, balance reactions and coordination

Balance training with the wobble board

are trained at a subconscious level, facilitating these reactions to become automatic. This helps to prevent injury and improve sport performance. Refer to Chapter 5, Balance Training, for further information.

RECONNECT THE CORE

Upper and lower core stability provide a stable three-dimensional power platform for the extremities to work off during multi-planar, multi-joint, and multi-muscle activities that involve acceleration and deceleration forces. Real life is three dimensional, and the activities of daily living and sporting activities challenge the body to dynamically react to the moving, changing environment in which we live and play.

As a tennis player, you need a strong core to maintain balance, stability, and alignment as you generate power. When moving laterally, the core muscles and hip stabilizers work functionally to control movement. Numerous muscles attach to the lower core's lumbo-pelvic-hip complex and spine and the upper core's spine, ribs, and scapular region. When activated and recruited properly, the stability of the upper and lower core forms the foundation or base to all movements. Dr. Ben Kibler defines core stability as, "the ability to control the trunk over the planted leg to allow optimum production, transfer, and control of force and motion to the terminal limbs." This is obviously something all tennis players need.

The first muscle to be recruited prior to any upper and/or lower body movements is the tranversus abdominus. Normally it fires in a pre-anticipation of any movement, but with dysfunction there is a timing delay, and studies have shown that without efficient and optimal recruitment, subsequent spinal dysfunction can occur (Richardson & Jull, 1995). Reconnecting the core with simple exercises that either close or partially close the kinetic chain for both

Pony Back. *Kneeling on all fours, allow the back to arch down like an old pony. Exhale and arch back up to neutral. Hold for eight seconds and repeat eight times.*

upper and lower extremities helps increase the three-dimensional core stability and ensure optimal recruitment, timing, performance, and injury prevention. Refer to Chapter 6, Upper and Lower Core Training, for further information.

Squat with ball and band. *Squating while squeezing a ball between your knees and pulling a stretch cord apart combines the upper and lower core. The legs perform a closed kinetic chain squat as the stretch band partially closes the upper extremity kinetic chain to improve three-dimensional core strength.*

RELEASE THE SOFT TISSUE

Post-training soft tissue release is a positive step towards relieving symptoms of trigger points, delayed onset muscle soreness, and muscle tension. Active trigger points that result from heavy training may reduce muscle strength. These problems can impair training and competition and can progress to injury if they are not resolved (Bruker & Khan, 2002). The effectiveness of massage or soft tissue techniques as an adjunct to stretching in order to facilitate flexibility have been demonstrated in the past (Witkorson-Moller, 1983). They have also been shown to promote mood enhancement and feelings of well-being by reducing tension, depression, anger, fatigue, anxiety, and confusion (Weinberg & Jackson, 1988).

The incidence of delayed onset muscle soreness is different with sex (gender), as females seem to be less susceptible to it (Tarnoplosky, 1990). Practical experience dictates that both men and women benefit from soft tissue release. Post-training or competition massage may enhance recovery by promoting the removal of metabolites, while at the same time helping the athlete relax or promote passive rest (sleep).

There are many well known soft tissue techniques used in treating sports injuries, including longitudinal stroking, strip and stretch or active release technique, transverse friction, transverse gliding, sustained myofascial tension, vibrational techniques, and digital ischemic pressure. Utilizing a variety of techniques based on an athlete's preference and experience can help promote recovery. Depending on facilities and expertise available, the post-training soft tissue work can be done either by a professional or by a training partner, parent, coach, or by the athletes themselves. For example, soft tissue techniques can be done on the upper and lower extremities when in the whirlpool. Self-massage can also be done in a relaxing atmosphere when players are in the bath, showering, watching television, or in the hot tub (Clews, 1990). These techniques combined with the pressure massage of the hot tub jets are especially good for the feet, hands, forearms, and rest of the upper and lower extremities, hips, and torso.

The myofascial system has received increased attention in the past few years and is an intricate system that surrounds all the muscles, nerves, and blood vessels in the body. It is a complex web-like system that separates muscles into compartments, and dysfunction is common. Because this system wraps around each muscle fibril in the body, it can become twisted and snagged in different places. It is like a nylon stocking surrounding your muscle, and with dysfunction, this stocking can become all twisted.

For years therapists and other health professionals have suggested to patients *Myofascial ball release—hamstring*
to use a tennis ball to release sore, tight muscles. Recently, in addition to using a tennis ball, small myofascial release balls are being used to stretch and soften tight muscles. Refer to Chapter 30 on myofascial ball release for further information.

Small ball body rolling is a great way to stretch and release tight muscles. The

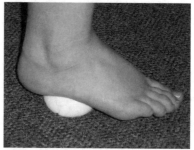

Myofascial ball release—foot

concept is very simple: Use the ball to "iron out" tight areas. By rolling on the ball along the muscle and at different angles to the muscle, you are trying to "untwist" the myofascial system. The fascia system responds best when gentle pressure is applied and sustained for more than two minutes. If an area is especially tight or sensitive, use the ball as a trigger point release tool and stay on the sore spot (Sirdevan, 2004).

REST—ACTIVE (CROSS-TRAINING)

Tennis players spend many hours per day pounding around the courts, so reducing the stress on weight-bearing soft tissues and joints using cross-training techniques makes sense. To help prevent injury and promote recovery, use techniques that are relatively nonweight bearing, including cycling, stairclimber, elliptical trainer, and water workouts, to maintain and improve aerobic and anaerobic fitness.

Whether you run in the pool, do pool exercises, or swim, the water offers many benefits to help keep you powered up and injury free, whether you are a professional athlete or hobby player. Water workouts are a refreshing way to change your usual routine, and they are an easy way to transfer land-based workouts into a nonweight-bearing environment.

Water run

Water is denser than air and supplies three-dimensional resistance that is 12 times greater than air for strength-type movements, but it provides the buoyancy necessary to make energy system training nonweight bearing. Benefits of water workouts include having your three-dimensional core working full time to maintain balance and upright position. Water also encourages a shorter recovery time than a similar workout on land, and the water's buoyancy, pressure, and cooling effect (provided you are not running in the hot tub) allow for a faster recovery time (Sirdevan & Petersen, 2003).

REST—PASSIVE

Rest is one of the most important principles of training. It is essential for coaches and athletes to realize that the body requires a certain period of time in order to recover from training-related fatigue or stress (Marion, 1995). Sleep is probably the best form of rest to aid recovery. Experts suggest that we need a minimum of eight hours per night. But high performance athletes may require up to 10–12 hours of sleep a night (Hawley & Schoene, 2003). Lack of sleep can be a potential problem. But be sure to check with your physician if your sleeping pattern changes as you may be sick or over-trained. The last time most people, including athletes, had a really good sleep was when they were still in school. As we mature there is always a reason to go to bed later, including text messaging, computers, homework, and television.

Sleeping

To ensure a good nights sleep, minimize caffeine in the late afternoon and avoid excessive alcohol. Also avoid hot showers and heavy exercise just before bedtime because a higher than normal body temperature makes it more difficult to sleep. Avoid long afternoon naps and try sticking to a schedule by getting up at the same time each day to avoid becoming sleep lagged. Refer to Chapter 29 Sleep Smarts for Recovery for further information.

RELAX

It is important to provide adequate time for recovery when planning the training program. This should include recovery days or rest days in the weekly training cycle and "easy weeks" in the longer term cycle (Brukner & Khan, 2002)

Following training one acquires fatigue. The greater the level of fatigue, the greater the training after-effects (i.e., low recovery rate, poor coordination, decrease in speed and power of muscle contraction, etc.). Normal physiological fatigue is often accentuated by a strong emotional fatigue, especially following competitions, from which it takes even longer to recover (Bompa, 1985).

After or between practice sessions and matches, give the body's systems a chance to relax. Learning to recover and relax is a great advantage for optimizing high performance. When you are in competitions, being calm and relaxed in tight situations are two of your best mental weapons. As long as you are in a relaxed state of mind, nothing can stress you. If you realize that something starts to stress you, you recognize it and have a technique or strategy in mind to respond to it. This will help you regain your physical and mental strength to train or compete at a high level again. It allows you to recharge the batteries or refill the tank.

There are a lot of different ways to relax and everybody has individual preferences. It is best to combine a couple of the favorite relaxation techniques and get into a personal routine.

- Court serendipity. Make no plans for the rest of the day. Instead have an adventure and explore the environment or the city you are staying in.
- Slow life down a little. Drive a little more slowly if you usually drive fast. Spend a few extra minutes listening to music in your car before rushing out. Eat more slowly and savor your food.
- Physical relaxation can include sauna, slow running or walking, massage, progressive muscle relaxation, yoga, stretching, or sleeping.
- Mental relaxation can include breathing exercises, meditation, or autogenic training.
- Emotional relaxation can include listening to music, daydreaming, or drinking your favorite beverage.
- Always shower after training and on-court practice to wash away the day.

Shower

The goals of physical, mental, and emotional relaxation techniques are to:

- Slow down your breathing.
- Slow down your heart rate.
- Decrease muscle tension.
- Relax your muscles.
- Gain control of your thoughts.
- Turn negative feelings and emotions into positive ones.
- Produce positive hormones.
- Block out everything that's interrupting you.
- Become aware of your body.

Refer to Chapter 20 for relaxation exercises to assist in relaxing the mind as well as the body and decrease stress related fight or flight chemicals. These exercises will also assist in acute and chronic stress management.

REFRESH WITH VARIETY

By using a variety of exercises or drills, sessions are made more enjoyable, and players are less likely to become stale and bored and more likely to improve performance in the given area being trained (Chandler & Chandler, 2003). From personal growth, enjoyment, and injury preventive perspectives, any training adage along the lines of "train, train, train" or "tennis, tennis, tennis" is undesirable (Reid, 2003).

The advantages of refreshing with variety are obvious because the adverse training changes are to an extent muscle specific, and daily hard workouts are less likely to result in specific musculo-skeletal injury when different muscle groups are worked out in different situations.

Keep the recovery sessions refreshing by using the variety of tools and techniques that are available to you to aid recovery. Also, take advantage of nontraining opportunities that present themselves, such as dining, the arts, or culture.

Recovery walk on beach

Variety benefits

- Variety is the spice of life, training, and on-court.

- Variety will help keep your body and mind balanced. Try taking a recovery walk on the beach.

- Variety increases fun and improves performance.

- Variety prevents boredom and maximizes the potential for improvement.

- Variety from day to day is important to allow recovery from day to day (Chandler & Chandler, 2003).

It is extremely important that young athletes (6–10 years of age) are exposed to a wide variety of different sport activities to ensure that the FUNdamentals of Agility, Balance, Coordination, and Speed (ABCs) are included in their long-term development (Balyi,1999).

Common activities to add variety

- Gymnastics, dance, and rhythm sports.
- Field sports such as soccer, ultimate, touch rugby, and field hockey.
- Pool workouts such as pool running, jumping, and swimming.
- Court sports such as volleyball, basketball, and netball.
- Pilates and various yoga types.
- Boxing and martial arts such as judo or tai chi.
- Cycling and inline skating.
- Other racquet sports such as squash, racquetball, badminton, and table tennis.
- Track and field sports.

REPLAY YOUR TRAINING OR MATCH

Replaying your training or match is a useful way to evaluate performance and aid in psychological and emotional recovery post-training or post-match. Some of the best lessons are those that you learn from a lost match. That's why you always have to sit down and replay and rethink the good and bad situations, points, and choices you made. A systematic and constructive approach that focuses on "process" rather than outcomes can provide players with achievable performance goals that they can manage and monitor (Hogg, 2002). It lets you objectively evaluate your performance and plan what changes are needed in training, practice, or match play.

Post-match analysis

Replay tips

- Make note of both the negative and positive aspects of your game.
- Work on the negative ones and don't allow them to affect you.

- Move on and look at the positive aspects of your game.

- Start a training diary and take short notes on what you practiced, what went well, what was critical, and what you have to work on in the next few days or weeks.

- You can only improve your game if you recognize your weaknesses, work on them, and stick to your strengths.

REINVIGORATE WITH RECOVERY MENU

Coaches and athletes alike need to be made aware of the importance of restoration and regeneration following heavy workloads and how to use the equipment, facilities, and modalities available to facilitate recovery (Petersen, 2005). These include adequate warm down; the use of whirlpools, spas, and massage; as well as nutritional and psychological techniques (Brukner & Khan, 2002).

Researchers have shown that when you compare lactate clearances following (1) passive rest, (2) light exercising (active recovery), and (3) contrast immersion techniques, that lactate levels were recovered equally fast by using either the contrast water immersion protocol or the active recovery protocol. Lactate recovery following passive rest was significantly slower (Calder, 2003). In addition, researchers have also demonstrated that underwater massaging (using the jets in a spa) following plyometric training helped athletes to maintain explosive leg power. In contrast, passive rest (doing nothing) after such training resulted in a significant reduction in leg power (Viitasalo et al., 1995).

It therefore makes sense that in contrast to passive rest, athletes might be best advised to use a combination of the three techniques—active recovery, soft-tissue release, and contrast immersion. Recovery workouts and soft-tissue techniques were discussed earlier in this chapter. Several contrast immersion techniques follow.

Contrast Immersion Techniques

Recovery sessions provide an opportunity for both player and coach to start to unwind, recover, and prepare for the next day. It is important for coaches to recognize that they also need to recover as they undertake large amounts of physical work and stress (Calder, 2003). The relaxed atmosphere fosters a good interchange of ideas that can be implemented into the training structure.

Try one or more of the following recovery techniques. Alternate stimulation with hot/cold makes you feel perky and pepped up and helps wash out waste products and metabolites and brings oxygen to the fatigued muscles.

- **Showers: use them to cleanse pores.**

  Shower promptly after training to clean the skin and help flush out waste products. Remember the skin is the largest organ in the body. Repeat often—especially on hotter days

Shower

- **Hot & Cold (A)**

  ‣ Hot (comfortable) x 2 min.

  ‣ Cold (as possible) x 10 sec.

  ‣ Repeat 6–10 times.

- **Hot & Cold (B)**

  ‣ Cold (as able to stand) x 1 min.

  ‣ Hot (as comfortable) x 30 sec.

  ‣ Repeat 8–10 times.

Ice and whirlpool

- **Water Pressure (Hose)**

  ‣ Cold Water hose—45 sec. each leg and 30 sec. each arm.

  ‣ Warm Shower—30 sec. each leg and 20 sec. each arm.

  ‣ Repeat 5–7 times.

- **Sauna/Cold Plunge (use at least one hour after training)**

  ‣ Shower warm-cool 3–5 min. (towel dry).

Water pressure

  ‣ Sauna x 7 min (RH 10–30% and temp 80–90 deg. Centigrade).

  ‣ Cold plunge or cold shower x 15–30 sec.

  ‣ Rest (feet up) x 5 min.

  ‣ Repeat x 3 before a day off from playing or training.

  ‣ Repeat x 1 before training or competition day.

  ‣ Finish with warm shower 3–5 min.

Sauna

RECORD AND REPLAN

It is important for the athlete and coach to monitor the training program carefully. A training diary should record details of all training sessions, rest days, amount of sleep, and early morning heart rate (Brukner & Khan, 2002).

Keeping a training log is an easy way to track your progress and watch for symptoms of overtraining. Let your coach and team doctor know early in the process if you have symptoms of overtraining. Prevention is the best cure (Hawley & Schoene, 2003). Refer to Chapter 22 for the Fit to Play™ training diary.

After taking time to follow both the physical and psychological high performance recovery tips and strategies outlined in this chapter, replan your daily, weekly, and monthly training, playing, competition, and recovery strategies to help you stay Fit to Play™ and optimize training and performance.

CONCLUSION

Training and competition fatigue experienced by players is a necessary part of the adaptive process. The challenge for most coaches and players is to identify which specific capacities are fatigued and then select appropriate recovery strategies to restore the player to a normal functioning state. Training for and playing tennis are both physically and mentally demanding, and recovery sessions must be incorporated into sports-specific training programs. Without the appropriate recovery techniques and time, the player will not adapt to the stress of training and will possibly experience overtraining or overuse injuries. (Chandler, Kibler, 2003).

The process of recovery depends on many factors, and a therapist who knows and understands these can selectively apply techniques and monitor on an individual basis to facilitate recovery and regeneration. Athletes, coaches, therapists, and parents all need to be more aware of the importance of restoration and regeneration following heavy workloads and how best to use the equipment, facilities, and modalities available to facilitate recovery.

Tennis Specific Recovery Tips

1) **If you arrive after a long flight over multiple time zones three days before your first match:**
   - Be tough on the day you arrive and do not nap as it will only take longer to adapt.
   - Do your jet-lag protocol (see Chapter 17).
   - Work on your core muscles and stretch your hip flexors, as you have just been sitting for a long time.
   - Stick to your normal routine for breakfast, lunch, and dinner times.
   - Wake up at the same time in the morning and go to bed at the same time as you would go to bed at home.
   - Eat light and drink lots of water or clear fluids.
   - Take it easy during your first practice session. Just try to get some touch, feel comfortable, and go through all your shots.
   - As soon as you feel comfortable, pick up the intensity and play out a few points to help prepare for match play.

2) **If you have traveled all day in the train or car:**
   - Try to have some light snacks before hitting or working out.
   - Don't rush onto the court. You won't enjoy practicing after sitting all day.
   - Make sure you loosen up your stiff muscles well before hitting. You need to activate your system and warm up well.
   - Eat a high carbohydrate meal at night.

3) **If your match ends late and you must play first on the next day:**
   - Make sure you do your post-match routine, no matter how late it is. Running and stretching will help you to shorten your recovery. It is easier to deal with a little less sleep than with stiff muscles.
   - Take some time to relax (use relaxation techniques, hot bath, read, music, etc.). Your system will need some time to wind down after a long and late match.
   - Try to eat a high carbohydrate meal that is not heavy (plain pasta), otherwise you might have trouble falling asleep.
   - Drink lots of water and clear fluids.

4)   If your match is interrupted by rain:

- Make sure you stay warm.
- Change out of wet clothes and put some pants and a sweatshirt on.
- Depending on how long the rain break is, make sure you're ready to go on court warmed-up.
- Stay loose, stretch, walk around, and do some jumps or skip rope.
- Try to find a quiet area and focus on your match. If you're down, take the chance to think about how to get yourself into the match again.
- If you are ahead in the match, make sure you stay focused and stick to your game plan.

5)   If your match is delayed for hours because of rain or long matches:

- Find somebody who checks the court you're supposed to play on (coach, friend, parents) and ask them to call you when the first set is over or the rain stopped.
- Relax, look for a quiet area, and try to focus on your match.
- If you have hours before you go on court, keep yourself busy without losing too much energy (i.e., don't go shopping or sight-seeing before a match; watching a movie or reading would be a better choice).
- Follow your pre-match warm-up routine.

6)   If your match is interrupted and you have to continue the next day:

- Follow your post-training and play recovery routine.
- Eat a high carbohydrate dinner and drink lots of water and clear fluids.
- Analyze your match with your coach; if you are alone, think about what happened so far, what went really well, what was not good, what are your opponent's strengths and what are his/her weaknesses, etc.
- Make an action plan for the next day; figure out what you have to do when you are up or down to win the match.
- Next morning, do a good dynamic warm-up and pre-match preparation routine.
- Make sure you are really well warmed up both mentally and physically because the match may already be half over. You have no time to ease into it.

Part 6 | Structured Recovery

References

Balyi, I. (1999). *Alpine Integration Model (AIM)*. Alpine Canada Alpin HPAC : 12.

Bompa, T. (1985). Theory and Methodology of Training–The Key to Athletic Performance. Dubuque: Kendall/Hunt.

Bar-Or O. (2001). Nutritional considerations for the child athlete. *Can. J. Appl. Physiol.* 26:186-191.

Brukner, P., & Khan, K. (2002). *Principles of Injury Prevention in Clinical Sports Medicine*. Roseville: McGraw Hill Australia Pty Ltd., :103-4.

Calder, A. (2003). Recovery. In: M. Reid, A. Quinn & M. Crespo (Eds), *Strength and Conditioning for Tennis*. London. ITF.

Chandler, T.J., Kibler, W.B. (2003). Training principles. In: M. Reid, A. Quinn, and M. Crespo (Eds), *Strength and Conditioning for Tennis*. London: ITF.

Clews, W. (1990) *Sports Massage and Stretching–Self Massage Techniques for All Sporting Activities*. Bantam.

Coyle, E.F. (1995). Substrate utilization during exercise in active people. *Am. J Clin. Nutr.* 61: S968-S97

Costill, D.L., Hargreaves, M. (1992). Carbohydrate nutrition and fatigue. *Sports Med.* 13(2): 86-92.

Enoka, R.M. (1994). *Neuromechanical Basis of Kinesiology*. Champaign, IL: Human Kinetics.

Hagan, R.D., Weiss, S.E., Raven, P.B. (1992). Effect of pedal rate on cardiorespiratory response during continuous exercise. *Med. Sci. Sports Exerc.* 24:1088-1095.

Hartig, D.E., Henderson, J.M. (1999). Increasing hamstring flexibility decreases lower extremity injuries in military basic trainees. *Am. J. Sports Med.* 27(2): 173-176.

Hawley, C.J., Schoene, R.B. (2003). Overtraining syndrome: a guide to diagnosis, treatment, and prevention. *Physician Sportsmed.* 31(6).

Hogg, J.M. (2002). Debriefing: A means to increasing recovery and subsequent competition. In: M. Kelleman (Ed), *Enhancing Recovery–Preventing Underperformance in Athletes*. Champaign, IL: Human Kinetics.

Kibler, B. (2006). Personal communication.

Lucas, R.C., Koslow, R. (1984). Comparative study of static, dynamic and proprioceptive neuromuscular facilitation stretching techniques on flexibility. *Percept. Mot. Skills* 58:615-618.

Marion, A. (1995). Overtraining and sport performance. *SPORTS, Coaches Report.*.

Petersen, C. & Nittinger, N. (2003). *Fit to Play Tennis: Practical Tips to Optimize Training & Performance (1st edition)*. Vancouver, Canada: Fit to Play/CPC Physio Corp. 108-116.

Petersen, C. (2005). Fit to play–practical tips for faster recovery (part 2). *Medicine & Science in Tennis.* 10(2), August 2005.

Reid, M. Quinn, A. & Crespo, M. (2003). Cross training alternatives. In: M. Reid, A. Quinn, and M. Crespo (Eds), *Strength and Conditioning for Tennis*. London: ITF.

Reque, J. (2003). Flexibility. In: M. Reid, A. Quinn, and M. Crespo (Eds). *Strength and Conditioning for Tennis*. London: ITF.

Richardson, C.A., Jull, G.A. (1995). Muscle control-pain control. What exercise would you prescribe? *Manual Therapy* 1995;1:2-10.

Schamberger, W. (2002). *The Malalignment Syndrome–Implications for Medicine and Sport*. London: Churchill Livingstone.

Signorile, J.F., Ingalls, C., Tremblay, L.M. (1993). The effects of active and passive recovery on short-term high intensity power output. *Can. J. Appl. Physiol.* 18(1):31-42.

Sirdevan, M. (2004). Myofascial release ball therapy. In: Petersen, C. *Fit to Ski: Practical Tips to Optimize Dryland Training and Ski Performance*. Vancouver: Fit to Play/CPC Physio. Corp. 165-168.

Sirdevan, M. & Petersen, C. (2003). Water recovery workouts. In: C. Petersen and N. Nittinger. *Fit to Play Tennis: Practical Tips to Optimize Training and Performance*. Vancouver: Fit to Play, CPC Physio Corp. pages:121-125

Tarnopolsky, L.J., MacDougall, J.D., Atkinson, S.A., Tarnopolsky, M.A., Sutton, J.R. (1990). Gender differences in substrates for endurance exercise. *J. Appl. Physiol.* 68(1):302-8.

Viitasalo, J.T., Niemala, K., Kaappola, R., Korjus, T., Levola, M., Mononen, H.V., Rusko, H.K. & Takala, T.E. S. (1995). Warm underwater water-jet massage improves recovery from intense physical exercise. *European Journal of Applied Physiology* 71: 428-43

Weinberg, R., Jackson, A, Kolodny, K. (1988). The relationship of massage and exercise to mood enhancement. *Sport Psychol.* 2:202-211.

Witkorsson-Moller, M., Oberg, B., Ekstrand, J., Gillquist, J. (1983). Effects of warming up, massage and stretching on range of motion and muscle strength in the lower extremity. *Am. J. Sports Med.* 11(4):249-52.

Index

Page numbers followed by "f" denote figures and "b" denote boxes

Index

Index

Index

Index

Index

About
the Authors

PRINCIPLE AUTHORS

Carl Petersen, BPE, BSc(PT), MCPA

Carl is a partner and director of high performance training at City Sports & Physiotherapy Clinics in Vancouver,
Canada (www.citysportsphysio.com). He is a physiotherapist and fitness coach with a variety of athletes ranging
from elite juniors to professionals on the men's and
women's tennis tours and World Cup Ski Circuit. He was
the physiotherapist for Alpine Canada Alpin at the
Olympic Winter Games in Calgary, Albertville, and
Lillehammer. As well, he has been the director of sport
medicine and science for Alpine Canada Alpin and traveled on the World Cup Ski Circuit from 1984-2003 as a
physiotherapist and fitness coach. He is a Level 2 Tennis Coach, Level 3 Ski Coach
(CSCF), and Level 4 National Coaching Certification Program (candidate). Carl regularly speaks internationally, most recently in Brazil, Australia, England, and the USA. He
writes regularly for a variety of peer review and lay journals (see www.fittoplay.com)
He stays Fit to Play™ with support from: Prince, Brooks, Ripzone, and Uvex.

Nina Nittinger, Dipl.KFFR/Sports Mgt

Nina is a former professional tennis player who spent
over six years full time on the tour. She is a certified tennis coach of the Swiss Tennis Federation and has attained
the highest level coaching certification in Germany. She is
also a mental trainer in sport psychology for professional
athletes. After finishing her masters in sports management, she published several articles and two books about
fitness and mental training in tennis. Currently she is
coaching and managing several young professional athletes in Switzerland, and she travels regularly both nation-
ally and internationally with tennis athletes. In Spring
2006, the second edition of Mental Tennis Training will be published in German. Her
website is www.mapp-coaching.com. She stays Fit to Play™ with support from Babolat.

About the Authors

CONTRIBUTING WRITERS

Joseph Brabenec Sr.

Josef captained several Czech national teams and was elected a member of Committee of Management of the ITF in 1969. Tennis Canada appointed him Canadian National Coach from 1975 to 1984. During this time he introduced the coaching certification program and started the junior development program. He was the players' choice as Davis Cup and Federation Cup coach and captain for six years. Since 1985, Josef has run coaches' clinics and junior training camps on behalf of the ITF. In this capacity he visited 60 countries, ran seminars for more than 5,000 coaches, and discovered several future ATP/WTA players. He was named a Level 5 Coach (the highest degree) by Tennis Canada in 1995. In Cairo, in 1997, the ITF awarded him a medal in recognition of his effort to develop tennis around the world. He has written several books including Tennis: Sport for Anybody, Tennis: The Decision-Making Sport and Tennis for Children.

Angela Calder, BA, MA(Hons), BApplSci(Sports Coaching)

Angela is a recovery and sports coaching consultant. She was the recovery consultant for the Australian Institute of Sport from 1990-2002. She compiled the Recovery Guidelines for the 2000 Olympic and 2000 Paralympic Games for all the Australian teams. Angie has also been a recovery consultant to over 50 non-Olympic teams, including tennis (Davis and Federation Cup). Currently she is undertaking a PhD, holds an adjunct senior lecturing position at the University of the Sunshine Coast in Queensland, and teaches post-graduate recovery modules for the University of Queensland. (www.ask.net.au)

Louis Cayer

Louis graduated from Université du Québec, Montréal, with a degree in Pedagogy (science of teaching and learning) in 1976. He present-ly works part time for Tennis Canada as consultant for the junior development and coaching certification system and as a consultant internationally with players, clubs, associations, and countries. Louis is the head national coach for junior club development in Canada. He currently coaches players in the top 50 on the ATP and WTA tour. He spent 12 years as Canadian Davis Cup coach and captain (1989-2000) and was Olympic coach in Atlanta and Sydney, coaching the men doubles gold medalists, Sydney 2000 (Lareau-Nestor). He has traveled with several top 100 ATP players from 1989-2000, including Grant Connell, Glenn Michibata, Daniel Nestor, Sébastien Lareau, Chris Pridham, Martin Laurendeau, and Greg Rusedski.

He has an active interest in coaching coaches and is currently (since 1989) the leader of the coaching certification in Canada. He served on the ITF coaching committee from 1995-2000 and has presented in more than 25 countries, including yearly presentations at the ITF worldwide workshop (since 1987).

Dr. David Cox, PhD, RPsych

David Cox is a clinical psychologist and a professor in the Department of Psychology at Simon Fraser University. Over the past twenty years he has established a reputation as one of Canada's top sport psychologists. He works extensively with athletes and coaches at all levels of competition from the grassroots to international levels. He has worked with many national sports teams including Tennis Canada and the Davis Cup, Men's National Rugby, Skate Canada, Men's National Soccer, Men's National Basketball, National Wrestling, Women's National Softball, Men's National Field Hockey, National Cross-Country ski, and Women's Olympic Curling. At the individual level, he has worked with many of Canada's top athletes and has served as a sport psychologist for Canada's athletes and teams at the Olympics. He is a Master Course Conductor in the Level 3, 4, and 5 components of the

National Coaching Certification program. He is also the president of the Sports Medicine Council of British Columbia.

Randy Celebrini, BSc(PT), RCAMT

Randy has been a physiotherapist in sports medicine for over 10 years and is a member of the medical team for Canadian Alpine, Canadian Soccer and Canadian Field Hockey. He is currently president of the On-Field-Clinic, a controlled rehab environment developed specifically for return-to-sport transition/sport-specific rehabilitation. (www.onfieldclinic.com or onfieldclinic@shaw.ca)

Patricia Chuey, MSc, RDN (Sport Nutritionist)

Patricia is a registered dietitian and sport nutritionist who has worked in the preventive health field for over 15 years. She is president of Eating for Energy, a nutrition consulting firm in Vancouver. Patricia has served as nutritionist for the Vancouver Grizzlies, BCTV's Noon News, and appears regularly in the media. She is the author of The 101 Most Asked Nutrition Questions. You can visit her on-line at www.saveonfoods.com or www.eatingforenergy.com.

Wayne Elderton

Wayne is the Head Course Conductor for Tennis Canada Coaching Certification in British Columbia. He is a certified Canadian national level 4 coach and a PTR Professional. For two consecutive years he was runner-up for Canadian national development coach-of-the-year, out of nominated coaches from every sport. He is a multiple winner of the Tennis BC High Performance Coach-of-the-year award. Wayne is currently tennis director at the Grant Connell Tennis Centre in North Vancouver. He has written coaching articles and materials for Tennis Canada, the PTR, Tennis Australia, and the ITF (www.acecoach.com).

Daniel Haggart, BSc(PT), BSC(HKin)

Daniel graduated with a bachelor's in human kinetics and a bachelor's in physical therapy

from University of British Columbia, where he played and captained the UBC soccer team. He also won a national championship as the captain of the Capilano Blues Soccer Team. He has completed his Level III Manual Therapy and is preparing for his Part A and Level II Sport Therapy certification. Dan was the physiotherapist and head athletic trainer for Capilano College Athletics as well as the physiotherapist for the U-16 BC Soccer Program, which won the 2005 national championships. He also worked two years as the head athletic therapist for the UBC soccer team. (www.citysportsphysio.com)

Dr. Bernie Lalonde, MD, Dip SM

Bernie has a 32 year history working with athletes in Canada, initially as a coach for six years in the '70s, and then head team physician from the '70s to the present. He is a sports physician in Ottawa and has worked every Olympic Winter Games from 1976 to 1998. He was head coach for Whitewater Slalom Team from 1982-1985, and worked at the Barcelona Olympic Games as physician and assistant coach with the whitewater team.

Dr. Donna Mockler, OD

Donna graduated with Doctor of Optometry degree from the University of Waterloo in 1983, where she was the recipient of the Award for Clinical Excellence. She currently practices with Pacific Eye Doctors in Richmond, B.C. She is a consultant to amateur and professional athletes, including tennis, skiing, cycling, shooting, and motor sports. She was the 2002 recipient of the BCAO Optometrist of The Year Award and is the clinical director for Canada for the "Opening Eyes–Healthy Athletes Program for Special Olympics." (www.pacificeyedoctors.net)

Phil Moore, BA, BPHE

Owner of Lady Sport since 1983. Footwear consultant to the Health Care Industry and author of The Shoe Update, a footwear directory since 1984 for podiatrists, physiotherapists, and sports medicine specialists. He also

About the Authors

lectures to college and university programs. (www.ladysport.ca)

Dr. Robert Morrell, BSc, MD, Dip SM

Bob is a sports medicine and family practice physician. He is also Medical Representative Canada FIS, Co-Director Canadian Alpine Ski Team, Medical Group Ski Patrol Whistler.

Dallas Parsons, Registered Dietitian, BSc(Hon), BA(Hon)

A sport dietitian committed to best practices, Dallas Parsons uses her personal experience, nutrition knowledge, and drive as an athlete to maximize the practicality and effectiveness of her strategic counseling.

As an energetic and creative motivator, Dallas guides many individual athletes and teams to eat an optimal sport diet that fuels athletic performance. In her private practice, Dallas delivers motivational nutrition seminars and one-on-one counseling to competitive and high performance athletes, many of whom compete at the international level. Dallas has also had the privilege of working with Olympic athletes in preparation for the 2006 and 2010 Winter Games. Dallas holds a bachelor of science in food and nutrition with honors from the University of British Columbia and is an active member of Dietitians of Canada. (www.dallasparsons.com)

Dr. John Peroff, OD

John is an optometrist with a special interest in sport vision. He is sports vision performance consultant for the Canadian alpine and freestyle ski team, as well as the speed skaters and equestrian teams. He is chairman of the Sports Vision Section of Canadian Association of Optometrists and worked at the Olympic Sports Vision Centres in Albertville, France and Lillehammer, Norway.

Martha Sirdevan, BSc(PT), FCAMT

Martha Sirdevan is a physiotherapist in Kelowna, British Columbia. She graduated from Queen's University in 1998 with a bachelor of science in physiotherapy. In 2003 she became a Fellow of the Canadian Academy of Manipulative Therapies. She is an avid runner and has completed five marathons.

Dr. Wolf Schamberger, MD, FRCPC

Dr. Schamberger is a clinical associate professor in rehabilitation medicine and consultant at the Allan McGavin Sports Medicine Centre at the University of British Columbia, Vancouver, Canada. A former 2:20 marathon winner, he continues to be active in sports, gathering first-hand experience on abnormal biomechanics and injuries caused by malalignment. (www.malalignmentsyndrome.com)

Dr. Bill West, BPE, MSc, MD, CCF(EM), Dip. Sport Med

Bill is an emergency medicine physician at Richmond Hospital, British Columbia, team physician for the Canadian Alpine Ski Team, consulting physician for the Canadian Women's Soccer Team, and team physician for Racing Yacht Movistar in the 2005-2006 Volvo Ocean Race Around the World.

Dr. Tim Wood, MD, ChB, FACSP

Tim has been the chief medical officer of the Australian Open since Sept 2001, medical consultant to Tennis Australia since 2002, and member of Tennis Australia Anti-doping review board since 2001. He has been a member of the ITF sport science and medical commission since 2004 and honorary doctor to the Australian Fed cup team since 2003. He was the convener of the 8th international congress of the Society for Tennis Medicine and Science in Melbourne January, 2006. Dr. Wood currently is vice-president of the Australasian College of Sports Physicians and practices as a sports physician in Melbourne, Australia.